CHOCOLATE

CHOCOLATE

Artistry

Elaine González

Techniques for Molding,
Decorating, and Designing
with Chocolate

CONTEMPORARY
BOOKS, INC.
CHICAGO

Library of Congress Cataloging in Publication Data

González, Elaine.

Chocolate artistry.

Includes index.
1. Cookery (Chocolate)   1. Title
TX767.C5G65   1983   641.7   83-14364
ISBN 0-8092-5544-8
ISBN 0-8092-5339-9 (pbk.)

Photography by Donald Link

Published by Contemporary Books, Inc.
180 North Michigan Avenue, Chicago, Illinois 60601
Manufactured in the United States of America
Library of Congress Catalog Card Number: 83-14364
International Standard Book Number: 0-8092-5544-8 (cloth)
                                    0-8092-5339-9 (paper)
Published simultaneously in Canada by Beaverbooks, Ltd.
195 Allstate Parkway, Valleywood Business Park
Markham, Ontario L3R 4T8 Canada

Contents

For Pepe . . . a gift of love.

Acknowledgments

I wish to express my love and gratitude to my family, each of whom contributed to my creative growth in very special ways:

To my husband Pepe, for providing me with the space that I needed to stretch, grow, and blossom.

To our children Jay, Carla, and Lisa for years of cooperation and creative stimulation.

To my mother Mary García, for inspiring me, supporting me, and assisting me in every possible way.

To my father Adenso García, in remembrance, for a lifetime of wisdom and guidance and for awakening within me the creative curiosity that ultimately charted my course.

I am also deeply indebted to Elaine Sherman for the integral part that she played in the development of my career and for the advice, comfort, and friendship that she has extended to me thoughout the years.

I am immensely grateful to Bob Bemm, who has taught me so much, stood by me so faithfully, and contributed so significantly to my professional accomplishments.

I am equally grateful to Eva Myers of Cora Lee Candies in Glenview, Illinois, for introducing me to chocolate as an art form and for sharing so much of her considerable knowledge and expertise with me.

I especially wish to thank Herb Knechtel, Paul Richards, Tom Treece, and Mary Domanski of the Knechtel Laboratories in Skokie, Illinois, for the enormous amount of technical information and sound advice that they gave me. Their generosity was matched only by the warmth of their hospitality.

I am also very grateful to many members of the chocolate industry for the assistance and encouragement that they have extended to me. In particular, I would like to thank Malcolm Blue, Frank Van Son, Marie-Claude Stockl, and Chris Klaiss of the Nestlé Company, and Robert Blommer of the Blommer Chocolate Company.

My appreciation also goes to Eloína Torre de Rivas of Mexico City, who, besides nurturing my infatuation with Mexico, has consistently provided me with an abundance of historical data regarding the origin of chocolate.

In addition, I would like to thank Kathleen Perry for rekindling my spirit, and Donald Link for capturing it all on film.

Finally, to Maida Heatter, Alice Medrich, John Clancy, and Chef Lutz Olkiewicz I offer my heartfelt thanks for the guidance, enrichment, and inspiration that I derived as a student in their classes.

Prologue:
The Legend
of Chocolate

It is written in the ancient chronicles that the gods one day looked down with pity on the Toltecs as they struggled to survive in the barren Mexican land in which they lived. They resolved that Quetzalcoatl-Tlahuizcalpanticutli, the god of light, should go down to Earth to teach the Toltecs matters of science and the arts to help them cope with life's hardships.

Quetzalcoatl, the plumed serpent god, assumed human form and descended into their midst on a beam of morning starlight. Startled by his luminous arrival, unusual fair skin, and glowing white beard, the Toltecs accepted his apparition as a godly one and worshipped him as they did Tlaloc, the rain god.

The god-man Quetzalcoatl was loved and admired by all and looked on as a man of virtue with high ideals and strong moral convictions. Together with the other gods, he taught the Toltecs to chart the movements of the stars and to measure time and the change of seasons. The Toltecs soon became able masters of their fields.

The unique religious doctrine that Quetzalcoatl preached was based on the existence of one supreme, creative god who was not only the giver of life and death but the creator of the sky, sea, and Earth; the lesser gods were but manifestations of him. Just as the supreme god was creative, so should man be, said Quetzalcoatl, creating things whenever possible. These teachings inspired among the Toltecs an artistic renaissance that spread throughout the central valley of Mexico. The gods high in the garden of Tecuhtli smiled down approvingly on the wise and artistic Toltecs.

As an act of love, Quetzalcoatl bestowed on his people a little shrub that had, until then, belonged exclusively to the gods. The cauhcacahuatl (cacao tree) was planted in the rugged fields high above Tula where Tlaloc saw that it was adequately nourished and Xochiquetzal, the goddess of love and happiness, adorned it with beautiful blossoms. Similar cacao trees—the mecacahuatl, xichicacahuatl, and tlcacahuatl—were also planted there.

The other gods witnessed the harvesting and

roasting of the fruits of the cauhcacahuatl with increasing displeasure. A chocolate drink, xocolatl, prepared with the roasted fruits and heretofore considered the sacred liquor of the gods alone, soon became the most sought-after drink among the priests and nobles of Quetzalcoatl's court as well. The fruits of the other trees were used as money and became symbols of a person's wealth. Enraged by these acts of sacrilege and Quetzalcoatl's betrayal, the gods sought retribution and the ultimate destruction of the Toltec Empire. They dispatched Tezcatlipoca, the god of night and darkness, on a mission destined to destroy them all. Dressed as a merchant, he descended to Earth on a black spider's thread to await a confrontation with his arch-rival Quetzalcoatl.

Though ominous dreams of vengeance and doom had forewarned him, Quetzalcoatl, an avowed abstainer, fell easy prey to Tezcatlipoca's evil scheme and drank of the fermented juice of the maguey, which Tezcatlipoca offered to him as an elixir to quiet his fears of reprisal from the gods. The effect of the potent pulque was devastating. Much to the delight of Tezcatlipoca and the other gods, a drunken Quetzalcoatl shouted and danced shamelessly before his scandalized people, behaving in the most outrageous ways. Exhausted at last, he fell into a long, deep sleep.

It was with dismay that he discovered upon awakening the following morning that he had dishonored himself in an irreversible way with such deplorable behavior and that he could no longer effectively rule the people he loved. The grief-stricken Quetzalcoatl set out on a long and perilous journey on foot in the direction of the evening star, his home. The cacao trees that he passed along the way reflected the impending doom that prevailed throughout the land. Once green-leafed and heavy with fruit, they now stood shriveled and dry, transformed into thorny cacti. He scooped up a few of the remaining seeds, held them tightly within his palm, and continued on his sorrowful way.

When at last he arrived at the shore of what is now Tabasco, he cast a handful of his precious cacao beans on the beach, the god of light's parting gift to mankind. He hesitated there briefly, promised to return in the year of Ce Acatl (1519), stepped onto the beam of the evening star that lay across the surface of the sea, and ascended to his home.

The thorny cacti still grow in the high regions of Tula, Mexico, painful reminders today of the demise of a great empire. But in the distant, low, tropical land where Quetzalcoatl spent his final hours, his remarkable gift of love, the cacao tree, also flourishes, a lasting memento of a golden era long gone but not forgotten.

Introduction

Chocolate! Now *that* is a word that conjures up describable ecstacies. Truffles, bonbons, peppermint patties, lollipops, cakes, cookies, and more. Breathes there a man, woman, or child who has not lusted after it, devoured it, and moments later dreamed of it still? Chocolate is, quite frankly, *it*.

It has captivated me for years. I am beginning to suspect, in fact, that my fate was cast in 1519, the year of Ce Acatl, when Hernán Cortés (mistakenly identified as the returning Quetzalcoatl) and his men touched Mexico's soil and sampled Moctezuma's precious brew. Those were, after all, my ancestors who sampled and later introduced chocolate to the rest of the world. It is indeed curious that I, who have always maintained a very strong Spanish identity as well as an infatuation with Mexico, the land to which my family emigrated from Spain, am now also linked indelibly with chocolate, the origins of which are so deeply rooted in my heritage. Can it be true, as some people say, that I *do* have chocolate in my blood?

Having the proper lineage is not a prerequisite to working with chocolate. Enthusiasm is. Patience is. Motivation is. The excitement of creating something made of chocolate that looks as good as it tastes will increase your enthusiasm, reward your patience, and motivate you to do more and more things with it.

This is a book about making a good thing better; it is about chocolate as an art form. Here, in layman's terms, you will learn to handle chocolate successfully and, subsequently, to use it artistically in ways that will amaze and delight you. An introduction to chocolate artistry requires little more than a trip to the grocery store for chocolate and a selection of a molding receptacle from within your own kitchen cabinets. Further experimentation will inevitably lead to a desire to buy chocolate in bulk form and an investment in some of the inexpensive chocolate molds that are available throughout the country.

My basic decorating instructions will enable you to create greeting cards, architectural extravaganzas, and a multitude of party favors and gifts. You will shine as a hostess when you entertain with chocolate placecards, chocolate baskets, and desserts decorated with chocolate accents. As a bonus, the same decorating techniques, when extended beyond chocolate, may be used to decorate other kinds of sweet or savory foods.

The popular nonchocolates, commonly known as *compound coating, pastel coating, confectioners' coating, summer coating, chocolate-flavored coating,* and *white chocolate* (a misnomer), are highly recommended as substitutes for real chocolate in any of the procedures presented in the book. **They are easy to use, require no special handling, and will do almost anything demanded of them.** While their taste, though certainly acceptable, is no match for that of fine chocolate, they are far superior to chocolate as a beginner's medium for the development of new decorating skills and for creative experimentation.

The first five chapters of this book describe in detail the fundamental techniques required to create the multitude of chocolate items that follow. Do not be intimidated by the length of any of the instructions. Imagine me at your side as you read them, guiding your hand, coaxing, cautioning, reminding, and applauding you as you work.

Be prepared for occasional disappointments in your earliest efforts. Some techniques, as their descriptions suggest, are more difficult than others. Be realistic and select the ones that best suit your current level of expertise; reserve the rest for later. I promise no quick road to proficiency here, only the academic know-how and creative stimulation needed to achieve it. Proficiency cannot be assimilated through the reading of any text; it must be earned—every single step of the way. A willing and eager student who practices diligently and with frequency can expect to achieve it in much less time than one who does not.

Just as practice will improve your decorating proficiency, so will the frequency of your efforts fuel the creative spirit that exists within you. Accept each new confectionery challenge readily, not only to awaken your creativity but also as a means of exercising your developing agility and to gain confidence and a sense of pride in your newfound ability. I can truthfully say that the demands placed on me by my enthusiastic students, discriminating clients, and admiring friends and family are unquestionably responsible for any success that I may have achieved as a teacher-decorator. Still, while it is they who continue to sustain my creative energy, it is my own sense of personal pride in each piece of chocolate that I decorate that determines the ultimate quality of my work.

Chocolate, the legendary gift of love, continues to be the confection most often associated with that sentiment throughout the world today. The endurance of chocolate's popularity is a fitting tribute to the god of light who lovingly bequeathed it to us long ago, along with the desire to create things with it whenever possible. **If chocolate inspires within you an artistic renaissance, as I hope it does, then surely Quetzalcoatl and I will both be pleased.**

1
An Introduction to Chocolate and Compound Coating

Fundamental to any pursuit of artistic prowess with chocolate must be an awareness of its unique physical makeup and its seemingly erratic behavior. It is a subject about which much has been written, to be sure. Unfortunately, many of the conclusions drawn by the average layman from such writings are mostly paradoxical: chocolate must be handled ever so carefully, with meticulous attention to detail, yet the techniques suggested for doing so and the degree of precision specified are so diversified as to confuse and disillusion, rather than enlighten, the eager student.

Over-simplified instructions found in other writings that suggest merely melting chocolate over "not-too-hot" water and then allowing the chocolate to cool "slightly" before using it must also be regarded with some degree of skepticism. This casual approach to handling chocolate may be acceptable for baking and cooking procedures, but it is totally unreliable for molding, decorating, and designing with chocolate.

It is, therefore, the intent here to describe the most reliable, most widely-accepted techniques for working with chocolate in an effort to dispel many of the doubts and fears that you may have regarding the subject.

There is an option open to the timid novice who prefers to acquire some manual dexterity before attempting to tame real chocolate's free spirit. That option is a nonchocolate product called *compound coating*. It is manufactured by most of the chocolate companies in this country and has become an immensely popular medium among laymen and members of the confectionery trade because of its ease of handling and much lower cost. (See pages 14–17 for a complete description and instructions for usage.)

Let us first examine the nature of real chocolate as an introduction to the discussion of its handling.

CHOCOLATE INGREDIENTS

Chocolate Liquor

The skillful blending of assorted types of cacao beans makes possible a wide range of distinctive flavors, colors, and degrees of smoothness in the chocolates that we enjoy. The cocoa nibs constitute the meat that is separated from the roasted cacao beans during the winnowing process. A dark brown liquor (nonalcoholic) is extracted from these nibs in the subsequent grinding procedure and is then used in the manufacture of chocolate in three different forms:

1. *Unsweetened baking chocolate.* The chocolate liquor, when solidified into blocks, is sold commercially as baking chocolate.
2. *Cocoa powder.* The liquor particles, when separated by hydraulic pressure from the cocoa butter fat in which they are suspended, are used in the manufacture of powdered cocoa.
3. *Coating and eating chocolate.* When chocolate liquor is combined with additional cocoa butter, sugar, milk products, flavorings, and emulsifiers, it becomes a chocolate coating or a related chocolate product.

Sugar

A highly refined grade of sugar with no traces of moisture is essential in the manufacture of sweetened chocolate.

Cocoa Butter

This natural fat base, derived from the processing of the cacao bean, is responsible for the fluid melting quality of fine chocolate and for the troublesome grey bloom that frequently appears on the surface of finished chocolate products.

The amount of additional cocoa butter that is added to the other ingredients in the manufacturing process is greatly determined by the individual companies, though European confectioners generally use more of it proportionally than do their American counterparts.

Butter Fat

Butter fat in the form of dehydrated unsalted butter is often included in the manufacture of milk chocolate and is sometimes used in dark chocolate as a bloom deterrent.

Milk and Milk Solids

Milk solids and milk fats are added to the chocolate liquor in the manufacture of milk chocolate. Minimum government standards require that no less than 12 percent milk solids or less than 3.66 percent milk fat be used. Milk solids are sometimes also added to semisweet chocolate but no more than 12 percent is allowed.

Lecithin

Lecithin, an emulsifier, is used to reduce the viscosity of the chocolate (it thins it) and serves to lessen the amount of cocoa butter required in the manufacturing process.

Flavorings

The development of distinct chocolate flavors is an art that is practiced by chocolate manufacturers everywhere. Combinations of several varieties of cacao beans, just the right roast, carmelization of milk products, and even aging of the finished product are just some of the natural ways used to produce full-bodied chocolates. The unique flavors are further developed through the addition of vanilla or vanillin (an artificial flavoring) and various essential oils (oil of lemon, orange, almond, etc.).

TYPES OF CHOCOLATE

The immense popularity of chocolate has made it readily accessible all over the country. It is a common commodity today even in warm, humid climates as a result of the widespread use of air conditioning.

You need venture only as far as your neighborhood grocery store to purchase the chocolate required for your first experiments. Most molded pieces described in this book can be made from plain, solid, chocolate candy bars or cooking chocolates found on the grocers' shelves or at fine candy counters. Even though some areas of the country may have limited access to the most superior grades of chocolate, there are several catalog sources that can fill that need. (See the Appendix.) Most decorative work, however, does not require the most expensive chocolate.

You will eventually want to purchase chocolate in bulk form for the sake of convenience and cost. Cake decorating supply shops as well as gourmet/kitchenware supply shops usually sell this type of chocolate. Consult your telephone directory for the names of confectionery and baker suppliers and for the names of other sources in your area.

Unsweetened Chocolate

This chocolate, made of pure chocolate liquor, is sold in retail stores by several chocolate companies, including Baker, Hershey, Ghirardelli, and Wilbur. Use this type primarily for baking and for piping designs that require extreme fluidity. Thicken it, if necessary, by cautiously adding drops of vanilla extract and stirring well.

Bittersweet, Semisweet Chocolate

The chocolate liquor used to manufacture these chocolates is sweetened mildly for the bittersweet type and more heavily for the semisweet and sweet cooking varieties. These chocolates are ideal choices for decorative piping, molding, dipping, and spreading as well as baking—and eating!

Look for this type of chocolate on grocery store shelves in the form of squares, morsels, or solid chocolate candy bars. Here are some of the most popular brands that are available:

Baker's German's Sweet Chocolate
Baker's Semi-Sweet Chocolate
Cadbury Dark Chocolate Bar
Callebaut (bittersweet)
Ghirardelli Eagle Sweet Chocolate
Hershey's Chips and Mini Chips

Hershey's Special Dark Chocolate Bar
Lanvin
Lindt Rod (bittersweet)
Maillard Eagle Sweet Chocolate
Nestlé's Semi-Sweet Toll House Morsels and Mini Morsels
Poulain (bittersweet)
Sarotti
Suchard Bittra (bittersweet)
Tobler Tradition (bittersweet)
World's Finest Chocolate

The sweetened bulk chocolates, often called *vanilla coatings* or *couvertures,* are usually sold in ten-pound slabs. The chocolates that I use most often are Nestlé's Burgundy and Viking, Ghirardelli Bittersweet, Carma Bourbon Vanilla Couverture, and Callebaut Bittersweet.

Note: The viscosity of all these chocolates when melted ranges from high (morsels and chips) to low (the European couvertures). Generally speaking, the more cocoa butter the chocolate contains, the lower its viscosity (the thinner and more fluid it is).

Milk Chocolate

The chocolate liquor is sweetened heavily in the manufacture of milk chocolate. The heavy additions of milk products make it more temperamental to work with than semisweet chocolate. I recommend that you use the latter in the beginning.

Here are some popular brands:

Nestlé's Milk Chocolate Morsels
Hershey's ½ lb. Milk Chocolate bar
Nestlé's Crunch bar
Cadbury Milk Chocolate bar

The bulk milk chocolates that I use are Nestlé's Broc and Glenmere, Carma Des Alpes couverture, and Ghirardelli Bay Bridge.

Cocoa

Pure, unsweetened cocoa is the result of the removal of much of the cocoa butter from the chocolate liquor by hydraulic pressure. The remaining chocolate liquor is subsequently ground and sieved, creating the fine powdered cocoa that we enjoy today; the cocoa butter is then used in the manufacture of other chocolate products. Some of it is also used pharmaceutically and in the manufacture of beauty aids.

The cocoa "dutching" process neutralizes the acidity in the powder, making it more digestible, more flavorful, and, if thoroughly alkalized, darker in color. The brand that I use is Droste, imported from Holland. Other brands include Guittard, Ambrosia, Hershey's, Wilbur, and Poulain.

White Cocoa Butter Coating

This cocoa-butter-based coating is closely related to the previously described chocolate products except for the absence of chocolate liquor. That omission prohibits it from being labeled *white chocolate*, the name frequently (and erroneously) used to identify it.

Its composition is similar to that of milk chocolate, with extra milk products and a mild-flavored cocoa butter replacing the absent liquor; consequently, it can be temperamental and requires the same attention as, or perhaps more than, milk chocolate. Contrary to what you may have heard, it must be tempered. (The term "temper" will be explained shortly.)

When available in grocery stores, this product is usually located amid the bars of imported chocolates (see the Appendix for other sources).

Cocoa butter coating is ivory in color, creamy, and has a very mild milk chocolate flavor. I use Nestlé's bulk Snowcap Coating, Tobler Narcisse bars, and Callebaut White. Other popular brands are Merckens Ivory Milk Coating, Van Leer's Van Wit White, and Wilbur's White Ermine.

STORAGE OF CHOCOLATE

Chocolate should be stored at 65°F.-70°F. in a room with good air circulation and a relative humidity of 50 percent or lower. Temperatures above 70°F. are likely to cause some of the cocoa butter crystals to melt and rise, giving the surface a grey appearance called *bloom*, a superficial defect.

Because chocolate is so susceptible to odors, it should be wrapped and stored away from foreign flavors. White cocoa butter coating is especially prone to these odors and will turn rancid if exposed to prolonged light. Do not stack bulk chocolate directly against walls or on floors.

Chocolate that is in "temper," a term used to describe its crystalization condition, has a conservative shelf life of 1-2 years. The dark, sweet chocolates that are stored under ideal conditions have the longest life, white cocoa butter coating, the shortest. Consider your storage facilities before you invest in large quantities of chocolate.

HANDLING CHOCOLATE

Water, Steam, and Extreme Heat—Chocolate's Greatest Enemies

When you are melting chocolate it must never be subjected to extreme heat; the warmest it should ever reach is 120°F. Drops of water or steam will tighten (thicken) it, so guard against dripping or splashing, especially when using a water bath to heat or cool the chocolate.

Grated or Chopped Chocolate Melts Faster than Chunks

Grating and chopping chocolate is no fun, but it melts much faster that way and makes it worth

The chunk on the left shows signs of gray strata and should be considered untempered. The chunk on the right is in a tempered state.

the effort. Break large pieces with an ice chipper (available in restaurant and bar supply stores), an ice pick, a heavy knife, or a candy scraper. To grate with a hand grater, chill the chocolate briefly, especially if the room is warm, and hold it between double thicknesses of wax paper so as not to melt it. To chop it in a food processor, break it into one-inch chunks and feed them gradually into the feed tube of a running food processor fitted with the steel blade. Chop half a pound of chocolate at a time.

How to Identify Solid Chocolate in a Tempered State

It is important to know if the chocolate that you plan to melt is in prime condition or not, because its crystalization condition will determine the temperature to which it must be melted. Examine all of its exterior surfaces; crack it into two pieces. All surfaces should appear dark, firm and uniform: most chocolate leaves the manufacturer looking like that—"in good temper." Improper subsequent storage conditions, however, may have altered its "tempered" state giving rise to bloom (gray shadows), crumbling, and/or gray strata on the chocolate's surface. This "untempered" chocolate is still fine to use, but it must be melted to exactly 120°F., a slightly higher temperature than that required for solid chocolate in a tempered state.

Ideal Room Temperatures for Chocolate Work

Dipping should be done in a dry room at 65°F. Warmer room temperatures will likely cause bloom to appear later on the final product. Molding should be done in a warmer room, approximately 80°F.

Equipment Used in Handling Chocolate

Thermometer

There is nothing more vital to successful chocolate tempering than an accurate thermometer. Yes, professional chocolate dippers temper by feel; but they had on-the-job-training to acquire their sensitive touch. To work toward that goal, determine the chocolate's temperature with the thermometer, then touch the chocolate with your finger and dot your bottom lip with some of it or touch the chocolate with the back of your hand. It should definitely feel cool to the touch if its temperature is below body temperature.

Not every thermometer will work for tempering. It must be one that covers the low 80°F.–120°F. range. I use the following Sybron/Taylor thermometers in my work. Any one of them is sufficient, though an extra one is convenient.

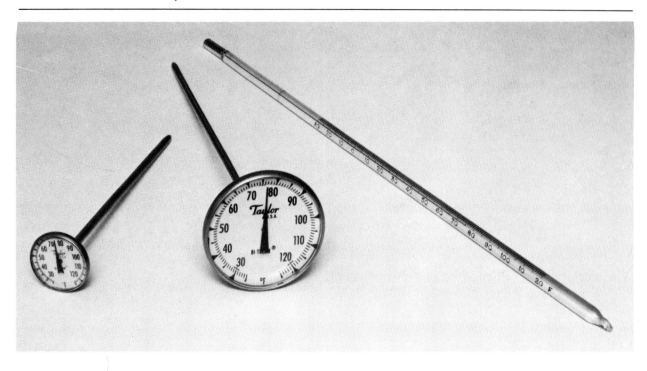

One-inch Dial Bi-Therm Thermometer (#6175-1); range: 25° F.–125° F.

Two-inch Dial Bi-Therm (#6212); range: 25° F.–125° F.

Superior Grade General Test Thermometer (#63116); range: 30° F.–120° F. (It resembles a large oral thermometer.)

Note: Another fine thermometer has been designed by Rose Levy Beranbaum. It is similar to the General Test Thermometer just mentioned. Rose's thermometer is 12 inches long and measures in easy-to-read, one-degree increments. The thermometer is available through Madame Chocolate.

Double Boiler

For melting chocolate, select a standard double boiler or a saucepan fitted with an appropriately sized bowl that will prohibit the splashing of water into the top. If possible, select one that will allow for the insertion of a thermometer into the water. I use a Leyse aluminum double boiler (3 quart insert with a 4⅜ quart bottom). I had a hole drilled into its side to accommodate a thermometer.

Stirring Paddle

An ideal paddle or spoon for stirring chocolate should have a broad, squared bowl rather than a concave, pointed one. I highly recommend the use of a plastic or rubber spatula. Or use a metal spoon rather than a wooden one, since the latter retains moisture and could possibly splinter. The stirring paddle should be free of old chocolate, so as not to contaminate the fresh batch, and perfectly dry.

Marble Slab

A marble slab (approximately 15 inches square or larger) makes short work of cooling chocolate, but it is clearly a luxury item for the novice chocolate handler. Substitute a metal cookie sheet (not really comparable but better than nothing).

Candy Scraper

A candy scraper is used to work the warm, melted chocolate across the surface of the marble slab during the tempering procedure. Mine has a three-inch-wide stiff blade that extends down through the full length of the wooden handle. Substitute a similarly sized wall scraper available in any hardware store or a five-inch dough scraper.

CHOCOLATE TEMPERING (THE CURSE OF MOCTEZUMA)

The tempering procedure is a classic battle of good against evil, of stable against unstable, of beta crystals against alpha crystals. The final stakes are high. Beta, you win: glossy, firm chocolate. Alpha, you lose: bloom, doom, gloom.

Real chocolate must be melted and cooled in a manner aimed at achieving a shiny, firm surface when it finally hardens. This is no simple task considering the fact that melted cocoa butter, present in liquid chocolate, is composed of a complex mixture of fat crystals that is capable of recrystalizing in stable and unstable forms. Tempering is the procedure used to achieve the stable beta form of cocoa butter crystallization within the fluid mass of chocolate.

To speak of "the state of temper" of a bowl of melted chocolate is to describe the quantity of stable beta crystals in it. If a bowl of warm chocolate is allowed to cool unattended, the cocoa butter fat will recrystallize in both forms. The resultant overabundance of unstable alpha (awful) crystals will produce a final product that is slow to set, granular in texture, and dull in appearance, with patches of grey bloom on its surface. We can say with certainty that "the state of temper" of that bowl of chocolate was poor. The challenge, then, is to produce a bowl of chocolate in a state of good temper.

Learning to temper chocolate can be exciting and rewarding, but do not be surprised if it is a little exasperating and humbling as well. It requires patience (it is a slow procedure), diligence, and determination. The price you will pay for success is high, but the reward is wonderful!

Tempering Procedures

Once real chocolate is melted (regardless of its original, solid, crystalization condition), it requires special handling to restore its tempered state.

The tempering procedures that follow are based on the following assumptions.
1. The chocolate to be melted is grated or chopped into small pieces.
2. The chocolate to be melted is in a tempered state. Untempered, solid chocolate must be melted to exactly 120° F. for best results.
3. At least one pound, and preferably three or four pounds (or more) should be melted at any given time. Working with several pounds of chocolate, even when you need very little, will provide you with a valuable reserve source of warm chocolate from

which to draw throughout the project. What is left over can be reused, and what is used up should be replaced before you need to melt chocolate again.

Melting the Chocolate

Double Boiler Method

1. Hold the bulb end of the thermometer under hot running tap water until it registers exactly 120° F. (or heat water on the stove to achieve that temperature). Fill the bottom of the double boiler with enough 120° F. water to touch the bottom and sides of the top vessel, adjusting the water level, if necessary, so that it does not float. Maintain this temperature reading throughout the melting procedure; don't let it get any higher.

2. Fill the top vessel with a portion of the grated chocolate. (Guard against splashing water into it!) After about five minutes, begin to stir the mixture. As it melts, add more and more of the remaining chocolate, stirring it frequently to assure uniformity of temperature throughout the chocolate mass.

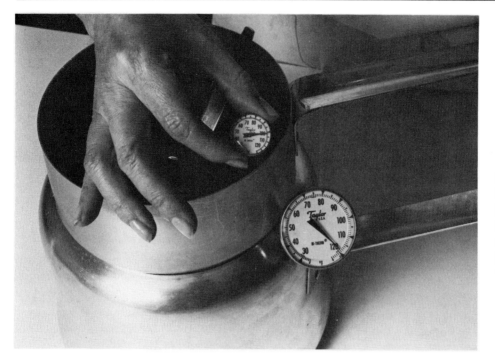

Check the chocolate's temperature frequently during the melting procedure and continue to warm it until it reaches 110° F.–120° F.

3. Test the temperature of the chocolate with a dry thermometer. Continue to heat it until it registers 110° F.–120° F. (White cocoa butter coating in good temper should be melted to 100° F. and untempered, solid chocolate to 120° F.)
Note: Chocolate may be melted using wet or dry heat. See "Alternate Melting Methods," described later in this chapter.

Tempering Method I

This is the most universally accepted method for tempering chocolate. It requires the cooling and reheating of the chocolate to precise temperature ranges.

1. Once the proper melting temperature is achieved, replace the 120° F. water in the bottom of the doubler boiler with 95° F. water. Position the top vessel filled with melted, virgin chocolate (all fat crystals are dissolved—stable and unstable ones) over this water and cool it, stirring occasionally, until it reaches 90° F.–95° F.
2. Withdraw a portion of the chocolate (½ pound, perhaps), and place it in a bowl or pour it in the center of a marble slab. Maintain the melted reserve over the 95° F. water throughout the work period. Monitor

the water's temperature and add warm water whenever necessary.

Cooling the Chocolate

It is important to stir the withdrawn portion of chocolate frequently during the cooling period to encourage the formation of minute fat crystals and to distribute those desirable crystals throughout the chocolate, discouraging the growth of unstable ones.

Bowl Method

1. Cool the bowl of chocolate until it reaches 80° F. and takes on the consistency of

2. Spread it across the surface with a candy scraper and begin to work it back and forth until it turns to paste and is 80°F.

chocolate paste. Use a rubber spatula to prevent the thickening of the faster-cooling chocolate along the walls of the bowl. Do not beat the chocolate at any time as that creates air bubbles.

2. If the temperature drops below 77°F., you must remelt it—this time exactly to 120°F.—and start all over again.

Note: The bowl of chocolate may be cooled more quickly by immersing it in a 70°F. water bath (a larger vessel filled with water) if desired. Be especially diligent about stirring if you use this method.

Marble Slab Method (faster)

1. Wipe the wet bottom of the melting pot and pour the desired portion of chocolate (½ pound, perhaps) onto a cool, dry, marble slab.

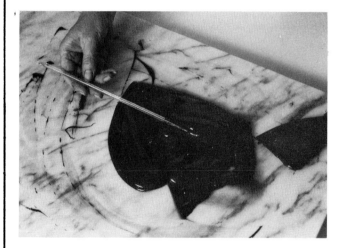

Note: To work it by hand, rather than with a scraper, use a circular motion. Occasionally use the scraper to clean the surface of the marble. Your hand will soon become accustomed to the changes in the chocolate's temperature. Before long, you will be able to temper by feel as professional hand dippers do. Use the thermometer until you can do it accurately.

3. Transfer the chocolate to a bowl or leave it on the slab for the reheating step.

Reheating the Chocolate

1. Add a spoonful of 90°F.-95°F. chocolate, drawn from the reserved supply, to the cool paste in the bowl or on the marble slab. Stir or use the candy scraper to blend it in well.

2. Continue to add small amounts only until the chocolate reaches the following temperature ranges: 86°F.-90°F.—dark chocolate; 83°F.-88°F.—milk chocolate and white cocoa butter coating. (To. ½ pound of chocolate paste, gradually add up to ½ pound of untempered, lukewarm chocolate reserve.) Monitor the chocolate's temperature frequently as you add to it so as not to exceed the given range. If you do

Add warm chocolate gradually to the cool chocolate paste (candy scraper method) to achieve the appropriate temperature.

When working chocolate by hand on the slab, add small amounts of warm chocolate and blend well.

exceed it, you must reheat it to 120°F. and begin again.

Note: Purists believe that the temperature of the reserved supply of chocolate should remain at a constant 120°F. for the reheating procedure, rather than cooled to 90°F.-95°F. as I have suggested. To use this more precise method: Melt the chocolate to 110°F.-120°F.

Withdraw a portion and cool it to 80°F. Maintain the reserve supply at 120°F. Cautiously begin adding the 120°F. chocolate by the tablespoon, remembering that it will take much less of it to achieve the correct temperature than suggested above. To ½ pound of cool paste, add 1½ to 3 tablespoons of warm chocolate. There is only a narrow margin for error.

Alternate Reheating Methods

Water Bath Method

If preferred, the bowl of 80°F. chocolate may be reheated to the appropriate temperature range by immersing it in a warm water bath. The water's temperature must not exceed the chocolate's maximum temperature range by more than 2°F.

Infrared Lamp Method

I love my infrared heat lamp (General Electric, Order Code 250R40/10). It is used in conjunction with a garage reflector shade that comes complete with a 20 feet cord and a clamp that I attach to a shelf at one end of my work table.

Place the bowl of 80°F. chocolate under the

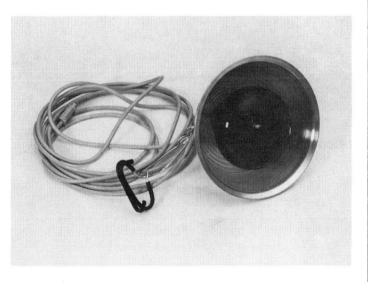

rays of the lamp at a distance of about 18 inches. Stir it gently and check its temperature frequently until you achieve the proper reading.

Testing Your Tempering Accuracy

The tempering procedure is now complete. Test the accuracy of your work by placing a dab

of the tempered chocolate on a small piece of wax paper and chilling it in the refrigerator for approximately three minutes. If, at the end of that time, the chocolate is still soft and tacky, the chocolate is probably not in temper. Chocolate that fails the temper test must be reheated to exactly 120°F. and the procedure begun again from step 1.

Tempering Method II

This popular method is faster than the one just described, though somewhat less reliable. Reserve a chunk of chocolate (or some of the grated chocolate) when melting the larger amount.

Cooling the Chocolate

1. Cool the pot of chocolate to 90°F.-95°F. as suggested previously by replacing the 120°F. water with 95°F. water.
2. Withdraw a portion of the lukewarm, melted chocolate and place it in a bowl. If necessary, continue cooling and stirring it until it reaches a temperature of 90°F.-92°F.
3. Add a chunk of chocolate in good temper (important) to the melted mass and stir well to continue to the lower the temperature.

4. When the chocolate reaches the appropriate temperature range (86°F.-90°F.—dark chocolate; 83°F.-88°F.—milk chocolate and white cocoa butter coating), remove what is left of the chunk and set it aside for subsequent cooling procedures. The chocolate is now ready to be tested and

used. It is not necessary to cool it to 80° F. as in Tempering Method I.

Note: Substitute several sprinklings of grated, tempered chocolate for the chunk, if desired. Add only enough necessary to achieve the required temperature. Anticipate some difficulty in blending the particles.

Maintaining the Temper in Chocolate

Once you have tempered your chocolate, you will want to keep it in that state for as long as possible. This is the preferred method. As you use a portion of the tempered chocolate, replace it with small amounts of lukewarm, melted chocolate (90° F.-95° F.) from your reserved supply. This will not only replenish your supply of tempered chocolate but will also maintain its proper temperature and fluidity. Caution: Guard against adding too much untempered chocolate at any one time (especially if you are adding 120° F. chocolate), or you will disrupt the balance and take the whole batch out of temper.

Alternate Methods for Maintaining the Temper in Chocolate

Chocolate may be kept in temper for short periods of time using the following methods, provided the chocolate is stirred occasionally and the temperature remains within the appropriate range. After about an hour, however, the chocolate will become increasingly thick and unmanageable.

Water Bath Method

Use a water bath temperature no more than 2° F. higher than the maximum temperature range

allowed for the tempered chocolate. Frequently verify the water's temperature with a thermometer and replenish it with warm water as necessary.

Infrared Lamp Method

Warm the chocolate briefly under the rays of the lamp each time it begins to cool. Stir frequently.

The Final Cooling

Once the chocolate has been used to mold, dip, etc., it must be cooled properly. Follow these simple steps to assure the high gloss and firm texture that you have worked so hard to achieve:

1. Place the chocolates on a cooling rack in a cool room (50° F.-55° F.) with good air circulation. Lacking that, chill them briefly in the refrigerator only until set. Some freezers can be used successfully if used in moderation, but it is a risky procedure that I do not recommend.

2. Remove the chocolates and allow them to warm to a moderate room temperature (65° F.-70° F.).

3. Store the pieces uncovered at that same room temperature for at least 24 hours before packaging them to prevent the entrapment of residual heat within the finished chocolates.

Leftover Chocolate

At the conclusion of each chocolate work day the question arises as to what to do with the leftover liquid chocolate. If you plan to work with chocolate the following day and have a way to keep it melted, at a temperature of about 110° F., then by all means do so. If not, it should be stored in a tempered, solid state, if possible. Doing so will assure a good shelf life and require less melting time the next time you use it. Simply spread a thin layer of the tempered chocolate on an inverted, wax paper-covered cookie sheet and cool it until set. Break it up, wrap it, and keep it stored under proper conditions until needed again.

The leftover hard chocolate scraps that accumulate throughout the work day should be kept separate from the reserved supply of melted, virgin chocolate lest they contaminate it. Store them properly until you need to melt chocolate again and include them in that batch.

Alternate Melting Methods

Compound Coating Warmer

I prefer to melt chocolate using dry heat. The compound coating warmer (available through International Leisure, Inc.), though designed primarily to fast melt and then hold compound coating, is well suited to do the same with chocolate. It is necessary to monitor the chocolate while the unit is in the "melt" position (mine heats to 122°F.–125°F.), but its "hold" position will keep chocolate at approximately 110°F. for as long as you wish.

Microwave Oven Method

Microwaves can be used to melt chocolate with considerable speed and accuracy. The instructions that follow are based on my experiences with my own Toshiba microwave oven, utilizing its full 650-watt output and melting 1 pound of chocolate at a time. Since all ovens vary so much, you may need to modify the power and time to fit your own unit. As a precautionary measure, use shorter time intervals than those given here to guard against overheating the chocolate. Be particularly cautious toward the end of the melting procedure. Once you can melt 1 pound successfully, work out a time schedule for melting larger quantities at a time.

1. Place 1 pound of grated chocolate, uncovered, in a microwave-safe bowl. Heat on high (650 watts) for one minute. Stir.
2. Heat for one minute more on high. Stir.
3. Heat for 30 seconds on high. Stir well and check the temperature of the chocolate. If necessary, continue.
4. Heat for 30 seconds (or less). Stir well. The temperature of the melted chocolate should be 110°F.–115°F.

Note: For smaller amounts of chocolate, use less wattage and time. Check the manufacturer's booklet for suggested time and setting for your unit. It is important, however, to heat the tempered chocolate to at least 110°F. and the untempered to 120°F. Reaching for the 120°F. temperature is risky in the microwave unless you know your unit very well. I suggest using a hot water bath to reach that final temperature.

Conventional Oven Method

1. Heat the oven to 250°F. Turn off the heat.
2. Place a shallow, ovenproof bowl filled with grated chocolate in the oven, uncovered, for five minutes.
3. Remove it and stir. Return it to the warm oven for five minutes more.
4. Continue in this manner until the chocolate reaches the required temperature (110°F.–120°F.). It may be necessary to reheat the oven. If so, be sure to remove the chocolate before you do!

Note: This method is particularly suited to melting large quantities of chocolate. Use a cake pan or roasting pan, if necessary.

Infrared Heat Lamp Method

1. Place a shallow, heat-resistant bowl filled with grated chocolate directly under the infrared lamp at a distance of approximately 18 inches.
2. Use a rubber spatula to stir the chocolate as it begins to melt and continue to do so at frequent intervals.
3. After approximately 20 minutes of heating and stirring, lengthen the distance between the lamp and the chocolate to about 24 inches. Continue to heat and stir until the mass reaches the desired temperature of 110°F.–120°F.

Salton Hot-Tray Method

My hot tray is an invaluable aid to me all day long. Before you use yours, however, test it to be sure that it has a low enough temperature setting for chocolate work. Turn it on low, position your palm directly on its surface, and count to 10—slowly. If you flinched, you will have to buffer

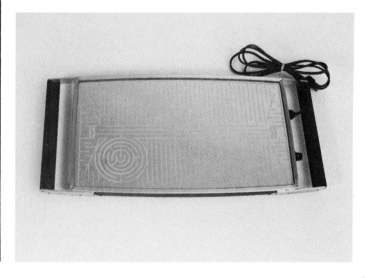

the heat with a thick piece of toweling or something similar before using it to melt chocolate.

1. Set the hot tray to its lowest setting. To melt chocolate, place a small bowl filled with grated chocolate in a water bath and position it on the surface of the hot tray.
2. Stir it occasionally throughout the slow melting period and monitor its temperature frequently.

Summary of Tempering Procedures

Method I

1. Melt to 110°F.–120°F., stirring frequently.
2. Cool to 90°F.–95°F.
3. Withdraw portion, cool to 80°F.
4. Reheat paste to 86°F.–90°F. for dark chocolate, 83°F.–88°F. for milk chocolate and white cocoa butter coating.

Method II

1. Melt to 110°F.–120°F., stirring frequently.
2. Cool to 90°F.–95°F.
3. Withdraw portion, cool to 90°F.–92°F., if necessary.
4. Add chunk of chocolate to lower temperature to appropriate temperature range (see above).

Untempered Chocolate

Melt to exactly 120°F. Temper as desired.

COMPOUND COATING

Compound coatings, sometimes called chocolate substitutes, are largely responsible for the resurgence of interest in candy making across the country today. They offer the novice a medium for self-expression that is easy to handle, good to eat, and attractively priced and the confectioner a line of coatings that complements his chocolates and stimulates the development of new products.

My interest in compound coating was aroused quite innocently when I began some creative experimentation with it for one of my food-decorating classes. It was love at first sight! My chocolate apprenticeship was served discovering the nuances of compound coatings, an experience that significantly affected the depth of my more recent artistic discoveries with chocolate. The challenges that I faced then were creative in nature, not technical, as they became when I began to work with real chocolate. The coatings were incredibly cooperative, rarely resisting the crazy whims of my imagination. That is why, when detractors label them as inferior to chocolate, I rise to their defense. Compound coating is an important confectionery product in a class of its own that should not be underestimated.

Many of the major chocolate companies produce a full line of multicolored, flavored compound coatings using the same kind of equipment that they use in the manufacture of chocolate. These products fail to meet the government's standards of identity for chocolate labeling because they do not contain cocoa butter or chocolate liquor. For that reason they may never be called chocolate, white chocolate, yellow chocolate, etc., but rather, chocolate flavored, wherever that flavoring description pertains.

Compound Coating Ingredients

Sugar

The high-grade sugar, which constitutes 45–55 percent of the product, is pulverized and low in moisture.

Vegetable Fats

Many of the top-quality compound coatings manufactured today are made with either hydrogenated or fractionated palm kernel oil, a lauric fat base. The nonlauric fat coatings containing Kaomel are produced from domestic soybean and cottonseed oils. There are some important differences between lauric and nonlauric fat coatings:

1. Though lauric-fat-based coatings technically require a simplified tempering procedure, most laymen use them successfully without tempering them. The nonlauric fat coatings never require tempering.
2. Lauric fat coatings are *not* compatible with cocoa butter; nonlauric fats are. Lauric fat coatings may never be blended with chocolate and will develop bloom if placed

in direct contact with any product containing high percentages of cocoa butter.

3. Nonlauric fat coatings are primarily suited for enrobing (coating) procedures, rather than molding.
4. Nonlauric fat coatings are most frequently available in chocolate-flavored varieties.

Nonfat Milk

Most compound coatings are composed of 15–25 percent milk solids.

Cocoa (Used in Chocolate-Flavored Coatings Only)

The lauric fat coatings must be flavored with cocoa, not chocolate liquor, to instill a chocolate flavor and color to the product. The cocoa butter content of the selected cocoa must be low. The chocolate liquor is what is most often used to flavor the nonlauric fat coatings.

Emulsifiers

A variety of emulsifiers are used, including glyceryl-lacto esters and lecithin, to reduce viscosity and improve gloss.

Flavorings

A variety of oil-soluble flavorings is used in the broad spectrum of coatings that are manufactured today. Besides vanillin, they include mint, assorted fruit flavors, butterscotch, and natural peanut flavor.

Color

With the exception of the white and chocolate-flavored coatings, the remaining multicolored ones are colored with U.S.-certified food colors in every color of the rainbow and beyond.

Types and Brands of Compound Coatings

There are many brands of compound coatings available in candy-making supply shops, gourmet/cooking school shops, craft stores, variety stores, some grocery stores, and various specialty catalogs. It is therefore important to be selective when choosing a brand; quality varies from good to horrible.

The coatings, once available only in 10-pound slabs or one-pound bags of chunks, can now also be purchased in quicker-melting chips, wafers, and rectangles. Look for them in these colors: ivory, yellow, pink, light green, bright green, peach, red, blue, orange, orchid, and tan (butterscotch and peanut butter). Choose between light and dark chocolate-flavored coatings as well. Some brands are kosher, and their manufacturers will supply documentation on request.

Here are some of the well-known brands (mostly lauric-fat-based):

Nestlé's Icecap Coatings—slabs and caps
Merckens Rainbow Coatings—wafers
Van Leer Chocolate Corporation—slabs and ribbons
Guittard Chocolate Corporation—ribbons, slabs, A'peels, and chocolate-flavored lauric and nonlauric fat coatings
Ambrosia Chocolate Co.—slabs and Diskins
Wilbur Chocolate Co.—drops, chocolate-flavored lauric and nonlauric coatings
The Blommer Chocolate Co.—slabs of lauric as well as nonlauric coatings
Wilton Enterprises—Candy Melts (wafers)

Things to Know about Compound Coating

There are many similarities between compound coating and chocolate. It should never be heated above 120° F. That is perhaps the single most common error committed by beginners. Also guard against steam or water contamination of the product. Very often the two problems are related. Those who "cook" the coating on the stove or over boiling water will necessarily suffer the double disappointment brought about by excessive heat and steam. It is impatience that generally precipitates the overheating of the mixture. Use the convenient easy-melting shapes or chopped coating to shorten the melting time.

Compound coating that has been stored improperly and/or subjected to excessive heat and humidity will show signs of bloom on its surface. It is usually a superficial defect. If, however, after following the proper 120° F. melting procedures, the mixture is still thick and lumpy, it may have deteriorated. In some cases the thick mass may be salvaged by forcing it through a fine sieve or by adding some fresh coating to it.

When all else fails, try adding the thick mixture to the bowl of a food processor fitted with the plastic blade. Process several minutes.

The coatings may be colored with food-safe paste or powdered food coloring products. They may be mixed together to produce color blends, provided they are made of the same fat base. To enhance the vanilla flavor of the white coating or to add a complementary one to the chocolate-flavored ones, add a few drops of oil flavoring, not extract (see Chapter 3).

Melting Procedures

The compound coatings are much simpler to handle than chocolate. The truth is, you merely melt them slowly without excessive heat and then use them. Technically, they should be melted to 115°F.–120°F., then cooled to 90°F.–110°F. and used in that range. I have found that they may be used at any time within a 90°F.–115°F. range. When you require fluidity for any given decorating procedure, use warm coating; for techniques requiring a thicker medium, use it when it is cooler. Below 90°F., the coating becomes increasingly viscous and will need to be reheated briefly. Failure to do so may result in a bloomed final product.

The same methods suggested for melting chocolate may be used for the compound coatings except for a lowering of the wattage to 470 watts in the microwave method. In addition, the use of thermostatically controlled electric appliances with low temperature ranges may be utilized. I particularly like my Wet or Dry Food Warmer (#557) made by the Medalie Manufacturing Co. (see Appendix). I use it as a source for dry heat, **setting it as low as possible. The most appropriate melter for compound coating is surely the compound coating warmer mentioned earlier, which fast-melts and then holds the coating at the proper temperature.**

The following modified version of the double boiler method described earlier may be used to melt compound coating, especially if you do not own a thermometer. It utilizes hotter water and a top vessel that is *not* submerged in the water until after the melting is complete.

1. Place approximately one inch of hot water in the bottom of a double boiler. Bring the water to *near* boiling. Remove it from the

source of heat and wait until the steam subsides before proceeding.

2. Fill the top of the double boiler with part of the coating; place it over the hot, but not steaming, water. The bottom of the vessel must not touch the water.

3. Stir the coating from time to time to speed the melting. Once it begins to melt, add the rest of the coating to it.

4. *Do not cook the mixture at any time.* If the water needs to be reheated, remove the top pan filled with the coating and repeat step 1. You may need to add more water as it boils away. Keep the coating over the hot water only until it is warm and creamy (110° F.–120° F.). Cool it slightly, stirring occasionally.

5. Refill the bottom of the double boiler with warm water (105° F.–110° F.), this time submerging the top pan into the water, as described for melting chocolate. This holding temperature will maintain the coating in an ideal, fluid state throughout the working period.

The Final Cooling Procedure

The acceptable cooling range for compound coatings is decidedly broader than that for chocolate and permits the conservative use of the freezer as well as the refrigerator to speed the cooling time.

Use these units to cool the coating, not to freeze it. Overchilled pieces that survive such careless handling without cracking will have sticky, dull surfaces when they return to room temperature. Never add such pieces to a fresh batch of melted coating; you may contaminate the whole mixture, if you do.

CHOCOLATE AND COMPOUND COATING AS AN ART MEDIUM

This chapter and the next four explain the basic techniques used in chocolate artistry. Use these chapters as reference pages to guide you through the hundreds of creative experiences that are described in the subsequent chapters.

To simplify the reading of the text, whenever the word *chocolate* is used in the directions, it should be interpreted to mean chocolate, cocoa butter white coating, or compound coating. Most techniques can be accomplished in any of those three media, and I believe that the choice should rest with the artist. In cases where a color is needed to create a special effect, the term *coating* may be used to imply cocoa butter coating or compound coating.

The incompatibility problem (coatings have a tendency to bloom when piped directly on chocolate surfaces) that exists between the popular lauric-fat-based coatings and real chocolate presents a dilemma of grand proportions to the artist who would like to combine the best qualities of both media in some decorative work. Here are some suggestions for getting around the problem:

1. Pipe the designs directly onto the real chocolate surface with compound coating that is 90°F. Higher temperatures are more likely to cause bloom to develop. Store the finished pieces in a cool room.

2. Pipe the compound coating designs onto wax paper as described in Chapter 5. Attach them to the chocolate surface with real chocolate or compound coating.

3. Pipe the designs directly onto the chocolate surface with white cocoa butter coating rather than compound coating. It can be dyed with powdered coloring and used exactly like compound coating. Remember to temper it, however.

4. Pipe the compound coating designs directly onto a compound coating surface rather than a chocolate one.

2
Molding Procedures for Chocolate and Compound Coating

Molding your first piece of chocolate is a magical experience. So is molding your 500th piece! Seeing that warm, creamy mass of chocolate quickly transformed into a cool, definable shape does indeed have an aura of mystery about it. Facts are facts, though. As magical a phenomenon as it may seem, with a little know-how, the process can actually be quite simple.

Successful molding is dependent on proper tempering of the chocolate. For that reason the previous chapter's lessons must be mastered first. When untempered chocolate is deposited in a mold it is noticeably slow to dry and extremely difficult to release; tempered chocolate, on the other hand, sets quickly and falls out of the mold with little coaxing. Until you are confident in your tempering skills, it is important to test your accuracy, as described in Chapter 1, before filling the molds. It will save you time and allow you to avoid an unproductive molding maneuver.

If you choose to mold with one of the compound coatings rather than chocolate, you will find the procedure as easy as child's play. Compound coating is so simple to use that it is indeed recommended for children's projects. Success in molding with it, even for the first time, gives child and adult alike a marvelous

feeling of satisfaction and a sense of real accomplishment.

Whether you choose chocolate or coating, you will find molding an exciting art form. It requires no previous candy-making experience and no artistic ability. Best of all, you need very little equipment to get started. Assemble a pot of tempered chocolate or melted coating, a spoon, and a molding receptacle of one kind or another, and you are ready to go.

GENERAL MOLDING TIPS

The following pages describe in detail a broad variety of procedures used to mold chocolate and compound coating. These general statements apply to all of them.

1. When real chocolate is used for molding, it must be in a tempered state.
2. If compound coating is used, it should be melted to a smooth and creamy consistency.
3. Mold in a warm room (80°F.), if possible.
4. Use a large spoon to deposit chocolate into large mold cavities and smaller ones for small cavities. Iced tea spoons and infant feeding spoons are useful small sizes.

5. Whenever possible, use a shiny, scratch-free surface for molding chocolate. Chocolate mirrors the finish used to mold it. Scratches on the mold's surface will not only appear on the face of the chocolate but may inhibit the easy release of the molded piece as well.

6. **All molding surfaces must be clean and dry. Buff them with a soft, lint-free cloth, if necessary.**

7. All molding devices (molds, cookie sheets, tart shells, etc.) must be at room temperature before chocolate is deposited in them. If the refrigerator or freezer is used for cooling, allow time for warming up in between repetitive molding procedures.

Note: A hand-held dryer may be used for quick warm-ups.

8. Always rap the filled mold on the counter several times to eliminate the air bubbles and flatten the chocolate. Remove the excess chocolate with a metal spatula.

9. Cool real chocolate as described in Chapter 1. Extend the normal cooling time in the refrigerator when molding chocolate in extra-large molds. Remove clips, if used, midway through cooling.

10. Cool compound coating in the refrigerator or freezer only until set. Remove promptly.

KITCHEN CABINET MOLDS

Your kitchen cabinets contain an endless variety of potential molds. Purists believe that chocolate should be used only in molds specifically reserved for chocolate use, because chocolate is susceptible to foreign odors and tastes that may have permeated multiple-use molds. There is a good deal of truth in this, but I believe that the lay person can find many articles in the kitchen that, though used for other purposes, are odor-free and taste-free.

MOLDING WITH COOKIE CUTTERS

I discovered a long time ago that cookie cutters could be used to mold chocolate in an endless variety of shapes to make lollipops, placecards, cake decorations, and more. Before I began

collecting the candy molds that I now use so often, cutters were the only things that I used. I continue to use them for many of my favorite projects.

The two types of cookie cutters that lend themselves to the molding of chocolate are the tinplate or plastic open-ended ones and the closed-top cutters that have a design embossed inside their cavities. The open-ended ones are easiest of all to use and certainly the ones that I would suggest you use in your first attempts.

Open-Ended Cookie Cutters

When molding with this type of cookie cutter, it is important to have a shiny, scratch-free surface on which to place the cutters. A new cookie sheet that shows no signs of wear and tear is perfect for molding. It should be slick, not non-stick-coated and sized to fit into your refrigerator or freezer. A sheet of wax paper cut to fit the bottom of a scratched cookie sheet is an acceptable substitute for a shiny, new one if you do not mind a matte finish on your molded pieces.

The first time that I molded with open-ended cutters I used some very large ones that did not lie flat on the cookie sheet. I worried that some of the chocolate would run out of the bottom (which it did) but was pleased to see that, once cooled and set, the excess runoff, along with any other drips or spills, broke off easily and could be remelted and used again.

Method: Spoon, Rap, Cool, Release

1. Arrange clean, dry, open-ended cookie cutters on a clean, dry cookie sheet.

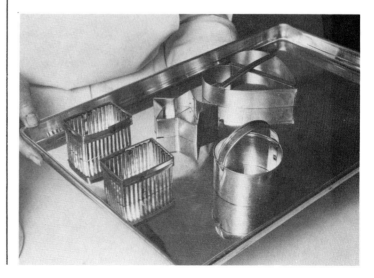

2. *Spoon* enough melted chocolate into the cutters to cover the bottoms of the cavities. Ease it into the corners with the tip of the spoon. The more you fill the cutter, the thicker the piece will be. It will take some experimenting to determine how much chocolate to deposit in each cutter. A two-inch molded piece should be about ¼ inch thick. If the molded piece is extralarge in diameter, additional thickness may be necessary to give it strength.

3. *Rap* the cookie sheet sharply on the counter several times. This will encourage the chocolate to flow into all of the crevices of the cutter and level itself to make a smooth surface. If it does not smooth itself out, the chocolate is probably too cool. Do not worry about it. The bumpy side is the back side of the finished piece. Just shave off the

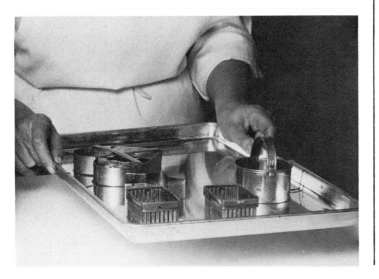

rough spots with a paring knife once the piece has set and been unmolded. Adjust the temperature of the chocolate according to the directions in Chapter 1 before continuing to mold more pieces.

4. *Cool* the filled cookie sheet until the chocolate is completely set. The time it takes to do this is determined by the size of the piece, the thickness of the piece, and the temperature of the freezer, refrigerator, or room. In the case of real chocolate the setting time is determined largely by proper or improper tempering procedures.

5. Once the chocolate is set, use the palm of your hand to press down firmly on the top of the cutter. This action will sever most of the surplus chocolate that has run out.

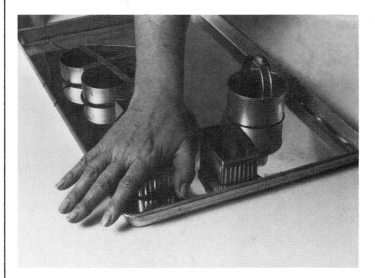

6. Grasp both sides of the cutter and pull up on one side only. The chocolate should release cleanly and rather easily from the cookie sheet. If it does not, it is an indication that it has not cooled enough. Continue to cool it for a few more minutes and try it again.

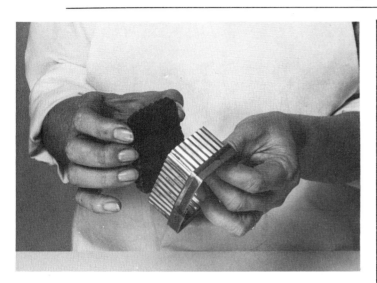

7. The molded surface touching the cookie sheet is the face (front) of the piece. Push the chocolate out of the cutter from its back side without fingering the face to prevent your fingerprints from showing and spoiling the shiny surface.

Closed-Top Cookie Cutters

The closed-top plastic or metal cookie cutters are not always easy to use. Some, with many deep, close-together grooves, cannot be used at all. Because these cutters will be filled with chocolate, examine them to be sure that no opening exists under the handle in the top before even considering molding in them. Pieces molded in these cutters are usually very thin, so they should never be allowed to get too cold in the freezer or refrigerator or they will crack even before they are unmolded. Do not try to unmold them before they have had time to set, however, or they will stick to the cutters. Therein lies the dilemma—they must be chilled enough to release from the mold but not chilled enough to make them crack.

The handle on the top of this type of cutter prevents it from lying flat, as it must, once filled.

Instead of placing these cutters on a cookie sheet, rest them directly on the metal refrigerator rack (or a cake rack). The handle will fit nicely between the prongs of the rack.

Method: Spoon, Scrape, Rap, Cool, Release

1. *Spoon* only enough chocolate into each cutter to come up level with its edges.

2. *Scrape* off the excess chocolate with a metal spatula, if necessary.
3. *Rap* the cutter on the counter once or twice to release the air bubbles.
4. *Cool* until set. If you use the freezer, be sure to remove the cutter promptly once chilled.
5. Invert the cutter and slap it into the palm of your hand once or twice. If it does not *release*, proceed with Step 6.

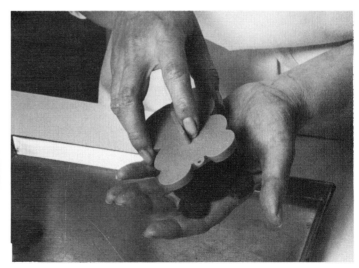

6. Allow the cooled piece to warm slightly at room temperature. Now grasp the sides of the cutter and gently pry them outward in several places. Gently ease the molded piece out. If it does not release, it may simply need more cooling. Need I tell you that patience is the key word in this particular molding procedure?

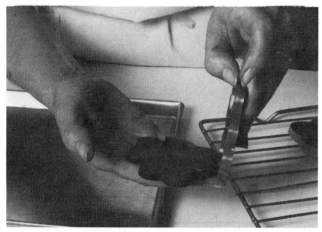

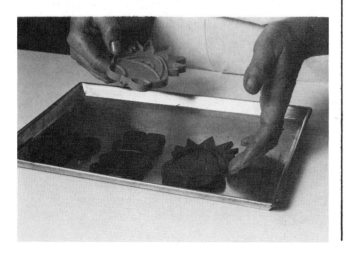

MOLDING WITH TART SHELLS

Another kitchen cabinet staple is the tart shell. These metal shells come in a wide variety of sizes, shapes, and designs. Depending on how they are ultimately to be used, they may be molded solid or hollow.

Method for Molding a Solid Tart Shell: Spoon, Rap, Cool, Release

1. *Spoon* the melted chocolate into the clean, dry tart shell, filling it almost to the top. Scrape off the excess chocolate with a metal spatula.

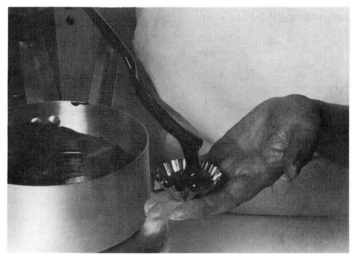

2. *Rap* the mold on the counter several times to release the air bubbles.

3. *Cool* it until set. Because of its depth, this type of molding will take longer to cool completely than the cookie-cutter-molded pieces.
4. To *release* it from the shell, invert the tart shell into the palm of your hand. It should release easily. If it does not, continue to cool it until it does.

Methods for Molding a Hollow Tart Shell

Method I: Spoon, Rotate, Invert, Cool, Release

1. *Spoon* a small amount of chocolate into the bottom of the tart shell.

2. *Rotate* the mold so as to coat its interior with chocolate; add more, if necessary. The back of a spoon or a small brush may be used to facilitate this step.
3. *Invert* the coated shell over the pot of chocolate to allow the excess chocolate to flow back into it freely. Vigorously shake it back and forth in that position until all but a thin layer of chocolate remains. Use your fingertip or a metal spatula to free the top rim of chocolate.

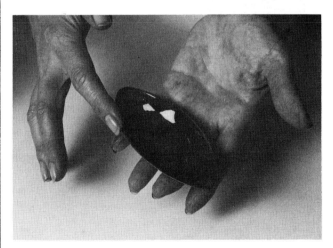

4. *Cool* the shell as desired only until the chocolate loses its wet look and appears set. Repeat the procedure for a second layer of chocolate whenever extra thickness is desired. Small shells usually require only one layer of chocolate and should be cooled to completion after the first application. In either case, guard against overchilling the thin layer of chocolate.

Method II: Fill, Cool, Invert, Cool, Release (for Thicker Shells)

1. *Fill* the cavity to the top with melted chocolate as if to mold a solid piece.
2. *Cool* compound coating pieces in the freezer and chocolate ones in the refrigerator or in a *very* cool room (50° F.–55° F.) for approximately five minutes. You will notice the piece beginning to set along the perimeter of the mold. The center will be noticeably loose and will shake when the mold is jiggled. Ideally, the set portion will be about ⅛ inch wide. Realistically, you may find that it has already set to a ¼-inch width. Freezer and refrigerator temperatures vary widely, especially if you are opening and closing the door often. Do not despair if the center does not jiggle. It is possible that a crust may have formed across the entire top of the mold. Puncture the center with a knife. You may find that under the top crust there is still enough loose chocolate to make the piece salvageable. Proceed with the next step.
3. For compound coating shells: *Invert* the partially set mold over the pot of coating and the loose coating will run into it freely, leaving you with a hollow shell. You may need to define the inner edge of the coating with a small knife.

4. For real chocolate shells: To avoid contaminating the pot of tempered chocolate, *invert* the mold over a marble slab or wax-paper-covered counter and let the surplus chocolate fall onto it. Shake the mold to speed the process. Once set, this surplus chocolate may be remelted.
5. *Cool* the shells without overchilling them.
6. To unmold, invert the shell into the palm of your hand and shake it gently. If it does not *release,* and you are sure that it has cooled long enough, use your index and third finger, pressed against the chocolate, to pull it up and out of the mold.

Method III: Freeze, Immerse, Push Down (for *Very* Thin Shells)

This unusual chocolate molding technique caused me to gasp in horror (and then in delight) when I first saw the chocolate queen, Maida Heatter, demonstrate it in class several years ago. It contains an element of risk, so please be careful.

1. Fill the tart shells with water and place them in the freezer. When the water is nearly frozen solid, stand a toothpick in the center of the ice. Allow the water to freeze hard.

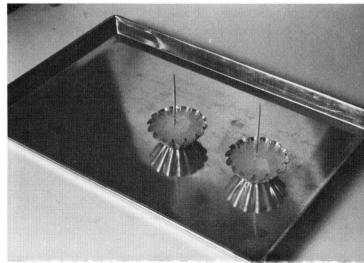

2. Grasp a filled, metal tart shell in the palm of your warm hand for several seconds. Then hold it by the toothpick and tap it lightly on the counter to release the "speared" ice cube from the shell. Promptly return the released cubes to the freezer and leave them there until needed.

3. Working with one cube at a time, grasp it by the toothpick and quickly plunge it (yes, I said plunge it) into a cup of melted chocolate, immersing it only up to its top edge. Do not allow the chocolate level to rise above the top edge of the ice. Lift the cube out of the chocolate bath immediately.

4. Hold the cube about one inch above the counter; use your thumb to push downward gently on the top edges of the chocolate in several places. A very, very thin chocolate

shell will drop off the ice. The floor of the shell's cavity may be wet, but it will air dry. It is sometimes possible to use the ice cube more than once, if you work quickly. The risk lies in getting water into the chocolate. Avoid that at all costs.

Note: Leftover chocolate from this procedure should never be added to the virgin stock or reserved for subsequent projects, as it is likely to contain some moisture.

MOLDING IN COOKIE SHEETS AND CAKE PANS

Molding slabs of chocolate in cookie sheets or cake pans is another technique that you will find most useful when you begin to construct large centerpieces and architectural extravaganzas. Best results come from molding in large, scratch-free, shiny, new ones. If more than one slab will be required to complete your project, it is wise to mold each sheet to the same depth. This is best accomplished by determining the weight of the first slab and molding the rest by weighing the chocolate as explained in the directions that follow.

Method: Fill, Smooth, Rap, Cool, Score Top Edge, Cool, Release

1. Place an empty cookie sheet or pan squarely in the center of a sturdy kitchen scale. Adjust the scale to the weight of the pan. Pour the chocolate into the center of the cookie sheet until the scale registers the predetermined weight of the chocolate required. A 12-by-18-inch cookie sheet usually requires approximately 2¼ pounds of chocolate.

2. Jiggle the pan to *smooth* out the chocolate and use an offset or bent metal spatula or spoon to spread it evenly across the pan.

3. *Rap* the pan on the counter several times and *cool* it briefly.

4. Once the top is firm, *free the top edge of the chocolate* from the sides of the pan with a sharp knife. Do not cut down to the bottom of the pan. Continue to *cool* the sheet. Watch carefully so as not to overchill it, or cracking will result. Even if a crack does occur, it is usually possible to salvage some portions of the slab, so do not be too quick to melt it down.

5. After approximately 30–35 minutes in the refrigerator (less time in the freezer), invert the pan onto a large, flat cardboard or an inverted cookie sheet. The piece should drop out of the pan easily. If it does not, do not force it out. Chill it for a few more minutes.

6. Once released from the mold, the slab should be allowed to return to room temperature before being used.

Note: Do not be alarmed to see a shadowlike blemish appear on the surface of your molded slab. It is an almost inevitable result of the "dead" spot found on flat-bottomed molds. To make it less noticeable, use a soft brush and horizontal strokes to buff the surface gently. It will diminish the shine, but leave a lustrous look of patina in its place.

MORE KITCHEN CABINET MOLDS

A quick look through your cupboards should convince you that many potential molds are there awaiting discovery. How many of the following items do you have stored away someplace? How many others can you add to this list?

1. Gelatin molds, especially the newer plastic ones
2. Metal pie pans and trays
3. Pizza pans, including aluminum, disposable ones
4. Stainless steel mixing bowls
5. Stainless steel platters
6. Cupcake pans
7. Plastic refrigerator or freezer containers
8. Toaster oven broiler pan (This item must be reserved solely for chocolate molding. Mine is used to mold a large greeting card and is sometimes used as a base for centerpiece extravaganzas.)

CAKE DECORATING MOLDS

In addition to the above molds, there are several cake decorating items normally used to mold gum paste that I enjoy using for chocolate projects. They are available through Wilton Enterprises and through cake decorating/candy-making supply shops across the country.

1. Baroque gum paste mold kit featuring seven thin designs, including wheat, a shell, a cameo, and a crest. (Wilton #1906-K-1299)
2. People molds. The kit includes a nine-inch man, an eight-inch woman, and seven-inch and six-inch children. I love them all! (Wilton #1906-D-5154)

You will think of more potential molds as your interest is aroused. Be open to new ideas and molding opportunities. Expect a failure now and then. One word of caution, though, before your imagination runs away with you: Be sure that the molding surface that you are using with chocolate is food-safe; many plastics (some toys, boxes, etc.) are not.

CANDY MOLDS

Sooner or later an insatiable desire to broaden your molding vistas will push you beyond your kitchen cabinets and into a never-ending search for "legitimate" candy molds. The search began for me in the dark corners of antique shops where, on hands and knees, I foraged through dusty boxes of metal molds looking for any that still had shiny, scratch-free insides with no traces of rust. Patience and perseverance are needed, but be assured that marvelous antique molds do still exist, not only in antique shops but also in Grandma's attic and in flea markets around the world.

There is something special about molding with an antique metal mold. It has nothing to do with any superiority over its newer plastic or metal counterparts. As a matter of fact, it may not be as good! Rather, it's a matter of sentiment, I suppose. Images of storybook candy shops and Willy Wonka come to mind whenever I use them. A mold that you know has been filling Christmas stockings and Easter baskets for years and is still capable of filling them for a long time gives it an almost ageless ability to link the chocoholics of old with those of today and tomorrow.

It is important, however, to temper your nostalgia with a little realism. Antique molds can be very expensive. Unless you are buying a mold strictly for its sentimental value as a collector's item, its molding surface should be examined very carefully. Does it show signs of rust or pitting? Does the molding surface shine? Is it dented or scratched? Hollow molds should be purchased with their original clips and should be checked for tight closures. Only then, after a thorough examination, should you purchase an expensive mold.

To the credit of modern-day ingenuity, many of these old metal molds are now being manufactured of high-quality plastic approved by the FDA and offered at more moderate prices than their metal counterparts. And, of course, the mold designers have taken us from the charming Kewpie dolls of old to whatever is currently in vogue. Collectors today include among their favorites the signs of our times—T-shirts, blue jeans, Snoopy, the "Sesame Street" characters, and others.

Advantages of Plastic Molds

Besides being less expensive, plastic molds have certain other advantages over metal ones. The transparent ones enable you to spot the existence of air bubbles, which, if undetected, would mar the appearance of the finished piece. The frosted look of the plastic tells you when the filling has dried enough to permit unmolding. In addition, there is a certain degree of elasticity in plastic that does not exist in metal. This means that the mold can be flexed for easier removal of the molded pieces. Most plastic molds cannot be dented, as metal ones can, even if they are accidentally dropped. They have well-defined designs, cool fast, and return to room temperature quickly. Best of all, they never rust! Though the food-safe gauge used in the manufacture of candy molds can vary quite a bit from company to company, most major manufacturers sell quality molds that give long and dependable service.

Care of Plastic Molds

Before using a mold for the first time, it should be washed by hand (not in the dishwasher) with very warm water (never higher than 140°F.); rinsed in clear, cool water; and wiped dry with a soft, lint-free cloth. A mild detergent may be used this first time, but it is very important to avoid the use of strongly scented soaps, as the odor may transmit itself to the mold and ultimately taint the candy molded in it. Following the initial use of a new mold, it should rarely be necessary to use soap to wash it ever again. Merely run warm water over the mold until all traces of adhering chocolate run off freely. Above all, *never* use anything abrasive when cleaning the molds as it will surely mar the molding surface permanently and forever produce imperfectly molded pieces of chocolate. Though it is not ordinarily necessary to wash the mold after each use, it may occasionally be necessary to buff the molding surface with a soft, lint-free cloth to rid it of any residue that may remain after unmolding a piece prematurely. If the residue is not removed, it will mar the face of the next piece molded.

When storing plastic molds, special care should be taken to set them down in such a way as to prevent them from bending out of shape. The molds will warp if stored haphazardly. Always store them in a cool, dry location. Treat them with loving care and they should last for many years.

Care of Metal Molds

Metal molds should be treated in much the same manner as plastic ones. In addition, special care should be taken to store them carefully to avoid scratching their molding surfaces. Because they are subject to rusting, they should always be perfectly dry when put away and stored away from excessive dampness.

Flat Molds

Molds, whether made of metal or plastic, are classified as being flat or hollow. Flat molds are sheets containing cavities of varying sizes and designs. They produce molded pieces that have a dimensional face (front) and a flat back. These are often molds that contain duplicates of one design or a combination of several different designs on one sheet. One sheet may contain four flop-eared bunnies or a six-bunny assortment, for example; other sheets may contain one large flop-eared bunny. Some sheets may even contain

the front and back of a figure to enable you to join them for a three-dimensional look. The latter type has the potential for being converted into a hollow-type mold, if you wish. This procedure is discussed on page 34.

Molding Procedure for Flat Molds

Method I: Spoon, Rap, Cool, Release

1. *Spoon* the chocolate into each cavity on the sheet, taking particular care to underfill slightly rather than overfill each one. Once unmolded, the "feet" on overfilled pieces may be trimmed with a knife, but it is a tedious task at best.

Note: Some flat plastic molds are manufactured with a bothersome plastic ridge along their edges. To eliminate the possibility of overfilling the cavities on such molds, remove the ridges with sharp scissors. After filling the cavities, draw a metal spatula across the perfectly flat surface of the mold to rid it of the surplus chocolate. The surplus may, of course, be reused.

2. Sharply rap the filled sheet on the counter

several times. Raise the plastic mold and examine the appearance of its surface. Do you detect any air bubbles? Work them out with a soft brush, if necessary.

3. Cool the filled mold until the chocolate has set and is hard. Do not allow the pieces cooled in the refrigerator or freezer to get too cold.
4. Invert the sheet onto a large cardboard or cookie sheet; the molded pieces should drop out easily. If they do not, rap the inverted mold on the counter. Plastic molds may be

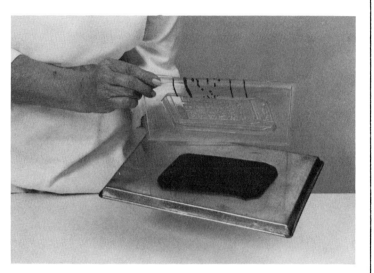

flexed, and the molded pieces will fall out. If they still do not release, continue to cool them until they do. Be suspicious of unsuccessful tempering if real chocolate pieces refuse to release.

Method II (Hollow Shells for Filled Chocolates)

1. Use a candy funnel or a spoon to fill the cavities.

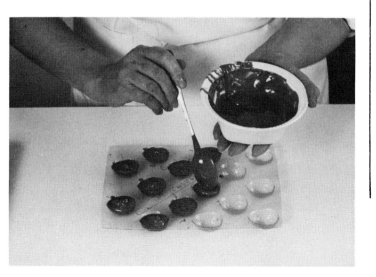

2. Vigorously rap the flat sheet on the counter to eliminate all of the air bubbles. Let the chocolate stand in the molds briefly.
3. Invert the sheet over a marble slab or a wax-paper-covered counter to allow the surplus chocolate to fall onto it. Shake the sheet in a circular motion to speed the process and to produce chocolate walls that are coated evenly.

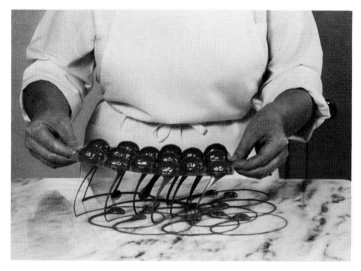

4. Turn the mold right side up and allow it to rest briefly. Use a metal spatula to scrape the top of the mold clean.
5. The coated cavities are then cooled and released from the mold or cooled, filled, sealed with more chocolate, cooled again, and released from the mold.

Flat Lollipop Molds: Spoon, Rap, Position Stick, Rotate Stick, Cool, Release

1. Follow steps 1 and 2 in Method I.
2. Position the lollipop stick so that it rests in the groove provided for it in the cavity.

3. Rotate it. This will automatically coat it with chocolate and assure a firm hold.
4. Cool and release from the mold.

Hollow Molds

Hollow molds, also available in metal or plastic, are comprised of two pieces with either a closed or an open bottom. They are often sold with accompanying clips, which securely hold the pieces together in their proper position. If your molds do not have clips, you may substitute paper clips for small, thin plastic molds, or metal stationery clips for larger, thicker ones. These are the molds that are responsible for the three-dimensional shapes (either hollow or solid) that we admire so often on candy shop shelves. When purchasing these molds it is important to be certain that the two pieces are mates and not duplicates; otherwise the front and back pieces will not match.

Hollow Molding with a Closed-Bottom Mold: Fill, Rap, Close, Rotate while Cooling, Release

1. Fill one half (the deepest side, if there is one) of a two-piece hollow mold with chocolate.

2. Rap the mold on the counter to release the air bubbles.
3. Attach the unfilled half of the mold to it, lining up the cavities perfectly and locking the alignment pins, if the mold has them. Securely clip the pieces together on all sides.

4. Now rotate the mold several times to coat the interior of the other half of the mold

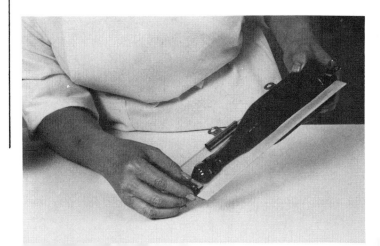

with chocolate. A plastic mold will enable you to see whether or not all parts of the mold are covered.

5. To cool, position the mold, newly-filled side down, for several minutes. After a few minutes, reverse the position of the mold and continue this frequent rotating until the chocolate appears firm on the surface. Release the clips and continue to cool it until completely set. Cooling times will vary.

6. To release the chocolate from the mold, remove the back piece first. Resistance may indicate the need for further cooling.

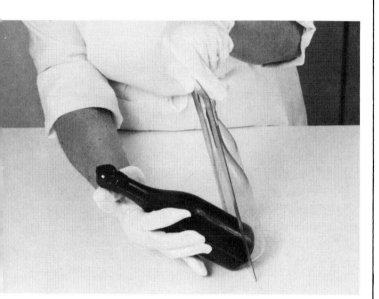

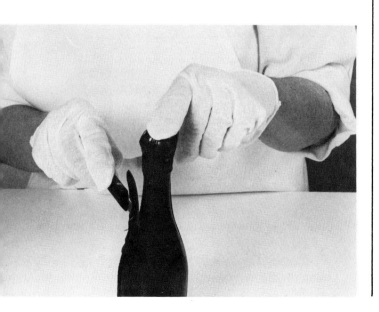

Solid Molding with a Closed-Bottom Hollow Mold: Fill, Join Mold, Chill, Release

1. Fill both sides of the mold to the top of the cavities with chocolate or *cool* coating. One side should be filled more generously than the other to prevent splits in the seams of the molded piece.

2. This step is not difficult, but it does take courage the first time you do it. Grasp the filled molds in the palms of both hands. Line up the inside edges of both pieces so that they are touching, paying particular attention to the alignment locks (if the molds have them) in each piece that come together for a good closure. Now calmly flip one mold half over onto the other, making sure that the locks are in place. It

sounds more difficult than it actually is. Trust me.

Note: If the mold has straight-sided margins, you may wish to tape the two pieces together to facilitate this step. See page 34 for taping instructions.

3. Squeeze the pieces together. This can be messy. But take heart: all the excess chocolate that has run out of the cavities and may even be running out of the molds and onto your counter will not affect the molded piece. Once cooled, all of those bits and pieces may be remelted. Secure the mold well with the clips.

4. Cool the mold front side down. Remove the clips when the chocolate's surface appears firm or midway through the estimated cooling period. Setting time will vary with this type of molding. Experience will be your best guide, but common sense will help, too. If the piece is small in diameter and depth, it could be ready in as few as 15 minutes. Larger pieces may take an hour or even longer.

5. To determine its unmolding readiness, first examine the surface of the plastic mold; it will appear frosted throughout. Lift off the back half of the mold. If it resists, cool it a little longer.

6. Handle the unmolded piece as little as possible (or use gloves) so as not to fingerprint its surface. Allow it to return to room temperature before trimming off any rough edges acquired during the messy molding procedure.

Solid Molding with an Open-Bottom Mold: Join Pieces, Fill, Cool, Release

1. Assemble the mold by securing the two pieces with as many clips as necessary for a tight closure.

2. Prepare a cooling place where the mold can stand without toppling. Because most inverted, filled molds do not have flat bases to stand on, a rack of some kind is helpful. I use the metal racks in my refrigerator or freezer. A cake rack may also be used. Or stand the mold in a deep pan or box that has been filled generously with raw beans, rice, or Spanish peanuts.

3. Fill the mold to the top with chocolate and rap it on the counter several times.

4. Cool it upright, propped if necessary. Release the clips midway through the cooling period.

5. To unmold, lift off the back side of the mold first. If the mold does not come away easily, continue to cool it until it does.

Three-Dimensional Molding with a Flat Mold

Sometimes a flat mold will contain the front and back of a figure. With this type of mold you can make a three-dimensional figure. Here are three ways to use the mold. The third method requires modification of the mold itself.

Method I

1. Follow the same procedure as previously described for molding with flat molds (Method I) paying particular attention to step 1. It is imperative that the cavities *not* be overfilled. I recommend scraping off the

excess filling with a metal spatula before cooling the pieces.
2. Once unmolded, allow the chocolate to return to room temperature.
3. Adhere the two sides—the front and back of the figure—with chocolate. Use this

chocolate "adhesive" sparingly, or it will ooze out of the sides.
4. Allow both pieces to set before handling.

Method II

1. Using a flat mold that contains a front and back, carefully fill one of the cavities with chocolate, being sure not to overfill it. Scrape off the excess with a metal spatula to be sure that the top is perfectly level.
2. Cool the filled mold until set and release the piece from the mold. Allow it to return to room temperature.
3. Fill the other half of the mold.
4. Lay the previously molded piece directly on the melted-chocolate-filled cavity. It may be necessary to press down slightly on the

previously molded half to be sure that it is aligned on all sides.

5. Cool and release from the mold. Voilá—a three-dimensional form from a flat mold!

Method III

1. Cut the plastic mold in half.
2. Remove the plastic ridge on the outside edge of the mold, if it exists, as described on page 28. Align the two cut pieces (the front and back of the figure) so that the cavities match up perfectly.
3. Trim the excess plastic surrounding the cavities to within one inch of them. One of the one-inch margins must have a straight outside edge. The cavities must still be aligned perfectly. *This is very important.*
4. Use a strip of heavy one-inch tape, cut the length of the straight-edged margin, to tape the two pieces together as if to bind a book.

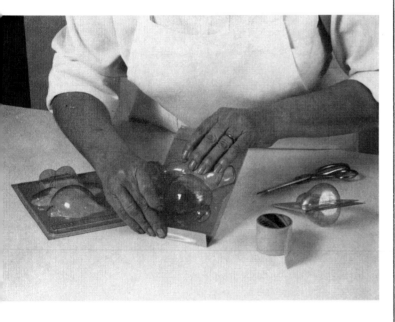

5. Check to see that the cavities still match up perfectly when closed. If they do not, remove the tape and repeat steps 3 and 4 until they do.
6. Follow the molding instructions for molding with a hollow, closed-bottom mold.

Painting Molds Prior to Molding

Once you have discovered the world of candy molds, you will surely want to take advantage of the following popular procedure for "painting" in the details of the molds with various-colored compound coatings prior to molding the finished piece. This is a simple way to mold and decorate a piece of candy without the aid of a decorating bag. It is particularly recommended for those without decorating skills and is a marvelous technique for children to use.

The Materials

Assemble the following:

1. *Several artists' brushes.* Be sure that they do not shed their bristles easily.
2. *A variety of colored compound coatings.* They may be purchased commercially colored, or you may prefer to dye your own. See instructions for coloring the coatings in Chapter 3.
3. *Several small containers to hold the colored coatings.* Widemouthed glass jars with lids work well and enable you to store the leftover coating for future painting projects. Ovenproof glass measuring cups and glass custard cups also work well.
4. *A shallow pan partially filled with warm water (which will need to be replenished from time to time) or an electric fry pan partially filled with warm water and set to its lowest setting.* To maintain the fluid, warm state of the coatings throughout your project, submerge the filled jars in either of these pans while you are working with them. For small painting projects you may prefer to hold your coatings in their fluid state in the sectioned compartments of an electric baby feeding dish or an egg-poaching pan.

Perhaps the most important piece of equipment that I own for my chocolate work is my Salton Electric Hot-Tray. I would select it without hesitation above all of the aforementioned choices for keeping compound coating fluid during my working hours. It is turned on early in the morning and serves me throughout the day by maintaining my individual cups and parchment bags of colored coatings in a melted state, ready to use at a moment's notice.

Method for Painting Molds

1. Dip a brush into the colored coating and carefully paint the interior of the mold in the appropriate areas. Use a different brush for each color.

3. Repeat step 2 with each subsequent color.
4. When all of the details have been painted in, fill in the remainder of the mold with the coating of your choice.
5. Cool and release from the mold.

Note: Decorators, proficient in the use of the parchment bag, may prefer to apply the various compound-coating color details with the bag, rather than with a brush. It is my personal preference.

2. Allow one color to set briefly before painting another color, if they touch each other in the design. This setting may be done in a cool room or *very briefly* in the refrigerator or freezer. Caution! If the painted area is allowed to get too cold, it will pop out completely, or it will contract and the rest of the coating will seep under it and spoil the appearance of the final product.

3
The Basic Tools of the Chocolate Decorator

Devotees of chocolate would most certainly agree that chocolate does not *need* to be prettied up to make it taste good. It is one of those rare culinary treasures that is inherently delicious. Chocolate decorators believe, however, that a flourish or two can make a good thing even better.

You cannot apply flourish until you assemble a basic inventory of decorating tools and learn the fundamental techniques explained in the following pages. Approach the next three chapters with an open mind; you *can* master these lessons. Refer to them often as you progress from one project to another, and soon, as your confidence builds, you will find that you need to look to them less and less for help.

A decorating bag is unquestionably the single most important piece of equipment used to decorate chocolate. It holds the icing or chocolate and enables the decorator to pipe out designs or accomplish some of the less creative maneuvers such as filling cups and/or molds neatly and quickly.

DECORATING BAGS

Ready-Made Bags

Ready-made bags are available in sizes ranging from small (eight inch) to large (18 inch) to superlarge sizes. I recommend the 10-inch size for most decorating jobs. A 12- or 14-inch bag is handy, though, for large batches of heavy mixtures such as truffles or ganache.

These bags are usually made of plastic-coated canvas, nylon, or polyester. I like lightweight polyester bags that are soft yet strong and very pliable. Wilton Enterprises' Featherweight Decorating Bags are my favorites.

Ready-made bags must be inverted and washed thoroughly in warm, sudsy water upon completion of each decorating project. It is not unusual for their interiors to become stained when they are used to hold strong-colored icing (pink, red, or black). Because the stain will affect light-colored icings that you later use in them, you may need to reserve the stained bags for dark-colored icing. A periodic soaking in a bowl of warm water and laundry bleach will remove most of the color from the bag. It is especially important after such a procedure to rinse the bags well in clear water. Always dry them thoroughly before storing or they will deteriorate quickly.

To utilize the polyester bag to its fullest is to use it in conjunction with a coupler—the decorator's ultimate time-saving invention. The coupler is a plastic nozzle that is inserted into the decorating bag in such a way as to protrude through the narrow opening of the bag. The decorating tube is then attached to it from the outside of the bag and held in place with a coupler ring. Being able to change tubes in the middle of a procedure without having to empty the bag is a real convenience!

When a ready-made bag is first purchased, its opening is too narrow to fit the coupler and must be cut. The cutting procedure follows.

Cutting Procedure for New Bags

1. Using a pencil and a ruler, mark off ¾ inch from the narrow end of the new bag. Cut off that piece with a pair of scissors.

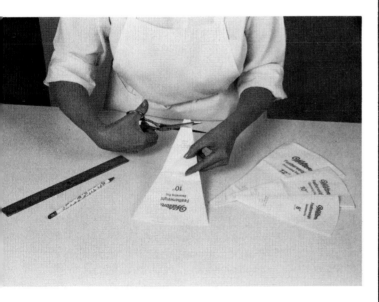

2. Insert the nozzle part of the coupler into the bag, pushing it down as far as it will go with your thumb. Check to see if any of the threads on the coupler show (they won't yet).
3. Remove the coupler and cut off another narrow piece. Push the coupler back into position. Do the threads show?

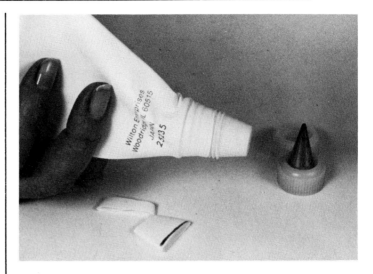

4. Continue these narrow cuts only until *one* or *two* threads of the coupler show. It is important to use restraint with the scissors, as too drastic a cut will leave an irreparably large opening. Should this ever happen, reserve the bag for other culinary purposes and use one of the large-sized decorating tubes in it to pipe whipped cream, mashed potatoes, etc.

Note: Once you have cut one bag correctly, it may be used as a pattern to cut others of the same size and brand.

How to Fill a Ready-Made Bag

1. Insert the coupler into the bag, pushing it down into position with your thumb.
2. Attach the appropriate decorating tube to the end of the coupler and secure it with the coupler ring.
3. Cuff the top of the bag to facilitate filling.
4. Use a metal spatula or spoon to *half-fill* the bag with icing. Pressing the spatula against the side of the bag as you pull it out each time will keep the icing deep in the bag where it belongs.

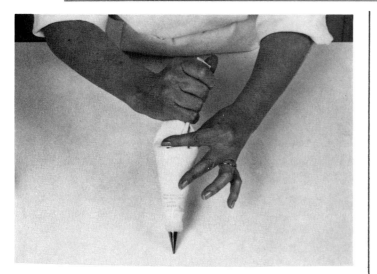

5. Push down on the outside of the bag to compact the icing and twist the top of the bag closed.

Note: It is important to "burp" the bag each time it is refilled with icing to release any air pockets trapped inside. To do this, hold the opening of the tube over the bowl and squeeze the bag until the air is expelled.

Parchment Decorating Bags

In chocolate art work, parchment decorating bags, or cones, are as important as polyester ready-made ones since they are used to pipe chocolate. Parchment is a grease-resistant, strong yet pliable paper that is used in a variety of ways in the kitchen. Perhaps you have used it to line baking pans to eliminate sticking and messy cleanups. The obvious advantage of the parchment bag over the nondisposable kind is that there is no cleanup. The used bag is thrown away. There really is no acceptable substitute for it, so please resist the temptation to use wax paper or butcher paper or anything else because you will likely be disappointed with the results.

Parchment paper may be purchased in rolls, rectangles, rounds, or precut triangles. The triangles are specifically meant to be rolled into cones; the other shapes may also be rolled, but they require a little more dexterity.

How to Shape a Parchment Bag

Courage, now. This simple procedure can be frustrating, discouraging, and downright demeaning until you get the idea. Awkwardness is in no way a sign of artistic deficiency, so keep trying until you are able to roll a cone easily.

1. Actually letter a practice parchment triangle as shown in the photo.
2. Hold the triangle between the thumb and index finger of your left hand at position D.
3. With your right hand, bring point A forward and position it on point C, curling the paper around as you do to form a cone.
4. Holding points A and C firmly with one hand, take point B and bring it over and around the cone so that all three points meet in the back.
5. To strengthen the back seam of the cone,

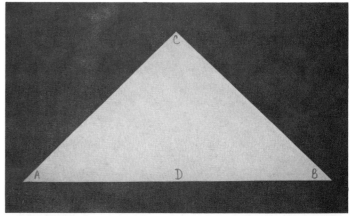

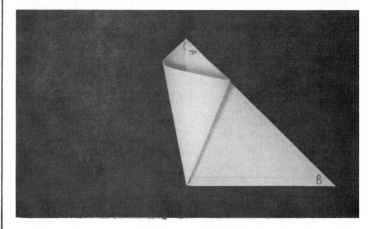

slide points A and B outward, in opposite directions, sharpening the point of the cone as you do. You should now have three distinct points—A, C, and B—visible at the back of the cone and no opening at the narrow end of the cone.

6. Secure the seam with two small pieces of cellophane tape, one piece placed about one inch from the bottom.

Note: To make small parchment cones when very little chocolate is required, cut the triangle in half from point C to point D. Roll as described.

How to Fill the Parchment Bag

Though parchment bags may be used for all types of decorating needs, I use them primarily to pipe chocolate and for some special icing techniques (see Run Sugar, Chapter 4). *To pipe with chocolate:*

1. Do not insert a decorating tube into the bag. Holding the bag in one hand, use a spoon with the other hand to fill it ⅓ full of chocolate.

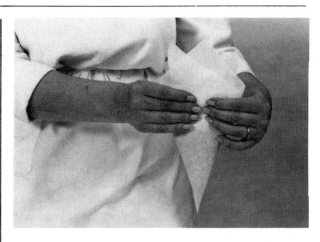
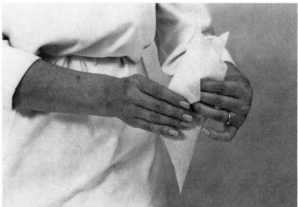
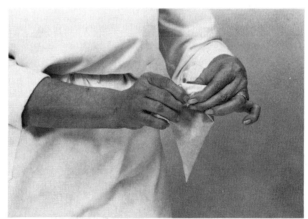

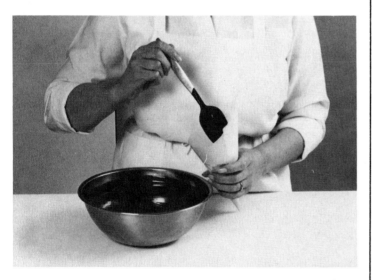

2. To close the bag, press the front and back flaps together. Fold one side inward and then the other as if to seal a package. Fold down the center and grasp the top of the bag firmly with your palm as if to hold a ball, scrunching it to conform its shape to your grasp.

3. With sharp scissors, cut the tip of the bag off to form the desired-size opening. The farther back from the tip that you cut, the larger the hole and the thicker the flow of

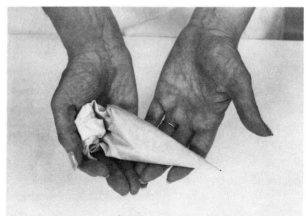

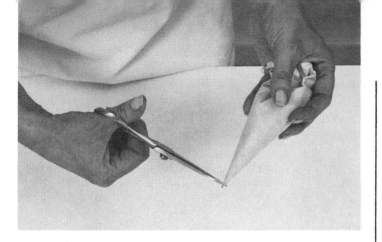

chocolate. Cut conservatively and test the flow by squeezing some chocolate out onto wax paper. It should flow easily and without much pressure on the bag. Cut off more, if necessary. If the opening is too large, or should the chocolate begin to leak out of the top, drop that bag inside a fresh parchment bag, close it up, and begin again.

Note: At the end of a decorating project, open the used parchment bag and the firm, cool chocolate will pop out of it easily. If it has not been overheated or subjected to high humidity while in the bag, the chocolate may be remelted.

DECORATING TUBES

Decorating tubes are small metal cones used to pipe out the designs that are the trademarks of the culinary artisan. With many more than 100 different tubes to choose from, it is important to know that not all of them are relevant to chocolate artistry. Actually, very few tubes are necessary to carry out the procedures in this book. Beginners would be well advised to purchase only a few basic tubes at first and add to their inventory as the need arises. The basic tubes should be drawn from the six categories described below.

The following is not a comprehensive listing of all the available tubes and their functions. It is, instead, a description of the tubes used most frequently in this book and their functions as regards the procedures herein.

As confusing as this all may seem to you now, you will soon be able to identify a tube and its function by merely looking at its opening. Tubes are further identified by a number printed on the outside. The number indicates:

1. *The size of the tube opening.* In most tube series the number sequence coincides with the size of the opening. Unless otherwise specified, within a series, the lower the number, the smaller the opening of the tube. In most decorating procedures given throughout the book, you may substitute one tube in a series for another provided they are not at opposite ends of the number sequence.

2. *The shape of the tube opening.* Except for the Drop Flower tube series, which follows no numbering pattern, and the Specialty Flower tubes series, which includes a diversity of shapes, most tube series are distinguished by a similarity of tube opening shapes. Consequently, a #4 tube, because it is part of the #1-12 sequence, is a plain-opening tube. A #16 tube is easily identifiable as a star tube along with others numbered 13-22.

Tube Types

The following tubes are classified as to usage.

Plain Tubes (#1s-12)

An *s* after the number indicates that it is smaller than the tube marked with the whole number.

Plain tubes are used for writing and for piping stems, dots, bulbs, beads, outlines, zigzag borders, and figures. The most important tubes in this series are #1, 2, 4, 6, 8, 10, and 12.

Star Tubes (#13-22)

Star tubes have jagged openings and are used to make shells, stars, rosettes, flowers, and zigzags. I recommend #14, 16, 18, and 22.

Leaf Tubes (#65s–70, 349, 352)

These tubes are used to make the basic leaf, the ruffled leaf, and the stand-up leaf. My personal favorites are #349, 352, and 65s.

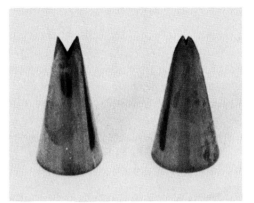

#352 is on the left; #65 is on the right.

Rose Tubes (#101s–104, 97)

Tubes in this category make roses, rosebuds, sweet peas, wild roses, pansies, and many other flowers. They also pipe ruffles and bows. The #97 tube pipes a curved-petaled rose. All of the tubes in this category are recommended.

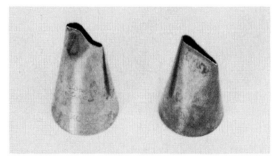

#97 is on the left; #104 is on the right.

Drop Flower Tubes

These are too numerous to list numbers. These tubes pipe "instant" flowers. Some of the most popular ones are #225, 191, 192, 177, and 106. Choose at least one of them to start.

Specialty Tubes

Use #59 for violets; #79, 80, and 81 (#79 is the large, #81 is the small) for chrysanthemums; and #75 for asters.

Left to right: #59°, #75, and #79.

Large-Size Tubes

The #7 tube is used for piping mushroom meringue cookies, among other things.

ROYAL ICING

Chocolate is a marvelous medium, to be sure, but when it comes to certain kinds of decorating, it has its limitations. For that reason one must learn to use Royal Icing. Sometimes called the decorator's "cement," this is a hard-drying, nonsmearing, very sweet concoction. In this country it is used primarily for its ornamental and adhesive qualities rather than to frost cakes.

Royal Icing, a meringue, is made with either fresh egg whites or meringue powder, a dehydrated egg-white product always found wherever cake-decorating supplies are sold. As in all meringue preparations, it is essential to use only grease-free utensils, regardless of which recipe you choose to make.

Many decorators—myself included—prefer to use the meringue-powder version of Royal Icing rather than fresh egg whites. We believe it to be more convenient to use (I would need a poultry farm to keep me in egg whites!) and more economical, considering the small amount used in each recipe. One batch continues to be usable throughout several days of an extended project and may be rebeaten to restore it to its original texture during that time, if necessary; the fresh egg-white batch will last only one day and cannot be rebeaten.

Most Royal Icing decorations are piped directly onto the chocolate surface and allowed to dry before handling. The length of the drying time depends on the size and thickness of the decoration and the humidity in the room. At times it will be necessary to pipe decorations on wax paper before using them. Once dried, these may be attached to the chocolate piece with a dab of chocolate, or they may be stored (covered) at room temperature for several months.

Bowls of Royal Icing should be covered tightly with heavy-duty aluminum foil at all times. Air contact will cause the icing to crust, and it will eventually dry to a hardness not unlike cement. This "cement," when soaked in hot water, will dissolve, so accidental carelessness will not ruin bowls or spatulas. The tips of decorating tubes filled with Royal Icing should be tucked under a damp cloth when not in use to prevent plugging. Should plugging occur, remove the coupler ring and the tube and unplug it with a toothpick or hat pin.

It was with dismay that I discovered that Royal Icing made with meringue powder was not compatible with chocolate. Almost immediately I found that the icing would not stick to the chocolate even if I scratched the chocolate's surface, added corn syrup, softened it, etc. To the rescue came my friend and early mentor, confectioner Bob Bemm, who endowed me with the special formula that quite literally changed the direction of my career. That formula was the impetus that led to the achievements I have made in developing these chocolate techniques. It is not 100 percent foolproof, but it is nearly so, which is

good enough for most situations. I believe that the following recipe is worth the price of this book—and then some!

Royal Icing with Meringue Powder for Chocolate Decorating

The magic ingredient that distinguishes this Royal Icing recipe from all others is gum arabic. This pharmaceutical product is available through some druggists, the Maid of Scandinavia and Madame chocolate catalogs, and many cake and candy decorating supply shops. It will be well worth the effort to locate it. The recipe for gum arabic solution can easily be cut in half.

Be sure to measure all the ingredients accurately, using *exactly* 1 pound of sugar and a liquid measuring cup, not a dry measuring cup (they are not the same), for the gum arabic-water mixture

- **1 pound** confectioners' sugar
- **3 level tablespoons** meringue powder
- **½ teaspoon** cream of tartar
- **1 tablespoon** plus 1 **teaspoon** gum arabic solution (see below) combined with ⅓ cup water

Combine the sugar, the meringue powder, and the tartar in a large, grease-free bowl.

Add the gum arabic-water solution mixture to the dry ingredients all at once. Beat slowly for about 1 minute until well blended and then at high speed until the mixture forms stiff peaks. Keep covered with foil.

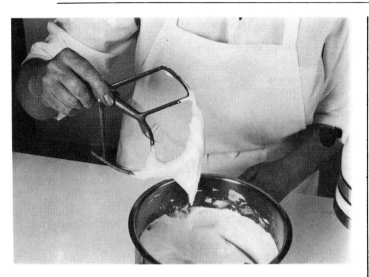

The icing will stand at room temperature for several days. It may be rebeaten, if necessary.

Note: Whenever it is necessary to soften small amounts of stiff icing, add drops of water very conservatively and mix well.

GUM ARABIC SOLUTION

1 ounce gum arabic powder
½ pint warm water

Dissolve the gum arabic powder in the water using a food processor or blender.

Pour through a fine sieve into a glass jar and keep covered in the refrigerator for up to three weeks.

The solution will look grey and generally unappetizing. It will have a distasteful odor as well. Ignore all of this and know that neither the color nor the odor will affect the icing in any way.

Royal Icing with Fresh Egg Whites

Royal Icing made with fresh egg whites must be used promptly, particularly if it is to be used for decorations requiring firm, heavy icing (such as flowers and some figure piping). Once made, it cannot be rebeaten.

3 egg whites (room temperature)
1 pound confectioners' sugar
¼ teaspoon cream of tartar

Separate the cold eggs carefully to avoid getting even a trace of yolk into them. Allow the whites to warm to room temperature before proceeding.

Combine ½ pound of the confectioners' sugar and the cream of tartar with the egg whites in a grease-free bowl.

Beat on low speed for one minute. Increase to high and beat for three more minutes.

Gradually add the remaining sugar and continue beating until the icing holds stiff peaks.

Cover the bowl with heavy aluminum foil when not in use.

FOOD COLORING

FDA-approved food coloring is available in three forms—liquid, paste, and powder. Liquid

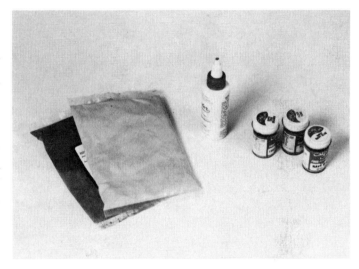

coloring may be purchased in most supermarkets as well as in many department stores, gourmet food shops, and cake-decorating shops. Of the three kinds of available coloring, however, it is the least acceptable. Though it does come in varying degrees of potency, it is still never as intense as its paste and powder equivalents when it comes to strong colors such as red, dark blue, and brown. In dyeing icing it often requires the addition of so much coloring as to change the texture of the icing, often breaking it down completely and as often giving the icing a very bitter taste. It is best suited to tinting icing in pastel shades. Most important, liquid food coloring must *never* be used to dye compound coating because the coating will tighten or thicken excessively in the presence of the liquid.

Paste coloring is the most popular material to use to dye icing as well as compound coating. It is intense, blends easily, and, if mixed correctly, rarely changes the texture or taste of the mixture. Usually sold in one-ounce jars, it is very economical because of its potency. Paste coloring has a very long shelf life if properly stored, but if it ever shows signs of drying, mix it with a few drops of glycerine and it will soften.

Powdered food coloring has many of the same advantages over liquid coloring as paste coloring. Because of its intensity, it achieves deep colors quickly, never affecting the consistency or taste of the icing or compound coating. Though I still prefer paste to powder for dyeing icing, the powdered coloring is often my choice for dyeing coating.

To build a basic inventory of food coloring, begin with the primary colors (red, yellow, and blue) and experiment with mixing and blending various colors. An artist's color wheel will help you. Or, for the less adventurous, buy two or three of your favorite premixed colors (one should be green) and add new colors as needed. Luckily for us, food coloring is available in a vast spectrum of colors today. My favorite brand of paste coloring is especially gel-like in texture, comes in scrumptious shades, and blends beautifully in icing and compound coating. It is manufactured by Cake Craft, a division of Nestelle's Inc. in Portland, Oregon. It is available in cake and candy decorating shops across the country, and through the Madame Chocolate and Maid of Scandinavia catalogs.

Principles of Color

As an intrinsic part of the design, color should invite attention, stimulate interest, and please the eye. Never forget that color should tempt the appetite as well. Avoid unappetizing colors such as grey and black and use gaudy or dark tones as accent colors only. Color should always be used with restraint. It should enhance the chocolate, not dominate it.

Some decorators seem to have a natural instinct for color. Others must acquire a sense of color perception by consciously working at it. Perhaps the greatest teacher is Nature herself. Nature is the ultimate artist's palette—a world of shades and hues that blend into a color-filled landscape that is picture-perfect in every way.

Our achievements in color blending are not always as successful as Mother Nature's. Too often the colors scream at the eye rather than entice it. Please be conservative when you dye icing or coating with potent food coloring. It is always easier to deepen the color than lighten it. Finally, when in doubt, use fewer rather than more colors in any given design. Too many colors can confuse the eye and detract from the overall continuity of the artwork.

Procedures for Dyeing Icing

Liquid Coloring

1. Place up to a cupful of icing in a small bowl.
2. Add liquid coloring to it one drop at a time, blending it well with a metal spatula until the desired color is achieved.

Note: Beware of pink, blue, and yellow—they are potent!

Paste Food Coloring

1. Place up to a cupful of icing in a small bowl.
2. Use a toothpick or a small, clean, metal spatula (so as not to contaminate the jar) to add a little paste coloring to the icing.

3. Work the coloring into a portion of the icing on the side of the cup. Now blend that into the rest of the cupful. Add more coloring, if necessary.

Note: Deep colors may require the addition of approximately ½ teaspoon of paste coloring.

3. Blend this into the reserved coating and blend well.

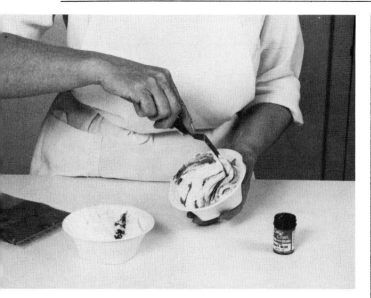

Powdered Food Coloring

1. Sprinkle a very small amount of the powdered coloring on the surface of a cupful of icing.
2. Blend it in with a metal spatula.
3. Continue gradual additions of powdered coloring until the desired color is achieved.

Procedure for Dyeing Compound Coating

(*Never* use liquid food coloring.)

Paste Food Coloring

Follow the same procedure for dyeing icing.
To dye large quantities of coating:
1. Melt the required amount of coating.
2. Remove a cupful and dye it several shades deeper than desired.

4. Repeat steps 2 and 3 until the correct shade is achieved.

Note: If the coating tightens (thickens) during the procedure, add a small amount of melted white coating and stir to loosen. Force it through a fine strainer if lumps remain or if specks of coloring are visible. *Never* add water to thin the coating.

Powdered Food Coloring

1. Follow the same procedures given for using paste food coloring, substituting a small amount of powdered coloring for the paste.
2. Repeat the procedure as often as necessary to achieve the desired shade.

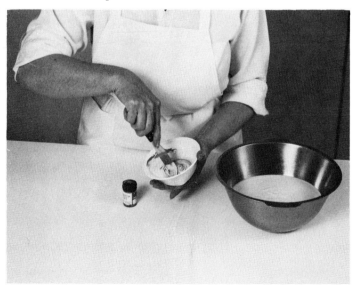

Procedure for Dyeing White Cocoa Butter Coating

White cocoa butter coating has a decidedly yellowish cast and reacts better to powdered coloring than to paste. Follow the same procedures given on page 45, substituting a small amount of powdered coloring for the paste. Repeat the procedure as often as necessary to achieve the desired shade.

OIL FLAVORING

Chocolate and coating may be flavored with one of the many oil-based flavorings that are sold in most gourmet shops. Do not use extracts to

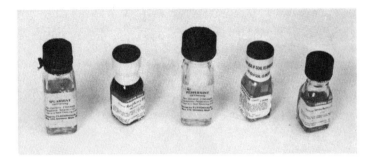

flavor them; the alcohol in extracts will tighten them immediately. Choose a flavor that is compatible with the color of the coating being used. For example:

red—strawberry oil
pink—raspberry oil
white—peppermint oil
yellow—lemon oil
orange—orange oil
green—lime oil

Use the oil sparingly. A few drops applied with an eye dropper will usually suffice to flavor one pound of melted coating. A cotton ball semisaturated with oil flavoring will flavor a small amount of molded chocolate if confined with it in a closed box. Remember that fact when combining strongly flavored mint patties with unflavored ones in a candy box; they may all taste like mint after awhile. Chocolate is very susceptible to odors.

THINNING AGENTS FOR USE WITH CHOCOLATE AND COMPOUND COATING

Generally speaking, the degree of viscosity of any given chocolate should be determined by the manufacturer. If you want thin chocolate, you should buy that kind. Minor fluidity adjustments may be made, however, with the following ingredients. Do *not* use cocoa butter to thin compound coating.

Cocoa Butter

Melt the cocoa butter and add in moderate amounts to viscous chocolate to thin it. Use ¼ teaspoon to one tablespoon per pound. Avoid excessive use for best results (Maid of Scandinavia #20346).

Lecithin

Soya liquid lecithin is available in health food stores. Excessive use of this product will cause the chocolate or coatings to tighten rather than loosen. Use no more than two drops per pound.

Paramount Crystals

These solid vegetable-fat pieces are preferred by some to thin melted compound coating only. It is important to melt the flakes before adding them to the coating. If you must use them (I do not), use them in moderation.

INVENTORY OF ESSENTIAL DECORATING MATERIALS

The following tools and other materials are those you'll find convenient and/or necessary for general decorating work.

Cake Cardboard Rounds

These corrugated boards, available in a variety of sizes, are designed specifically for cake use. Place the white side against the cake.

Conduit Wire

This heavy-duty, plastic-coated wire is used to

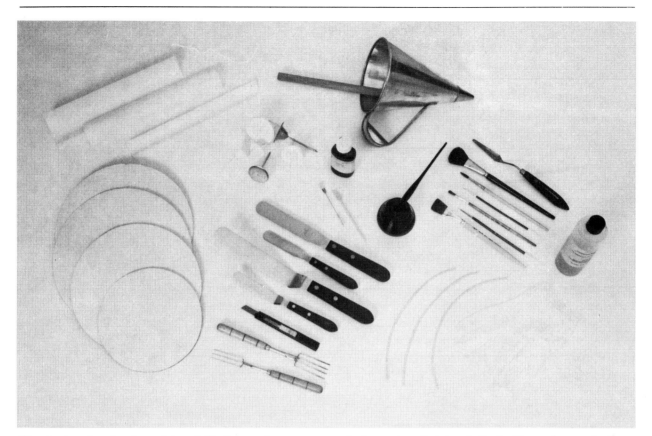

Clockwise, beginning at top left: flower formers, candy funnel, artists' palette knife and assorted artists' brushes, confectioners' glaze, editing gloves, conduit wire, dipping forks, utility knife and assorted metal spatulas, and cake cardboard rounds. Center: concave lily nails, flat #7 nail, glycerin, tube brush, Dipco stick, ink well filled with confectioners' ink and pen holder fitted with sketching nib.

make handles on chocolate baskets. It is too thick to be accidentally bitten into two pieces, so it poses little danger when used in chocolate work. Ask for 14- or 12-gauge TW solid wire for use in conduit house wiring. It may be purchased by the foot in hardware stores. Wash and dry thoroughly before using.

Confectioners' Glaze

This edible glaze may be brushed onto molded chocolate pieces to preserve them and impart a bright shine resembling shellac. I use it only on very rare occasions. (Maid of Scandinavia #62006).

Tube Brushes

To clean the tubes, soak them briefly in a bowl of warm, sudsy water. Special brushes are available (electric shaver brushes work, too) to

scrub their interiors. Rinse the tubes well and stand them on a soft towel until thoroughly dry.

Flower Nails

A flower nail is really a miniature turntable used to make certain multipetaled flowers. It is turned slowly to facilitate the placement of each petal. Nails are available in a variety of shapes and sizes. I particularly recommend the #7 flat nail.

For making cup-shaped flowers, it is important to use a lily nail. These nails are available in a very practical plastic set of four—½ inch, 1¼ inches, 1⅝ inches, and 2½ inches in diameter. A 1⅝-inch metal lily nail is also available.

Flower Formers

Flower formers are curved strips of plastic used to curve the petals of freshly piped chocolate or icing flowers. Available in a set of nine, they are 11 inches long and 1½, 2, and 2½ inches wide.

Metal Spatulas

Metal spatulas are invaluable when it comes to the many menial tasks involved with chocolate decorating. They are used for mixing, spreading, scooping, lifting, and numerous other chores that require an extension of your hand. They are available with straight or offset blades in short or long lengths.

Artists' Brushes

An assortment of camel hair and sable hair brushes will enable you to smooth away imperfections as well as apply realistic finishing touches to your decorations. I also use a ¾-inch soft-as-silk squirrel's hair brush to clean and buff chocolate surfaces. Select a #00 brush for fine detail work and a brush ½ inch wide for all-purpose jobs. Buy other sizes as needed.

Artists' Palette Knife

A palette or painting knife is used artistically to smooth large figure-piped forms and functionally to spread icing or chocolate into hard-to-reach areas. Buy one with an offset handle and a flexible blade approximately 3½ inches long.

Sketching Pen Set

A new dimension in confectionery writing is achieved when you use a penholder fitted with a sketching nib (point) to write on Run Sugar icing plaques (see Chapter 4). Add about ½ teaspoon of *soft* food coloring paste to two tablespoons of warm water to make a highly concentrated edible "ink." Do *not*, under any circumstances, use real ink, of course!

Retractable Utility Knife

High on the list of essential tools for chocolate artistry is a sharp knife with a thin blade. I recommend a retractable knife commonly used for hobbies that has either a "sheepfoot" or "utility" blade. These blades are suitable for digging in with the point as well as for scoring and cutting. You will use the knife to trim chocolate edges and for the pattern work used throughout the book.

Practice Board

You'll never outgrow the need for a practice board! Use a few dabs of icing or chocolate to attach a sheet of wax paper to a sturdy, flat surface—perhaps an inverted cookie sheet or a piece of cardboard. Keep the practice board handy and use it often.

Glycerin

Glycerin is another pharmaceutical product frequently used in confectionery work. Use it to thin paste coloring as well as to thicken chocolate for decorative piping.

Gloves

Lightweight, noncumbersome gloves, worn whenever chocolate art work must be handled excessively, will prevent smudges on its surface. I use inexpensive editing gloves purchased in camera shops or gloves similar to those worn by members of the local marching band. Clean gardening gloves or work gloves may also be used.

Optional and Advanced Materials

As you become increasingly involved in chocolate work, you will need to add many of the following items to the already-mentioned inventory of equipment and ingredients.

lollipop sticks
fluted paper candy cups (assorted sizes)
gold foil candy cups
toothpicks
scissors
cellophane tape
dipping forks
candy funnel
eye dropper
colored sugars
cookie trims (sprinkles, dragées, candy confetti, chocolate vermicelli, etc.)
assorted candies (spearmint leaves, M & Ms, cherries, licorice, jawbreakers, life savers, peppermint sticks, etc.)
assorted nutmeats (almonds, cashews, pecans, peanuts, filberts)
coconut
liqueurs
confectioners' foil paper

SWEET 16 FIGURE

CUPID CENTERPIECE

CHOCOLATE RECORD CENTERPIECE

BOX OF DOMINOES

FIGURE-PIPED LOLLIPOP FACES

DECORATIVE CHOCOLATE LOLLIPOPS

ALL-OCCASION LOLLIPOPS

SPORT LOLLIPOPS

WINTER HOLIDAY LOLLIPOPS

CHOCOLATE STRAWBERRY TREE

candy boxes
sateen ribbon
plastic wrap
wooden dowel rods—¼ inch and ³⁄₁₆ inch in
   diameter
glassine-coated, paper lace doilies
cloth-covered floral wire
Styrofoam

THE CREATIVE TOOLS OF THE CHOCOLATE DECORATOR

A skilled chocolate artisan is to be admired for creativity as well as handicraft. I believe that there is an artist in everyone—dormant, perhaps, but there. If you have the desire and the determination to work with chocolate, then be assured that the creative potential is there, too—dormant, perhaps, but there.

It is difficult to say how long it will take before you feel the artist in you begin to stir. Certainly the more actively involved in chocolate you are, the faster the juices will begin to flow. I sometimes find my inspirations in the strangest places, and so will you. Here are some examples.

Magazines

Sometimes just leafing through a magazine will spark your imagination. I must admit to being a collector of magazines featuring crafts and holiday ideas. Things that don't catch my eye one year often do the next.

Books

Those of us who lack an art background can profit from the information found in books dealing with design and cartooning. A calligraphy textbook can set the standards for your penmanship. What does the flag of Spain look like? Don't guess. Find out by checking an encyclopedia; it is indispensable for factual information. Party books will give you theme ideas for favors. Comic books, coloring books, and children's storybooks have simple designs that easily carry over to confectionery designs. The ads in the yellow pages of the telephone book are full of great ideas, too. Have you ever seriously looked at company logos with an eye to chocolate ideas?

Catalogs

Flower and vegetable seed catalogs are excellent reference books for finding new flowers to pipe. When I need to be reminded of what a lawn mower, a bicycle, or any other household item *really* looks like, I reach for the Sears catalog.

Paper Goods

Paper plates make perfect patterns to use for cake decorations. The ever-popular stickers are the right size for lollipop patterns. Gift wrapping paper, with its repetitive design, is a natural for pattern work, too.

Greeting Cards

This is perhaps my favorite idea source. Sometimes a drawing—a face, a posture, a situation will catch my attention. Often it is the sentiment expressed that will set my mind spinning. Whether contemporary or traditional, greeting cards are filled with whimsy and warmth that you will want to use in your chocolate designs.

4
Basic Decorating Skills—Royal Icing

A filled decorating bag can be an awesome handful for the inexperienced decorator. Horror stories of first efforts abound—aching, icing-smeared hands coupled with frustrating hours spent on a "simple" project turned complicated, and all of this ending in less than satisfying results. I know because I've been there.

What you need before you take on the chocolate-decorating challenge is information. A little of it will go a long way toward averting the disillusionments that so many of us have experienced when we tried to "run" before we could "walk"—tried to decorate before we could manipulate the bag. Learning to handle the bag and what is in it is the logical place to begin this chapter on basic decorating skills.

HOW TO HANDLE A POLYESTER DECORATING BAG

Note to lefties: Though most lefties ultimately develop their own style of decorating,

generally their movements are mirror images of the right-handed decorator's movements.

1. Prepare a practice board by attaching a sheet of wax paper to the bottom of an inverted cookie sheet or board with a few dabs of icing or chocolate.

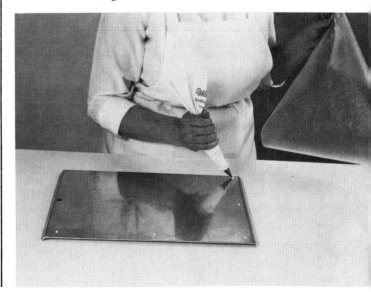

2. Attach a #4 decorating tube to a polyester bag half-filled with icing. Use your fingers on the outside of the bag to periodically push down any icing that creeps up toward the top of the bag.

3. Twist the bag closed above the filled portion; cradle it there between the thumb and forefinger, leaving the rest of the fingers and the whole hand free to press on the bag.

4. Position the bag at a 45-degree angle to the practice board with the tube pointing to your left and your fingertips visible on the top of the bag. Steady your working hand by placing the index finger of your free hand near the coupler end of the bag and keeping your elbows tucked in close to the body.

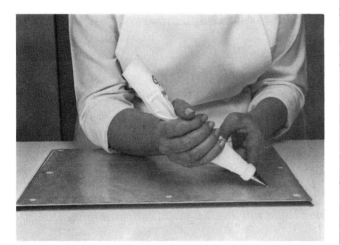

5. Practice squeezing the bag between your fingers and your thumb. Move your hand across the paper, touching the surface lightly as you do. Try to go from the left side of the paper to the right with one long squeeze of the bag. Do this several times, alternating between light and heavy pressure on the bag. Observe the reaction of the icing to the different kinds of pressure and the movement of your hand.

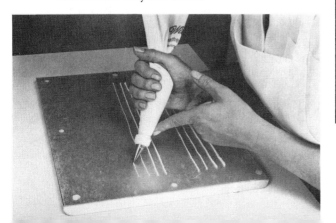

6. Replace the #4 tube with a #2 tube and experiment with pressure and movement again. As the icing flows out you will begin to notice that:

the larger the opening of the tube, the easier the icing flows;
the softer the icing, the easier it will flow;
the more filled the decorating bag, the more strength required to squeeze the bag.

The conclusions drawn from such observations are keys to handling a decorating bag:

1. To pipe delicate designs with small-opening tubes, use soft icing and a less-then-half-filled bag. Refill the bag as necessary.
2. To pipe designs requiring stiff icing, use a half-filled (or less) bag and medium- to large-opening tubes.

STAR TUBES

Star tubes are unquestionably some of the most fundamental tools of the decorator's trade. They are also among the easiest of the decorating tubes to use and a good place to begin these lessons on piping techniques. They are particularly useful to the beginner who has not yet learned to pipe flowers. Star flowers and rosettes are easy enough for children to make and may be made in a variety of sizes by using small, medium, or large tubes.

A flip of the wrist and the star tube becomes the sophisticated tube used to pipe scrolls and the classic shell border. Ideally shaped so as to texturize the surface it pipes, it seems a natural for filling chocolate cups with ease and flair.

Stars

1. Prepare a half-filled bag of medium-consistency icing and fit it with a #18 star tube.
2. Position the bag at a 90-degree angle to the practice board so that the tube barely touches the surface.

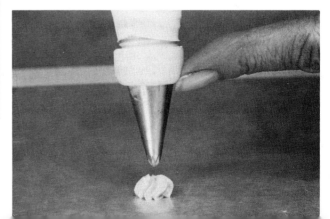

3. Squeeze the bag firmly. Elevate the tube slightly as the icing builds up, or the presence of the tube will smash the star shape as it is piped.
4. Keep the tube partially submerged as you cease pressure and pull straight up.

Rosettes

1. Position the bag as if to pipe a star, with the tube barely touching the surface.
2. Squeeze the bag gently but steadily. As the icing flows out, lift the tube slightly so as not to distort the design and move the tube in a counterclockwise, circular motion, returning to the center before releasing the pressure on the bag. Pull straight up and away.

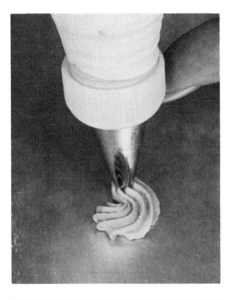

Shell Border

The shell is perhaps the most misunderstood of all decorating techniques and is more often poorly executed than any other. It requires attention to detail and a good deal of patience and practice to master it. Be proud when at last you do!

1. Prepare a bag fitted with a #18 star tube and medium-consistency icing. Point the tube to your left with the fingers visible on the top of the bag. Touch the tip of the tube to the surface at a 45-degree angle.
2. Squeeze the bag. The force of the icing will lift the tube off the surface. Maintain a steady pressure on the bag, holding that elevated position as you continue to squeeze the bag. The icing will fan out as you do so, forming the shell.
3. Release pressure rather abruptly and pull the end of the shell downward to a point and pull away.
4. Start the next shell approximately ¼ inch behind the previous one. The icing will move itself forward to join it.

PLAIN TUBES: CONFECTIONERY WRITING

Writing on chocolate is a lot like writing on unlined paper. It has its ups and downs! Once you know a few tricks of the trade, however, I think you will feel less intimated by it.

Each decorator should have his own personal

style of writing, based on his regular penmanship. There is nothing more artificial looking than writing that looks forced or contrived. I am very much opposed to imitating another person's handwriting, so I am not suggesting that mine be used as a model for yours. The theory behind my style, however, is one that may be helpful in developing your own unique confectionery signature. It is based on a combination of cursive script and block printing.

In normal penmanship a word is written in one continuous flow without lifting the pencil. The same practice is possible with a decorating bag, but because certain letters—b, d, f, g, h, j, k, l, p, q, t, y, and z—have both ascending and descending strokes, they become bulky looking when written in icing or chocolate. To maintain the same thickness in all written letters, I prefer to print those that require double strokes. This combination of cursive script and block printing is slower, but the end result is neat and professional looking.

This writing style will mean that some letters will be joined in a word and some will not. There are no specific rules for this; simply join those that can be joined easily. You will find that you need less space for this type of writing—an important point, to be sure.

The curse of writing on an unlined surface is the difficulty in staying on a straight line. Penmanship teachers tell us to concentrate on the top line being straight and that the rest will follow suit. When writing on a piece of chocolate that has a straight top edge, use it as a guide, keeping your words all equidistant from it. Otherwise, place a ruler or string about ¼ inch above your writing to serve as a point of reference.

Spacing is another writing problem. In your early efforts it may be worthwhile to take the time to calculate whether the words will fit into the allotted space. Write your message on a narrow strip of paper using icing, not pencil, and place it on the chocolate to see how it looks.

Care must also be taken within the word to see that proper space is left between letters to allow for the crossing of *t*s. All of these skills are acquired through practice. The more experience you have, the more precise your script.

Before you begin to write, find a comfortable position—whether standing or sitting. Unlike pencil writing, confectionery writing involves moving the whole arm, not just the fingers. To steady your hand, remember to support the narrow end of the bag with the index finger of your free hand. You will find that holding your breath as you write will give you better control. Inhale and exhale only when you are not pressing on the bag. Most important, don't talk while you write—and don't look up. You will lose your perspective if you do, and your script will begin to drift upward or downward. The ultimate success of your writing will depend on hand control, pressure control, and practice.

How to Write with Icing

1. Prepare a polyester bag fitted with a #2 decorating tube. The icing should be soft in texture, as lump-free as possible, and the bag less than half-filled. To soften icing, add drops of water very conservatively and mix well.
2. Position the bag at a 45-degree angle, with the tip of the tube touching the practice board. As you press on the bag, pipe out a line of attached *c*s, dragging the tube lightly across the board's surface as you do. Notice that your *c*s stop when you release pressure on the bag. If the lines in your script break often, the icing is too stiff. Soften it as explained in step 1.
3. Pipe a row of *m*s, this time briefly touching the tube to the surface and then, with steady pressure on the bag, lifting it slightly, pulling a thread of icing as you write.
4. Practice writing some words now. Touch the tube to the surface, lift slightly as you write, and touch down again to stop the flow of icing. Never raise the tube more than ⅛ inch off the surface.

Zigzag Border

Writing skills are used to pipe this versatile border.

1. Position the bag at a 45-degree angle to the practice board, tube facing left, palm and fingertips up.
2. Rest the tube lightly on the surface while you practice. As you press steadily on the bag, pipe a series of continuous up-and-down strokes, ¼ inch high, moving from left to right across the surface. To complete the maneuver, stop pressure and pull away.

PLAIN TUBES: CONFECTIONERY STEMS

Icing stems are piped similarly to the way words are piped—using a less-than-half-filled bag of soft, lump-free icing fitted with a plain tube (#1, 2, or 3).

The arrangement of stems is the skeleton upon which the whole floral design is based. For that reason, one should give definite thought to its position and shape rather than piping lines indiscriminately. You have only to observe flowers in their natural habitat to realize that stems curve, giving you an impression of life, growth, rhythm, and grace. So, too, should your icing arrangements display the easy flowing movements of the natural ones. A large flower (or several smaller ones) set in the central focal point of an arrangement should be balanced on both sides with subsidiary blossoms and leaves as it would in a garden. To maintain the graceful, uncontrived look of the floral spray, the curve of the auxiliary branches should correspond with that of the main stems in the design.

Drawing a simple sketch is probably the best way to assure the proper placement and balance of your floral spray. If words are to accompany the spray, they may determine where you position it. Be sure to include them in your sketch.

Procedure for Piping a Spray

1. Determine the placement and design of your spray.
2. As in writing, position the bag at a 45-degree angle to the surface. Squeeze the bag gently as you *lightly* skim across the chocolate piece, pulling a thread of icing as you do. It is easier to control the natural curve of each stem if you pipe one-half of it at a time, beginning at its center point and moving outward; then pipe the other half in the same way.
3. Once the main frame of the spray is piped, auxiliary branches may be added as needed. Holding the bag at a 45-degree angle with the fingertips on the top of the bag, touch the stem with the tip of the tube. Press very lightly on the bag as you begin to move outward to form the branch. Every effort should be made to join the branch to the stem as inconspicuously as possible.

PLAIN TUBES: FIGURE PIPING

Figure piping is the art of piping three-dimensional shapes with a decorating bag. It is really exciting to discover what a squeeze of the hand here and a twist of the wrist there can accomplish in terms of confectionery caricature and realism. You will be pleased to know that you do not need drawing skills to be a successful figure piper. What you *do* need is described below.

Proper Icing Consistency

A creamy, fresh recipe of Royal Icing beaten to a medium consistency is perfect for piping stand-up shapes; soft icing may be used for flat shapes. The figures are piped directly onto the chocolate pieces, or they may be piped in advance on wax paper and attached to the chocolate with more chocolate when needed.

Proper Equipment

Most of the relief work done on chocolate is piped with plain-opening tubes—in small, medium, and large sizes. Many decorators prefer to use parchment bags for figure piping, cutting their points to different-sized openings as needed. Common sense will tell you what size opening you will need for any given situation. No equipment list would be complete without a few soft artist's brushes. Dipped into hot water, these brushes do a remarkable job of smoothing bumpy surfaces on the piped figures. An artist's offset palette knife is useful in smoothing larger piped surfaces.

Proper Control of the Decorating Bag

Of all the decorating techniques discussed in this chapter, none is more dependent on control of the bag and the icing within it than figure piping. Control is determined by the texture of the icing, the size of the tube's opening, the degree to which you press the bag, the speed with which you move your hand, and the height above the surface that you hold the tip of the tube. Good hand control is hampered by an overfilled bag, which is hard to squeeze, and an undersized tube opening, which causes rippling in the surface of the piped icing.

Proper Bag Position

In order to pipe a three-dimensional shape, the tip of the tube must be clear of the surface, allowing space for the icing to swell. The higher you raise the tip and the longer you continue to squeeze the bag, the higher the piped form. The angle of the bag will vary between 90 and 45 degrees.

Practice, Practice, and More Practice

The success that you enjoy in your early figure-piping attempts will motivate you to experiment with more challenging shapes. The more often you practice, the more skillful a figure piper you will become.

Many of the personalized chocolate pieces in this book are decorated with figures that are piped according to the directions that follow. Specific piping instructions will be given as each situation arises. Most of the figures are variations of one another. A facial expression may be varied, a hairstyle changed, a posture altered, but the basic figure-piping technique remains the same.

The versatility of the plain tube or cut parchment bag is evident in its ability to pipe three-dimensional shapes as well as delicate lines and curves. The following exercises have been devised to enable you to appreciate its capabilities as well as your own.

Piping Balls and Dots

1. Half-fill a polyester bag fitted with a #10 plain tube. If you prefer to use a parchment bag, cut off a ¼-inch piece from its tip.
2. Hold the bag at a 90-degree angle (perpendicular to the surface) and slowly

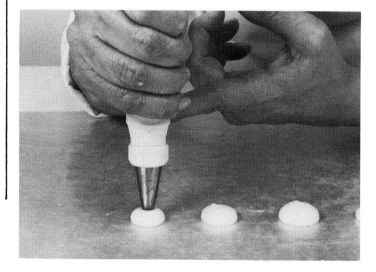

but steadily press on the bag, allowing the force of the icing to lift the tube off the surface. The diameter and depth of the ball will be determined by how high you lift the tube off the surface and how long you continue to squeeze the bag.

3. Keep the tip partially submerged the whole time, stop squeezing, and push in slightly to break off the flow.

4. Smooth the surface of the ball with the tip as you pull away with a circular movement.

5. Further smoothing of the surface may be done with an artist's brush dampened with hot water or a damp fingertip.

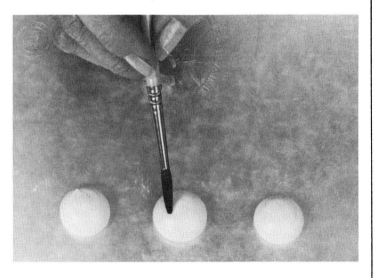

6. Substitute a #4 tube for the #10 and do the exercise again, this time piping dots instead of balls. Adjust the opening of another parchment bag accordingly.

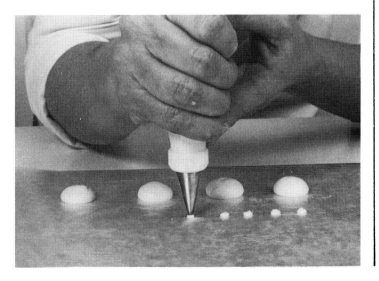

Piping Faces

Here is a figure-piping technique that will surely become a favorite of yours. Not only are confectionery faces easy enough for a beginner to master, but they are fun to make and will inspire you to depict people you know and love in icing. Once you realize the potential here for personalizing chocolate, you will look at everyone with an eye to caricature. Would not Uncle Harry delight in seeing his mustache and balding head memorialized on a slab of chocolate as a remembrance of some special occasion? Yes, there are some physical features that are absolutely *perfect* for figure piping. Balding heads, mustaches, beards, pigtails, and freckled noses are but a few of them.

Faces may be piped directly onto the chocolate piece or conveniently mass-produced for future needs. One bag of icing will make enough of them to keep you stocked for a very long time. Invert a cookie sheet and attach a sheet of wax paper to it with several dabs of icing. Beginning at the top left corner, pipe rows of faces, leave them to dry for several hours, and store them in a covered container for many months.

Method

1. Prepare a flesh shade of icing using a combination of pink and yellow coloring toned with brown to the desired darkness or use flesh paste food coloring by Cake Craft, Inc. See dyeing directions in Chapter 3. Place a minimal amount of this icing in a bag fitted with a #2 tube to be used for piping the nose and ears on each face.

2. Though faces may be piped with medium consistency icing using instructions given for piping balls and dots, they are even easier to make with very soft icing. To a cup of flesh-colored Royal Icing, add about ¼ teaspoon of warm water and stir well. It should be very soft but not runny and transparent looking. Adjust the icing with more water if it is still too stiff or add more medium icing if it has gotten too soft.

3. For a variety of faces, position the bag fitted with a #6 tube at a 90-degree angle to the surface and pipe balls, ovals, or any sort of semiround shape previously mentioned. The soft icing balls will flatten to a somewhat

larger diameter once piped. Tapping the surface board will usually eliminate ripples in the icing.

4. Allow the balls of icing to dry thoroughly at room temperature. They may be stored (always at room temperature) without further details or completed and then stored.

Piping Features on Faces

1. Pipe two white dots of icing in the center of the dried face for the eyes, using a #2 tube.

2. Halfway between the eyes and the bottom of the ball, paint a smile line. This is done with a dampened #00 artists' brush dipped in red paste food coloring.

3. Pipe a dot nose between the eyes and mouth with the medium-consistency flesh-colored icing and a #2 tube.

4. Use the same tube and icing to pipe ears on either side of the face, forming a *c* on one side and an inverted *c* on the other. The top of the ear should be level with the eyebrows (whether or not you pipe them on) and the bottom with the bottom of the nose.

5. Using a dampened #00 brush and black paste food coloring, paint the irises on the white eyeballs, once they have dried slightly. There is room for creativity here, so have fun.

6. Using appropriately-colored icing in bags fitted with #2 tubes, pipe strands of hair. Straight hair is piped by touching the surface, squeezing, and lifting the tube slightly as you pull the icing from "root" to "end." Hair may be curled by piping curlicues (a series of continuous circles).

A variety of emotions and reactions may be expressed with these confectionery faces by simply changing a smile line to a frown, raising an eyebrow, tilting the head, or directing a glance here or there. A more mature face may be created by increasing the separation between the facial features and centering them on the entire face rather than on the lower half of the face as described previously. Blushing, squinting, freckles, and other facial details may be painted on with #00 brushes and appropriate paste food coloring. Hats and other trims may be added using figure-piping techniques described in this chapter and thoughout the book.

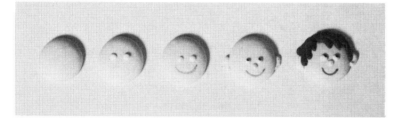

The sequence for piping features on faces.

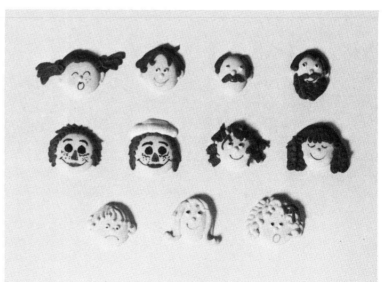

Piping Bulbs and Beads

1. Position a bag fitted with a #8 tube and medium icing at a 45-degree angle to the practice board.
2. Touch the surface, squeeze, and allow the force of the icing to lift the tube slightly off the surface. Hold that elevated position, pressing steadily on the bag, as the icing flairs. Relax pressure as you touch down again.

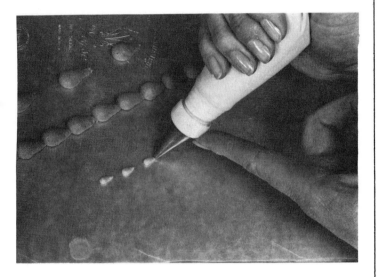

3. Draw the icing to a modified point as you pull away. A series of bulbs may be made in this manner by beginning one bulb on the "tail" of the previous one. This constitutes a shell border done with a plain tube.
4. To pipe beads, use a smaller-sized plain tube and follow the instructions given above. To pipe a bead-technique heart, pipe two vertical, side-by-side beads. Angle one to the left and the other one to the right, drawing their tails to a point.

Piping Elongated Shapes

1. Position a bag filled with medium icing and fitted with a #8 tube at a 45-degree angle to the practice board.
2. Squeeze gently but steadily on the bag, lifting the tube off the surface as you move it slowly across the board. Keep the tube submerged until pressure is released and then pull away. The width of the elongated shape will approximate the size of the tube's opening.

3. Pipe another elongated shape, this time exerting heavier pressure and elevating the tube somewhat higher than before and moving the bag even more slowly across the board. The extra pressure and slower movement will substantially increase the width of the figure. Release pressure and pull the tube away.

Piping People and Animals

To pipe many animals and people, use an upside-down bulb for the torso and elongated shapes for the limbs. These are the essential shapes required in most figures. The tube numbers will be determined by the size of the figure.

A stick figure drawing may be used as a guide in figure piping. Pipe the figure directly on the chocolate with a #4 plain tube. Using those lines as a guide, with a larger tube superimpose bulbs and ovals on them to give the figure its appropriate girth.

Figure piping over a pattern.

Figure Piping over a Pattern

1. Select a simple sketch from a comic book, coloring book, or pattern book and attach it to a flat board or an inverted cookie sheet with cellophane tape. Cover the pattern sheet with wax paper. Secure with tape.
2. Outline the sketch with appropriately colored icing and a #4 tube by touching the tube to the surface, lifting slightly to outline, returning to the surface, releasing pressure, and breaking away.
3. With heavy, extended pressure fill in the outlined sketch with a #6–12 tube, depending on the size of the figure.
4. Use an artist's palette knife or a soft artists' brush dampened in hot water to smooth the surface. Use water sparingly.
5. The figure must be thoroughly dry before it can be released from the paper and attached to the chocolate. The thicker the figure, the longer the drying period.

Special Effects

Ballooning

This technique is used to pipe puffy parts of the body such as cheeks, breasts, muscles, and stomachs.

1. After piping a figure that is decidedly too flat in any particular area, insert the tip of the tube *into* the icing in the appropriate spot.
2. Squeeze the bag and feel the icing swell within the previously piped form. Elevate the tube as the icing achieves the necessary degree of puffiness but do not withdraw it from the icing.
3. Release pressure on the bag and pull away in a circular movement, smoothing the surface with the tip of the tube as you do.

Carving

A pointed skewer is used in figure piping to carve openings into an icing form to add interest or realism. The most commonly used type of wooden skewer is available through many cake-decorating suppliers or through the meat department in some supermarkets. A makeshift skewer can be whittled from a narrow wooden dowel rod purchased at hardware stores. A metal skewer used to barbecue meats and even large sanitized nails may be substituted.

1. Grasp the skewer as you would a brush. Dip into hot water, shake off the excess, and insert it into the freshly piped icing form. It will slide in easily and deepen or enlarge the opening simply by moving it one way or another.
2. To complete the procedure, twirl the skewer as it is withdrawn from the icing.

Sometimes a challenging new figure-piping situation will arise that will test your ability and challenge your creativity. Over the years my reference file of possible figure-piping subjects has grown considerably. It is filled with many illustrations, pictures, logos, and insignias from magazines, program covers, greeting cards, advertisements, and a multitude of other sources that provide me with the details and ideas that I need to trigger a bright idea. You would be well advised to begin compiling a similar reference file. My determination has sent me on more than one research trip to the library, and I must say that friends and family are now well trained to be on the lookout for good subject material for me.

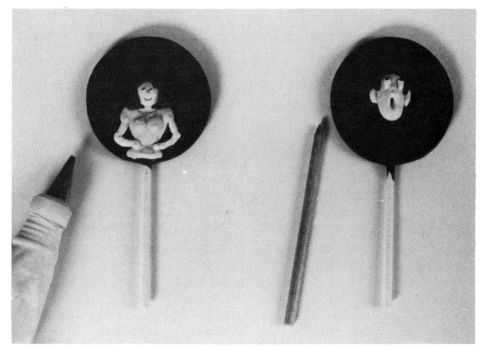

Left: The ballooning technique. Right: The carving technique.

CONFECTIONERY LEAVES

Having sampled the versatility of the plain tubes, you are now ready to meet the highly specialized leaf tubes (#65s–70). The traditional tubes have inverted V-shaped tips with a short slit down the center. Hold the leaf tube with its inverted V-shaped tip touching the surface, the slit in its center facing up. Held in this way, the icing will flow out through the sides of the V opening, and the slit in the center will define the center vein marking on the leaf.

Less well known, but considerably simpler to use, are tubes #349 and #352. Their appearance is distinguished by a very obvious *V* cut out of their point. When held correctly on the surface, the cut-out V should not be visible from the top.

The parchment bag is well suited to piping leaves when its point is flattened and then cut with sharp scissors to conform to the inverted V-shape of the traditional tubes. It too can provide the leaf's center vein marking by cutting a very short slit in its center with scissors. Position it on the piping surface as you would the traditional tubes.

A variety of different types of leaves can be piped with any given leaf tube. Changes in pressure and hand movement can produce short, long, or ruffled leaves. Miniature leaves, so often required for chocolate work, are best piped with tubes #342, 65s, or 65 or with a V-cut parchment bag. A simulated tiny leaf may even be made with a plain tube (#1) using the regular leaf-making technique.

The proper consistency of icing is as important to leaf making as is tube selection. Attempting to pipe a leaf with stiff, heavy, dry icing is an exercise in frustration. Rather than achieving pointed leaves, one is left with blunt ends—heavy, unattractive stubs. These may be corrected by dampening the thumb and forefinger and pinching the stub to a point. In order to achieve the desired point at the end of a leaf, always use icing that is medium to soft in texture. Do not, however, be overly zealous in softening the icing, for icing that is too soft will not hold its shape.

How to Pipe Confectionery Leaves

1. Hold the bag at a 45-degree angle to the surface, tube pointing left and fingertips visible on top of the bag.
2. Lightly touch the surface of the practice board with the tube. As you squeeze the bag, allow the force of the icing to lift the tube slightly as the icing fans out to the desired width. Gently stretch the leaf to a point as you pull it upward, simultaneously relaxing the pressure on the bag.

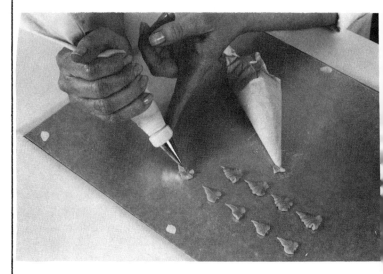

How to Pipe Leaf Variations

1. To vary the length of the leaves, press lightly and pull away quickly for some leaves and exert more pressure and hesitate longer for others.
2. For a ruffled effect, jiggle the tube in and out in several quick motions before pulling it to a point.
3. For another ruffled look, jiggle the tube quickly from side to side several times before pulling the leaf to a point.

CONFECTIONERY FLOWER MAKING

It is the goal of most would-be decorators to achieve a degree of proficiency in confectionery flower making. Unfortunately, many set their early sights on flowers (the rose, in particular) that are far too advanced for most beginners. What a pity when there are so many other beautiful flowers that are well within the capabilities of a novice.

Royal Icing flowers may be made many months

in advance and attached to molded chocolate pieces with a dab of chocolate when needed, or they may be piped directly onto the chocolate and allowed to dry before handling. One batch of icing will produce a great many flowers, so take advantage and make them in several colors, storing those you don't need immediately.

Drop Flowers

This unique series of tubes (#129, 136, 190, 193, to name a few), is designed to facilitate flower making in every way. The metal pin that protrudes through the opening of the tube rests on the surface at precisely the correct elevation to allow instant flowers literally to drop out of the bag with just a squeeze and a twist of the hand. These flowers may be mass-produced on wax paper or piped directly onto the molded chocolate piece.

To ensure success with this procedure you should examine the teeth in the opening of the tube to be sure that none is bent. Misshapen ones may be corrected with the point of a knife. Use a medium to stiff icing for piping these flowers as soft icing will not hold the petal impressions. It is also important to exert a moderate degree of pressure on the bag. Too little will prevent the flower from sticking to the surface, and excessive pressure will result in a blob instead of a flower.

Plain Drop Flower

1. Rest the bag, fitted with a drop-flower tube, at a 90-degree angle (perpendicular) to the surface.
2. Squeeze the bag until a full-petaled flower is clear of the tube. Release pressure, hesitate briefly, and, in a swift motion, lift the tube straight up so as not to distort the flower's petals.
3. Use a #2 plain tube to pipe a dot (or two or three) in the center of each flower in a contrasting color.

Swirled Drop Flower

1. Position the bag as above but with the right hand turned so that the fingertips are parallel to the body.
2. While squeezing the bag, rotate your hand as far to the right as possible, pivoting on the tube's pin as you do.

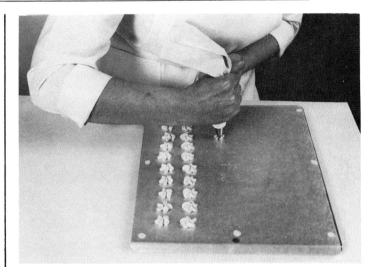

3. Release pressure, hesitate briefly, and lift as described in number two under "Plain Drop Flower."
4. Complete the center with a small plain tube as desired.

Dot Flowers

Call these what you may (forget-me-nots, dog roses, or whatever), they are still nothing more than dots piped in the shape of a flower. Their simplicity belies their delicate beauty— reminiscent of dotted swiss fabric. Use them alone or as an accent color in an arrangement of other flowers.

1. Prepare two bags fitted with small-opening plain tubes (#1 or 2). Half-fill them with medium-consistency icing dyed two different colors.
2. Following the directions for piping dots on

pages 56–57, pipe a circular arrangement of five dots, each one barely touching the other.

3. Pipe a center dot in a contrasting color.

Sweet Peas

This is an easy flower that lends itself to mass production either on wax paper or directly on the chocolate's surface. Use it when you need a speedy, small flower or as a filler in a floral spray.

The rose tubes (#101s–104) used to pipe sweet peas are distinguished by their wedge-shaped opening—wide at one end and narrower at the other.

1. Mark three dots in a horizontal line on your practice board with icing or pencil, positioning them as close together as possible without touching. A pattern sheet of multiple sets of dots, spaced an inch apart and placed under wax paper on your practice board, may also be used for this lesson.
2. Prepare a half-filled bag of medium-consistency icing fitted with a #102 tube. Position the tube on the middle dot at a 45-degree angle, wide end down.

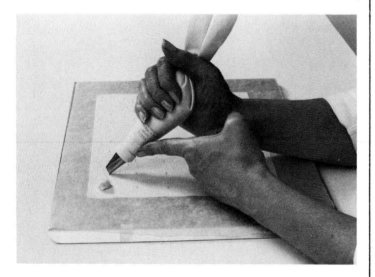

3. Squeeze the bag and, as the icing flows out, raise the tube ⅛ inch straight up off the surface without relaxing the pressure. Briefly hold that position before lowering the tube to its original position on the middle dot. Release pressure and pull away.
4. The two side petals are formed in the same

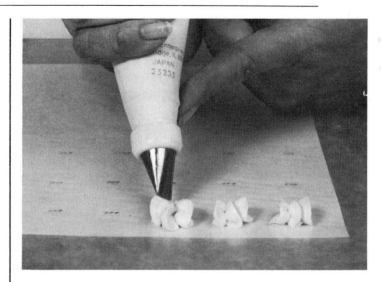

way using the remaining dots as the starting and stopping points. Angle the tube to the left to form the left petal and to the right for the other.

Rosebud (#101s–104)

The rosebud is a frustrating lesson in perseverance. It is, however, a lovely flower that should be an integral part of every chocolate decorator's repertoire. Resolve now to learn it, and with patience you will. The directions that follow are rather unorthodox, but they do work.

1. Mark two dots in a horizontal line on the practice board, ⅛ inch apart, or prepare a pattern sheet of dots.
2. Prepare a half-filled bag of medium-consistency icing fitted with a #102 decorating tube.
3. Position the wide end of the tube on the left dot at a 45-degree angle to the surface.
4. Squeeze the bag, lifting the tube ¼ inch off the surface with the flow of the icing and

moving the hand slightly to the right as you do. Continue to squeeze on the bag until the petal completely lays itself down on the surface. Relax the pressure on the bag as you touch down on the second dot. Release pressure completely and pull away. The right edge of the cupped petal should be standing straight.

5. To form the second petal, position the tube on the right dot, angled so as to barely touch the inside of the standing edge.

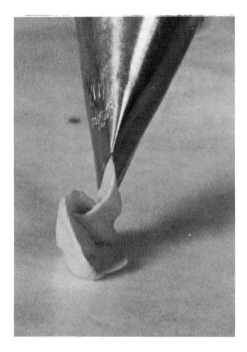

6. Squeeze the bag lightly, lifting the bag ¼ inch off the surface as the icing catches the standing edge, pulling it inward. Continue squeezing the bag until the second petal lays itself down, forming another cupped petal— a mirror image of the first.
7. Relax pressure as you touch down between the two marked dots. Pull away.

Half Rose

The rosebud may be embellished with two extra petals and it becomes a half rose.

1. Center the wide end of the #102 tube at the base of the rosebud.
2. Pivot the tube to the left. Squeeze the bag and lift the tube slightly as you move inward to the center of the bud. Relax pressure and pull away.

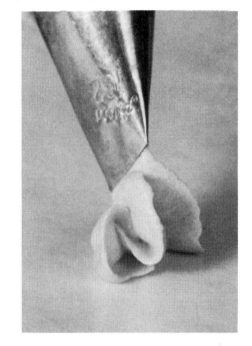

3. Pivot the tube to the right and repeat the above procedure.

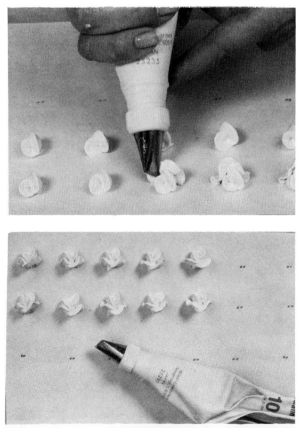

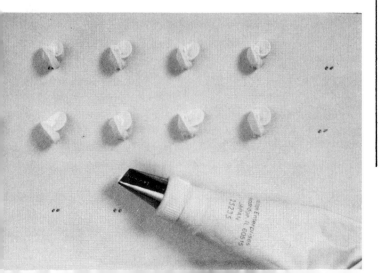

THE FLOWER NAIL

Learning to rotate a flower nail will enable you to create the multipetaled flowers that follow. After an initial period of awkwardness you will be able to manipulate it instinctively.

1. Hold the bottom half of the nail's pin in the thumb, forefinger and third finger of the left hand.

2. Use a dab of icing to secure a 1½- to 2-inch square of wax paper to the nail's head.
3. Practice turning the nail slowly, counterclockwise, as far as possible. Reverse the rotation to return the nail to the starting position. In practicing these movements it will occasionally be necessary to reposition the fingers on the pin to maintain a comfortable position that keeps you in control.
4. Now practice the counterclockwise turns, stopping after each quarter-turn and starting again. Reposition the fingertips as necessary.
5. To remove the wax paper square from the nail without damaging the completed flower, slide it onto an inverted cookie sheet. The flowers must then be dried before storing them or attaching them to molded chocolate pieces.

MULTIPETALED FLOWERS

Wild Rose

The same piping techniques used to pipe the wild rose are used to make many of the popular flowers in bloom today. Once you can pipe a wild rose you should be able to pipe any of the following flowers with a little improvisation: apple and cherry blossoms, impatiens, primroses, violets, pansies, and daffodils, plus many others. You can use the same piping technique to pipe your own versions of the wild rose, changing the size, color, and the number of petals to accommodate the situation.

1. Attach a wax paper square to a #7 nail. Hold the nail in the left hand. Position the wide end of a #102 tube in the center of the nail with the narrow end elevated about ¼ inch off the surface.
2. The next three things must happen simultaneously. Rotate the nail a quarter-turn counterclockwise as you squeeze the bag and slide the wide end of the tube outward about ¼ inch and back to the center again. This completes the first petal. Whew!

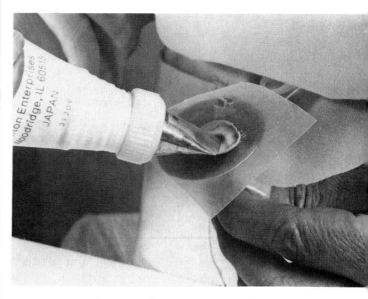

3. To pipe the second petal, position the tube as before, tucking it under the right edge of the first petal. Proceed as in step 2.

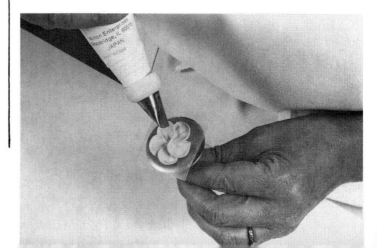

4. Pipe three more petals.
5. Use tube #1 to pipe several dots in the center of the flower in a contrasting color.

Wild Rose Variations

Violets

Here is a variation of the wild rose that is traditionally piped with the #59° F. tube, a curved version of the #101s rose tube. Its curved, wide end automatically cups the petal as it is piped. Use the regular rose tube, if you prefer, along with medium-consistency icing.

1. Attach a square of wax paper to the flower nail with a dab of icing.
2. Position a half-filled bag of dark purple icing fitted with a #59° F. tube (or 101s or 101) with the wide end touching the center of the nail and the narrow end up about ⅛ inch off the surface. The tube should be pointing left with the fingertips facing you.
3. Turn the nail as you pipe the first petal. Repeat for the second petal.
4. Turn the nail halfway around. Pipe three more petals—these slightly longer than the first two.

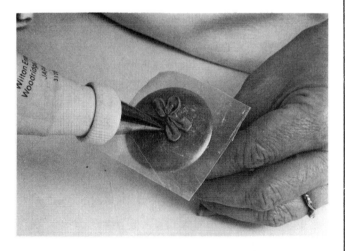

5. Pipe two tiny yellow dots in the center with a #1 tube.

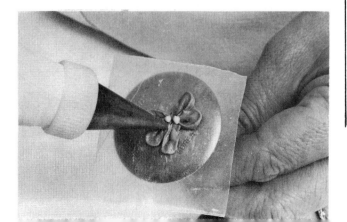

Note: Since these flowers are so small, you may be able to pipe more than one per wax paper square.

Pansies

Two bags of different-colored icing and two rose tubes (preferably #104) are required for piping this lovely flower. It seems like an ideal way to use up leftover icing.

Much of the pansy's beauty lies in the painted details that are added once the icing has dried. These little touches are simple but add so much to the realism of the flower.

1. Half-fill two bags fitted with #104 rose tubes with yellow and purple icings.
2. Pipe two large petals with the yellow icing on the wax paper-covered nail. It will be necessary to extend the tube out farther and into a wider curve than was required for the smaller flowers.
3. Pipe two slightly smaller petals on top of them.

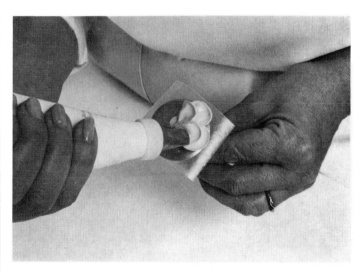

4. Turn the nail halfway around. To complete the pansy, pipe one very large petal, going from the left side to the right, using a back-and-forth motion for a ruffled effect.

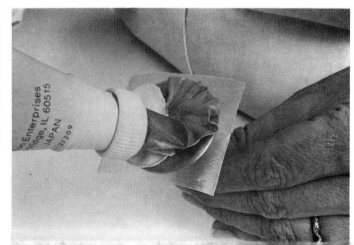

5. Once the flower has dried, paint veins on the petals using a dampened #00 artists' brush and brown food coloring.

6. Pipe a yellow oval-shaped line in the center. *Note:* Pansies grow in a broad spectrum of colors. Be sure to experiment with other color combinations.

Chrysanthemums

This is an ideal large flower to add to your confectionery bouquet. The mum is easy to master and fills the void that the full rose will ultimately fill. Though it is usually piped in fall colors, you'll find that pastel versions of it are nonetheless beautiful.

1. Half-fill two decorating bags with medium to stiff icing of the same color and fit them with #8 and #81 tubes.
2. Position the bag with the #8 tube in the center of the wax-paper-covered nail at a 90-degree angle to the surface. Squeeze slowly and steadily to form a round mound. The depth and diameter of that mound will determine the ultimate size of the mum.
3. Depending on your perspective, the #81 tube resembles a smile—or a frown. Position it— smiling—parallel to the nail's surface, touching the bottom edge of the mound.
4. Squeeze the bag with moderate pressure. As the petal emerges, relax pressure and pull the petal out a distance of no more than ½ inch. Completely surround the bottom of the mound with petals.

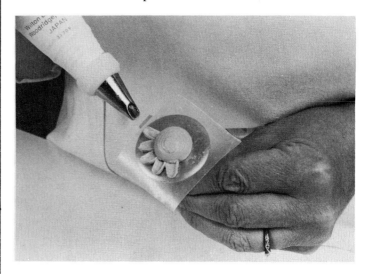

5. Begin the second row and all succeeding rows by positioning the tube between two petals of the previous row. It is not necessary (and indeed impossible) to follow

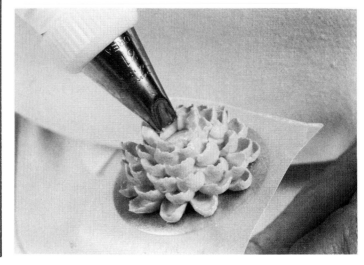

that pattern throughout the whole row. The petals of each row should become increasingly shorter and angled upward more and more.

6. The center of the mum may be filled with petals placed at a 90-degree angle to the mound or with tiny dots made with a #1 tube.

Chrysanthemum Variations

The potential for creating many other flowers based on the mum formula is enormous. Some of these are legitimate—actual known species—and others are fantasy flowers, figments of my wild imagination.

Asters

Made with vibrantly dyed icing and a #75 tube instead of the #81, these flowers are made in much the same manner as mums. The #75 tube resembles a star tube that has been stepped on. Hold it with the flattened side up. The petals will look like concave leaves—very pretty.

Bachelor Buttons

Bachelor buttons are perfect for decorating chocolate requiring a neat, tailored look. Pipe the mound with light blue icing and the pulled star-shaped petals with a #14 tube and darker blue icing. Fill the center of the flower with a cluster of light blue dots piped with a #2 tube.

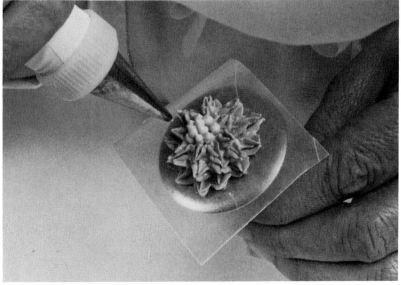

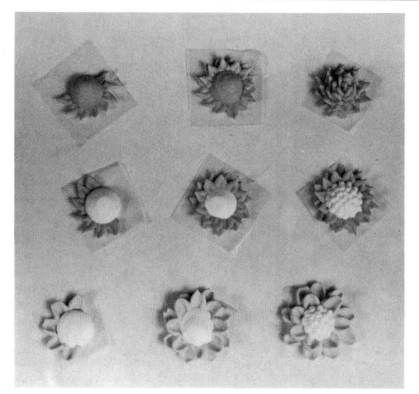

Top row:
Fantasy Flower #1.
Middle row:
Fantasy Flower #2.
Bottom row:
Fantasy Flower #3.

Three Fantasy Flowers

1. For smaller versions of mums or asters, pipe the mound with a #6 tube and the petals with the #349 leaf tube.
2. Pipe the mound with white icing. Surround its base with only two rows of pink petals, using a #349 leaf tube. Completely cover the remaining portion of the mound with pulled dots of white icing using a #2 plain tube.
3. Substitute one of the mum tubes (#79, 80, 81) for the #349 used above. Change the color scheme, and you have a completely different fantasy flower from the one just described.

The Classic Rose

It is no mere coincidence that the rose has been left until the end in these confectionery flower lessons. It is the most difficult lesson of all because it is based on the culmination of several acquired-through-experience skills, an understanding of pressure control, facile use of the decorating nail, and agility of hand movements.

I am convinced, after many years of teaching this lesson, that artistic prowess has less to do with it than simple know-how. It does not take an artist to pipe a rose, but rather someone who can follow directions—*well*. Do not be deterred by the length of these instructions. They are written in as thorough a manner as possible in lieu of my being able to personally guide your hand as I would do in my classes.

Before we begin, you must be aware of certain realities that exist concerning rose making. It requires freshly made, very firm icing! You may have to make a special batch for this lesson using slightly less water. An experienced decorator may be able to get by with a semifirm mixture, but the beginner doesn't stand a chance unless the icing is right for the job.

You must have the proper equipment. I believe that the beginner can achieve better results by using the #97 tube as opposed to the classic rose tubes #101s–104. This is not to say that the traditional tubes should never be used. On the contrary. It is just that the #97 tube hides a multitude of errors. A #7 decorating nail with its broad surface and a stack of approximately 1½-inch wax paper squares are also required.

The cone on which you pipe the rose petals is as important to success in this lesson as is firm icing and proper equipment. It must be broad at the base for support and completely stable throughout to withstand the repeated jabs of the tube, the turns of the nail, and the weight of the petals. To assure that these conditions exist, I strongly recommend that you prepare some Royal Icing practice cones (see step 2 below) on a sheet of wax paper in advance, allowing a day for drying time. After these practice sessions it will no longer be necessary to use hardened cones. The practice cones may be attached to the wax paper squares with a dab of icing.

1. Half-fill two bags with firm icing, fitting one with a #12 plain tube and the other with the #97 (or #104) rose tube.

2. To pipe the cone: Position the bag with the #12 tube at a 90-degree angle to the securely attached wax paper square covering the nail. As in figure piping, squeeze the bag firmly but steadily as you elevate the tube slowly—the tip always partially submerged. Gradually decrease the pressure on the bag as you reach a height of approximately ¾ inch. The cone should be stocky, not tall and thin.

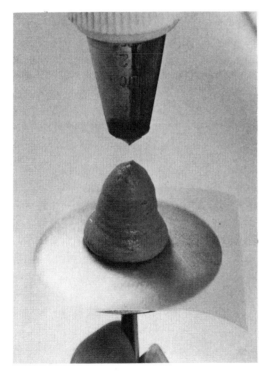

3. For good control, keep both arms close to the body and hold the nail about even with your chin. Gently touch the #97 tube, wide end down, against the top quarter of the cone with the narrow end angled in sharply.

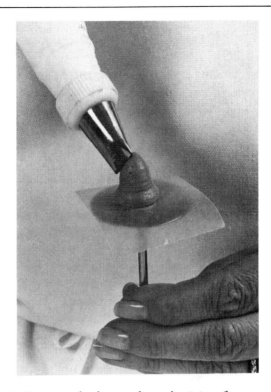

4. Squeeze the bag and, as the icing flows, turn, turn, turn the nail, counterclockwise, as you pull a ribbon of icing all the way around the top of the cone, encasing it in a teepee with a small hole in the center. The harder you press on the bag, the faster the flow of icing and the faster you must turn the nail. Check the opening in the teepee. If it is larger than ⅛ inch in diameter, the narrow end of the tube was not angled in sufficiently.

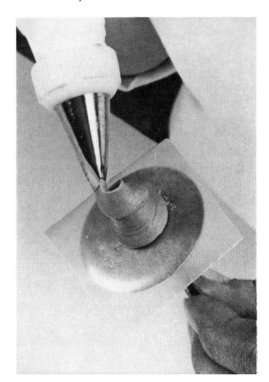

5. It is important to note that from here on the tip of the tube must always be in contact with the cone; otherwise, the petals will not attach properly to it. Examine the profile of the #97 (or #104) tube. It is significant that the wide end extends out farther than the narrow end. It is that extended point that should make the contact, not the entire full-wedged surface.

6. Position the extended point of the tube against the cone about halfway up. The angle of the tube should be parallel to the cone and at a 90-degree angle to the nail. As you squeeze the bag, turn the nail counterclockwise and move the extended tip of the tube across the surface of the cone in an up-and-down direction to pipe an arc. Check the appearance of the first petal. A half-moon shape should be visible. If it isn't, it means that you didn't move in an up-and-down direction. If the petal is rippled, it means that you didn't turn the nail quickly enough.

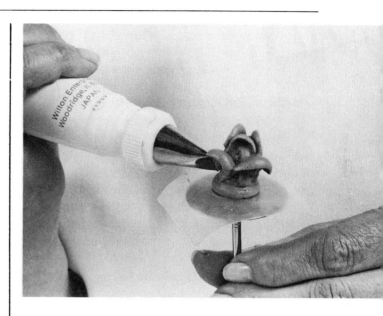

about a 45-degree angle to the cone. This angle will produce an opening effect of the petals. Gently place the extended tip of the tube against the cone under row 1. Rotate the nail as you pipe these petals as before—in an up-and-down movement and always in touch with the cone. Begin one petal where the previous one ends.

9. The final row of seven petals is opened completely. To achieve this look, the opening of the tube must be placed at an angle that is almost perpendicular to the cone and parallel to the nail's surface. The palm of the hand holding the bag should be visible as it faces up. Place the tip against the cone under the last row of petals. It is

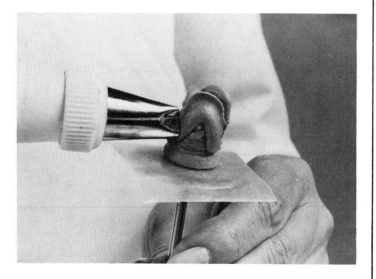

7. Pipe the second petal next to the first in exactly the same way, remembering to draw the tip of the tube up and down across the cone's surface as you turn the nail. A third petal completes the first row.

8. The first petal of the second row should be centered between two petals in row 1. A total of four or five will be required for this row. Whereas the tube was angled inward for the teepee, and straight up and down for row 1, it now begins to angle outward to

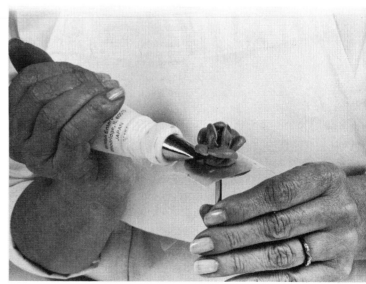

no longer necessary to move up and down with each petal. As you squeeze the bag and rotate the nail, a petal will form. Stop turning the nail and pressing on the bag to terminate the petal.

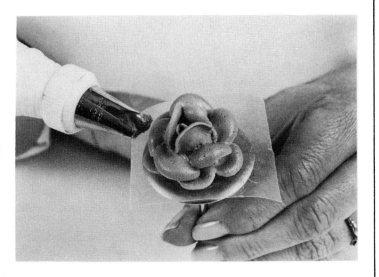

Miniature Roses

1. Push a toothpick through a tiny square of wax paper (about ¼ inch square) to expose a ½-inch point.
2. Using a bag fitted with a #101s rose tube, wide end down, pipe a spiral ribbon of icing on the point of the toothpick, rotating it as you do the flower nail, to form the bud.
3. Proceed as above for piping a full rose, piping two rows of petals instead of three.
4. To remove the rose from the toothpick, pull up on the paper square. Set aside to dry.

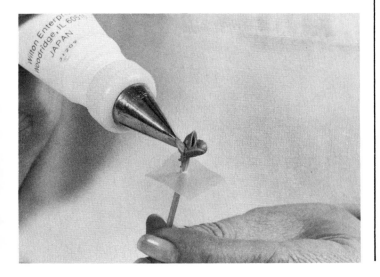

WIRED FLOWERS AND LEAVES

For obvious reasons it is important to use good common sense when combining wires of any kind with food products. Use wires only when no edible substitute is feasible and where they will never be mistaken for food.

To wire flowers and leaves made of Royal Icing, use green, covered floral wire in gauges 18 (heavy) through 22 (thin). This wire is available in most arts and crafts stores. It may be cut to any desired length with wire clippers.

Piping Calyxes

1. Prepare a bag of medium-to-stiff green icing and fit it with a plain tube. The size of the tube will depend on how large a calyx is required for any given flower. Use #2 for tiny ones, #6–8 for most others.
2. Center the tube at a 90-degree angle to a wax paper square. Squeeze the bag steadily, elevating the tube as you do, to pipe out a small cone.
3. Insert a short piece of floral wire into the top of the cone.

4. Grasp the wire and lift it upright. Use a dampened finger or artists' brush to taper the point of the inverted cone to assure a solid attachment of wire to cone.

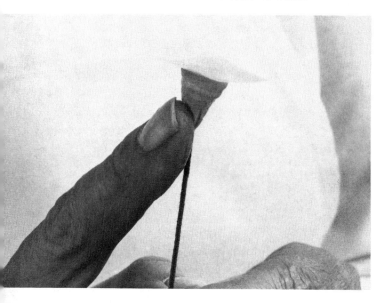

5. Insert the wires into a piece of Styrofoam and dry the cones thoroughly. Remove the wax paper square and attach the calyx to the prepared flower with a dab of icing.

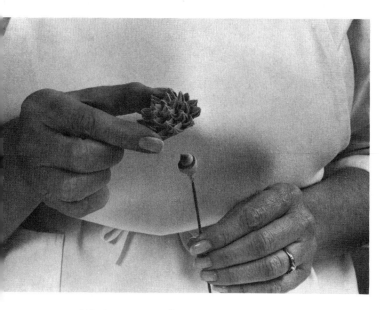

Piping Wired Leaves

1. Lay the end of a covered floral wire on a square of wax paper.
2. Using a #352 (or #67) leaf tube and green icing, pipe a leaf over the wire as if it were the leaf's stem.

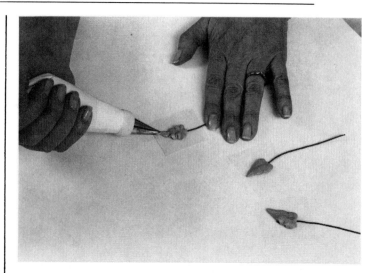

3. Dry thoroughly. Turn the leaf over and paint the exposed wire with softened green icing. Dry.

RUN SUGAR WORK

Run sugar—otherwise known as *Color Flow, run out, flow in, flood work*—is a technique that uses Royal Icing to outline and flood designs. Unlike the figure-piping techniques described earlier, these designs dry perfectly flat as though they had been painted on the chocolate piece with a marvelous icing paint.

1. Mark the outline of the pattern directly on the surface of the molded chocolate piece with a toothpick or hat pin.

2. Gently brush away the chocolate debris with an artists' camel hair brush.
3. If the icing needs to be dyed, do it now. Set

aside a portion of the icing to be used for flooding purposes.

4. Outline the pattern with a #1 or #2 plain tube, taking particular care not to leave breaks in the lines.

5. Begin adding ½ teaspoon of water at a time to the reserved icing, stirring it until the icing achieves the texture of melted milk chocolate—soft but not runny. Test a glob of it on wax paper. It should lose its ripples but still retain some body.

6. Pour the soft icing into a parchment bag, taking care not to overfill it. Cut a small opening in the tip and begin to flood the outlined area, beginning along the outside edges. Don't be afraid to press on the bag. The icing will not overflow the outline unless it is too runny. Ease the soft icing into any tiny crevices with a toothpick or a small brush.

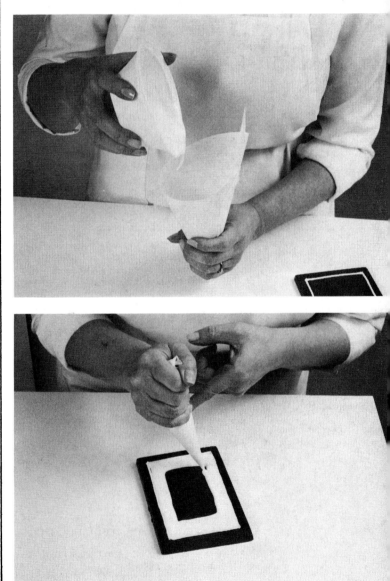

7. Examine the surface of the flooded area for air bubbles. Puncture them with the tip of a toothpick or hat pin before the icing crusts.

8. The run sugar work must dry several hours—overnight, if it is a large piece—before finishing touches are applied to it.

5
Basic Decorating Skills—Chocolate and Compound Coating

Decorative piping with chocolate is an exciting departure from the standard methods described in the previous chapter. Many newcomers find that using a bag full of chocolate is an easier introduction to decorating craftsmanship than icing, because it demands less expertise with the decorating bag, less familiarity with tube numbers and their uses, and less emphasis on proper texture of the piping medium. Most of the skills described in this chapter involve chocolate in an unadulterated, melted (and tempered, if real chocolate is used) form. A special section is devoted to piping skills that require a heavier, thickened form of chocolate.

Remember that whenever the word *chocolate* is used in the directions, it should be interpreted to mean chocolate, cocoa butter white coating, or compound coating. Unless specified, you may choose the medium in which you work most comfortably. In cases where a color is needed to create a special effect, the term *coating* may be used to imply cocoa butter coating or compound coating. Again the choice is yours.

Decorations piped in chocolate are decidedly easier and faster to make than those piped in Royal Icing, and they taste better, too. Designs done in icing take longer to dry and often break just when it is time to use them. Because chocolate sets so quickly, errors or breakage, if

they occur, are less painful. Our investment in time and labor is considerably less, and the flawed pieces can be melted down again and the procedure repeated. As frustrating as icing work can be at times, however, it is still a remarkably versatile medium for artistic expression.

You will come to realize as you experiment with both chocolate and icing that one is better suited than the other for certain situations. The preferred medium for the various designs throughout the book will be specified whenever it is imperative to use one or the other. At other times you will choose the one that best fits your needs.

The prerequisite to successful chocolate piping is a perfectly rolled parchment bag with a pinpoint opening. It is used without the insertion of a metal decorating tube to eliminate the constant plugging of its opening as the chocolate within the bag begins to set.

HOW TO HANDLE A BAG FILLED WITH CHOCOLATE

1. Always either hold the opening of the bag pointed upward as you move with it or cover the hole with your finger. The

chocolate is fluid and will run out of the hole freely even without pressing on the bag.

2. Grasp the closed end of the bag as you would a ball, touch the wax paper with the open end, and gently squeeze the bag. If a great deal of pressure is required, the opening may either be obstructed or too small, or the chocolate may be too cool. Make the appropriate adjustment.

3. To halt the flow of chocolate from the bag, stop pressing on it, and quickly angle the bag so that its opening is almost parallel to the surface. Backtrack over your final flourish to avoid dripping chocolate on the design.

The tip of the cone must be cut to the desired size opening just prior to using it. For procedures requiring a very small opening, special attention must be paid to the chocolate being used to assure that it is smooth enough to pass through the hole without plugging it. Force the chocolate through a very fine sieve before filling the bag, if necessary, to rid it of small lumps.

If the tip of the bag should ever plug (and it will), pinch the opening between your left thumb and forefinger and force the obstacle out. If the opening plugs because the chocolate has cooled and set, hold the tip of the bag flat against a warm heating tray or a warm pan just until the chocolate is melted enough to flow freely again. An optional method containing an element of risk is to pass the tip of the bag back and forth several times a few inches above an open flame, taking care not to scorch the chocolate—or your fingertips!

Decorating bags filled with coating should be kept warm and fluid throughout the piping procedure. This may be accomplished in several ways: place them on a hot-tray set at its lowest setting, on a metal pie pan placed over a bowl of warm water, in a turned-off gas oven, or under an infrared lamp, or use a unique system of your own.

Bags filled with real chocolate must be treated with greater care to maintain the temper of the chocolate throughout the piping procedure. Because most methods are generally unreliable, prepare only as much chocolate as you can use at one time without trying to keep it in temper for any length of time.

Dedicated decorators, determined to find a way, may wish to use the infrared lamp's rays to maintain the proper temperature in the chocolate-filled bags. Monitor the temperature of several small bowls of water positioned within the lamp's range until you find a spot that is warmed to the proper degree. Position the bag there accordingly.

WRITING WITH CHOCOLATE

Writing on chocolate with chocolate follows the same basic procedures as those described for writing with icing on chocolate (see Chapter 4). Because it is more fluid than even the soft icing that is used for writing, it is important to cut a very small opening in the bag and to use very light pressure on the bag; otherwise the letters will be thick and run together.

1. Use a parchment bag about ⅓ full of chocolate.

2. Cut a very small opening at the end of the bag—equivalent to a #1 tube. Test the flow on the practice board. Adjust the opening, if necessary.

3. Gently squeeze the bag, and the chocolate will flow out. The harder you press on the bag, the faster the flow and the faster you must write. Practice a row of *c*s, holding the bag at a 45-degree angle to the wax paper.

4. Practice a row of *m*s, lifting the bag slightly off the surface of the paper. In that position, pull the string of chocolate across the board as you write. Touch the surface to complete a letter or word, ceasing pressure on the bag as you do.

CHOCOLATE PATTERN WORK

One of the techniques that I personally find to be the most rewarding is pattern work done with chocolate. These paper patterns are placed on a flat, portable surface, covered with wax paper and traced over with chocolate or coating. Once you discover the potential that exists for this type of work, you will delight in it as much as I do.

Any of the patterns suggested here and throughout the book may be done in chocolate or in Royal Icing using the run sugar method described at the end of Chapter 4. Icing pattern work requires hours of drying time, however, and breakage of the thin, fragile pieces is not uncommon. It is so much simpler to pipe the patterns in chocolate and have them ready in minutes. Besides, broken pieces are often reparable when done in chocolate.

Patterns suitable for chocolate use may be found in coloring books, in embroidery and craft books, in the Sunday comics, and in greeting card illustrations. Potential patterns are everywhere! Company logos are often suitable, as are athletic team logos and insignias of all kinds. The best of all to use, of course, are those that you draw yourself—your very own unique designs. You need not be an artist to do this. Simple line drawings work best.

1. Attach a pattern sheet with cellophane tape to a flat cookie sheet or board that will fit into your refrigerator or freezer. I occasionally use a square of Plexiglas. Sometimes patterns are attached to a curved surface. Those will be dealt with specifically where necessary.
2. Tape a smooth sheet of wax paper over the pattern and set it aside.
3. Prepare as many parchment bags as needed for color changes for any given pattern. Fill the bags with chocolate or coating and keep them warm until you need them.
4. Cut an opening in the parchment bag the equivalent of a #2 tube. Hold the bag at a 45-degree angle and squeeze it gently to start the flow of chocolate. Adjust the opening, if necessary, to assure an even flow. The outlining may be done with the tube barely touching the pattern's surface or slightly elevated.

5. If the pattern is a filigree one, chill the piece once outlined and carefully remove it from the paper—either by loosening it with a metal spatula or by releasing the wax paper and peeling off the piece. Large fragile designs should be strengthened on their back sides by overpiping the filigree here and there.

Butterfly pattern for filigree chocolate work.

6. To fill in the various areas of the pattern, cut an opening equivalent to a #4 tube in a prepared parchment bag and begin flooding the perimeter of the open space. The still-wet outline will act as a wall and contain the loose chocolate. Continue to flood the center until the entire space is filled.

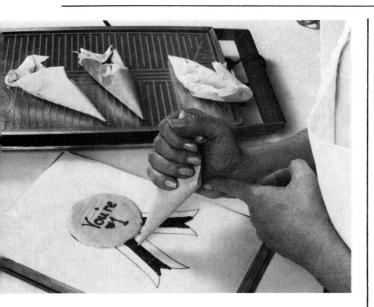

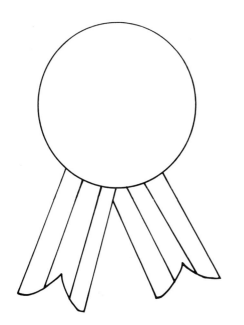

Pattern for a solid
chocolate design.

7. To smooth the bumpy surface of the flooded
   area, either gently tap the bottom of the
   board or jiggle the tip of the bag lightly
   over the surface of the loose chocolate.
8. Chill the completed piece and release it as
   explained in step 5.

CHOCOLATE BORDERS

The same skills used to write and outline
patterns are used to embellish the edges of cakes
and chocolate pieces with borders. Borders
convey a sense of unity—a completeness in
relation to the overall chocolate design.
Unfortunately, the inexperienced hand will be
evident in this type of work because it requires
precision and patient attention to detail. As a
beginner you can conceal your inexperience
considerably by piping the border in the same
color as the background.

The examples that follow are in no way
intended to teach the standard borders of the
classic school of decorating. Rather, they are
modified to blend the formal elegance of the past
with the delicate innovations of our
contemporary designs.

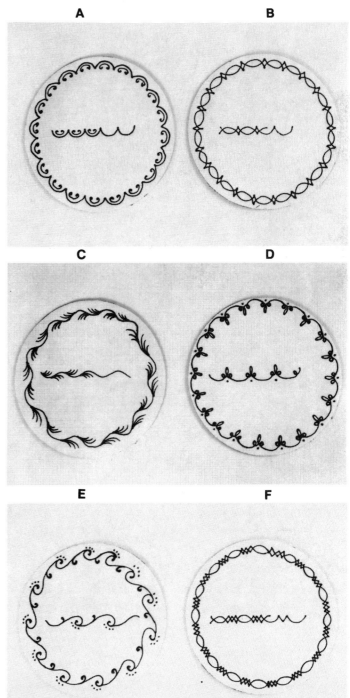

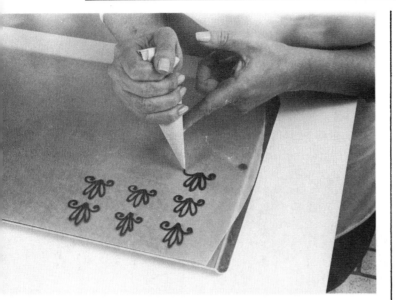

These borders are often piped on the sides of cakes and chocolate pieces. This technique is more easily accomplished with slightly thickened chocolate (see pages 91–92). Keep the tiny opening of the bag close to the surface at all times.

CHOCOLATE STEMS

Stems are piped using the writing techniques described earlier in this chapter and the procedures used to pipe icing stems in Chapter 4. If you use chocolate to pipe the stems, it is important to use chocolate for the leaves as well.

CHOCOLATE LEAVES

When you see how easy it is to make them, you will surely want to use chocolate leaves to finish off your luscious arrangements of chocolate or icing flowers or as a simple, dramatic touch on a special dessert. Here are three different ways to make leaves. Choose the type that is best suited for each situation.

Method I: Coating Fresh Leaves with Chocolate

These chocolate leaves are the most natural-looking ones of all because they are, in fact, chocolate carbon copies of fresh leaves from your own garden (or purchased from your florist). The ideal leaves for this technique are thick and shiny with distinct vein markings on their backsides. This is not to say that other kinds may not be used. Try a variety of them. To facilitate handling, leave a bit of stem on the leaves when they are clipped.

Though most leaves are harmless, some are toxic to differing degrees and can pose a health hazard if eaten or used in contact with chocolate or other food products. Even leaves that are considered safe to use can be potentially toxic if they have been treated with either spray or systemic insecticides. The following lists of safe and poisonous plants are incomplete. Consult an authoritative source (listed on page 81) if in doubt as to a leaf's classification.

Safe Leaves

Rose
Lemon
Gardenia
Magnolia
Grape ivy

Toxic Leaves

Poinsettia
Lily of the Valley
Mistletoe
Dieffenbachia
Oleander
Delphinium (Larkspur)
Caladium
Hydraegea
Amaryllis (jonquil, daffodil, narcissus)
Holly
Rhododendron (laurel, azalea)
Poppy
English ivy

STAND-UP PLACECARDS

RAGGEDY ANN, ANDY, AND CLOWN STAND-UPS

PECAN CUPS

HOUSEWARMING GREETING CARD

CASHEW BASKETS

TEACHER CARD

FLORAL SPRAY GREETING CARD

SOCIAL SECURITY CARD

HOLIDAY GREETING CARD

BONBON COOKIES

FOIL CUPS

ANNIVERSARY CARD

SHALOM GREETING CARD

BIRTHDAY CARD

BIRTH ANNOUNCEMENT

BIRTHDAY LOLLIPOPS

SEASONAL LOLLIPOPS

Sources

Hardin, James W., and Arena, Jay M., M.D. *Human Poisoning from Native and Cultivated Plants.* 2nd ed. Durham, NC: Duke University Press, 1974.

Kingsbury, John M. *Deadly Harvest (A Guide to Common Poisonous Plants).* New York, Chicago, San Francisco: Holt, Rinehart and Winston, 1965.

Muenscher, Walter Conrad. *Poisonous Plants of the United States.* rev. ed. New York: The Macmillan Company, 1962.

1. Wash the freshly picked, flawless leaves and pat them dry on both sides with a towel.
2. Prepare a few ounces of the chocolate of your choice.
3. Paint the back side of each leaf (because the vein markings are clearer there) with chocolate using an artists' brush (if the leaf is small) or a metal spatula. Do not allow the chocolate to overflow onto the front of the leaf or it will be difficult to peel it away once set.

4. Chill the coated leaf on a curved surface, if desired, until set.
5. Beginning at the stem, gently pull the fresh leaf away so as not to break the chocolate

leaf. Fresh leaves are sometimes reusable, so try not to tear it as you pull it away.
6. Keep the chocolate leaves refrigerated until needed unless your room is cool.

Note: To give the leaves a shine, they may be painted lightly with Confectioners' Glaze, but I really prefer them in their natural state. (see page 47).

Modifying the Leaf Size

When small fresh leaves are unavailable, use the large leaves in the following manner to make medium and small sizes.

1. Use a parchment bag to pipe the outline of the smaller leaf in the middle of the leaf's back side, directly over the vein in the center. Fill in the outlined area with chocolate. Do not make it too thin or the leaf will be difficult to remove.

2. Tap the leaf on the counter to smooth out the chocolate.
3. Briefly chill the leaf to set the chocolate and then peel away the fresh leaf carefully.

Method II: Molded Leaves

A variety of leaf molds is now available to decorators. These molds have all the markings of true leaves but are much thicker than real ones. For a thin leaf, follow the instructions for flat molding on pages 28-29, using as little chocolate as possible simply to cover the bottom of each cavity.

Method III: Piping Thin Leaves in a Mold

Most floral arrangements require large, medium, and small leaves. By piping them freehand in a standard leaf mold, you can make leaves sized to fit every floral design.

1. Half-fill a parchment bag with chocolate or coating.
2. Cut the tip off the bag, leaving an opening equivalent to a #4 decorating tube.
3. Pipe the outline of a small leaf within the cavity of the leaf mold. Use the cavity's point and the vein in the center for the smaller leaf's point and vein. Taper the leaf's bottom into a short stem.

4. Flood the outlined area using moderate pressure on the bag and working from the perimeter in toward the center. Gently rap the mold on the counter to flatten the chocolate.
5. Chill and unmold the small, thin leaf.
6. Pipe more leaves in a variety of sizes.

CHOCOLATE FLOWERS

When I discovered this technique of chocolate flower making, a new realm of possibilities opened up for me. The excitement that I felt then has not diminished one bit over the years. Prepare yourself! I think that you are going to enjoy this.

Dot Flowers

Let's begin with the simple chocolate version of the dot flowers described in Chapter 4.

1. Prepare two parchment bags with coatings or chocolate—in contrasting colors. Cut a small opening in each bag—the equivalent of a #1 or #2 tube.
2. To pipe a chocolate dot, hold the bag at a 45-degree angle to the chocolate piece, lift the tip slightly and squeeze the bag until a ball forms. Release pressure and pull away with a circular movement of your hand in order to control the drip.
3. Continue to pipe a circle of dots, spacing them so as not to touch one another, or they will run together.
4. Add a center dot in a contrasting color only after the other dots have hardened.

Note: Chocolate dot flowers must be piped directly onto the chocolate piece.

Chocolate Daisies

I have named these daisies, but really they are just nonspecific flowers. Change the shape and the number of petals, the size, and the color of the flower and call them whatever you wish. They are made on a square of wax paper using the #7 flower nail. Chilling them on a curved surface (such as a flower former) makes them look quite realistic.

1. Cut a small opening equivalent to a #2 tube in the tip of a chocolate-filled parchment bag.
2. Secure a wax paper square to the nail with a dab of chocolate. Hold the nail in your left hand.
3. Position the tip of the bag at a 45-degree angle to the outer edge of the nail. Squeeze the bag to pipe an elongated petal, moving in toward the center point of the nail.

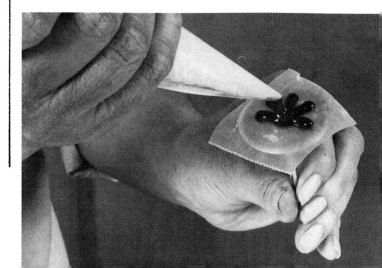

4. Continue piping more petals until the flower is complete.
5. Place the wax paper square on a curved surface until the petals are firm.
6. To decorate the center of the flower, pipe one or two dots of coating in a contrasting color.

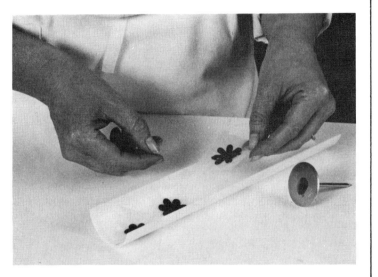

Full-Bloom Nonspecific Flowers

The flowers in the following series are assembled after their petals are individually piped and chilled. The shape of the petals may be created freehand or with a pre-drawn pattern as a guide. Do them weeks in advance or minutes before you need them. They are quick, beautiful, and delicious.

1. Prepare a pattern sheet by drawing or tracing the desired number of petals on the dull side of a 3- by 11-inch strip of freezer paper. That size fits the large flower former. Adjust the width and length of the paper to conform to any other curved surface you

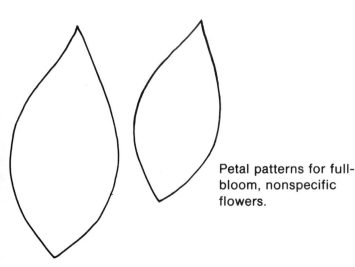

Petal patterns for full-bloom, nonspecific flowers.

might choose to use. If the flower requires large and small petals, draw a second pattern sheet.
2. Turn the pattern sheet over. The lines should be visible on the shiny side of the paper. If they are not, retrace them with a pen. Lay the strip inside the curve of the flower former with the shiny side up. (Sometimes you will want to curve the petals downward instead of upward. In that case the freezer paper should be attached to the outside of the flower former with cellophane tape.)
3. Outline the first petal. Flood its interior, using a side-to-side motion and firm pressure on the bag. Use the tip of the bag to skim the very surface of the chocolate lightly to flatten the ripples. Continue to outline and then fill each subsequent petal on the pattern sheet.

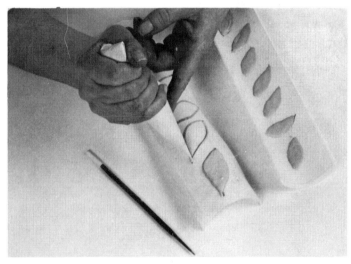

4. Gently tap the bottom of the flower former to flatten the ripples in the chocolate further. A small brush may be used to define the points on the petals, if necessary.
5. Chill the piped petals on the flower former until they are cold and firm.
6. Peel the petals from the paper and assemble them while they are still chilled.

To Assemble the Petals

1. Pipe a ball of chocolate about ½ inch in diameter on a small piece of freezer or wax paper. Begin positioning the blunt ends of the larger petals in it. Add dabs of chocolate

as needed to be sure all petals are attached securely. Allow this row of petals to firm up completely before continuing.

2. Pipe a smaller ball of chocolate in the center of the flower and add the smaller petals as above.

3. Decorate the center of the flower with dots of a contrasting color or as desired.

Jonquils

After you have made a few of the flowers just described you might want to modify the shape of the petals, the color, or the number of petals. The artist in you will surely begin to stir when, at last, you are able to pipe petals freehand, without a pattern, creating original blossoms at will.

Even when you think that you have exhausted all of the possibilities for modifying the basic flower, consider the next idea to stretch your

creativity even further. The lily nail's concave shape (see Chapter 3) is ideal for molding the trumpet that is necessary to convert the nonspecific flower into a jonquil, daffodil, or a narcissus. Begin by following the petal instructions given above and finish it off this way:

1. Hold the 1⅝-inch lily nail by the pin with your left hand.

2. Coat the bottom half of its interior with coating, using an artists' brush or a parchment bag. Keep the top edge of the coating as even as possible. Gently tap the nail's pin on the counter once or twice to smooth the surface of the coating.

3. Wait a minute or two before piping a zigzag border over the top edge. To do this, use a coating-filled parchment bag cut to a #2 tube size opening. Move back and forth in a tight zigzag all the way around the top of the trumpet.

4. Chill it until it is very cold (about five minutes in the freezer).

5. Gently tap the edge of the nail on the counter in various places. The molded trumpet will pop out and you will feel very proud of yourself!

6. To shape the jonquil, assemble a nonspecific flower using one row of large petals. Attach the trumpet to its center with a little coating.

Lily Nail Flowers

1. Prepare a coating-filled parchment bag cut to a #2 tube opening.
2. Hold the 1⅝-inch lily nail by the pin with your left hand.
3. Beginning deep in the cavity of the nail, pipe an outline of a petal, reaching up to the lip of the nail and back into the cavity again.
4. Immediately flood the outlined petal using a side-to-side motion. Pipe and then flood about five more of these petals. Flood the center of the cavity.

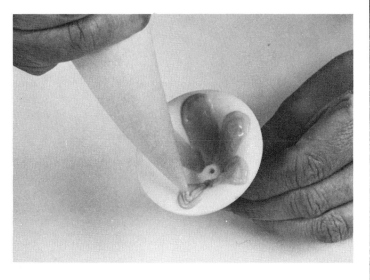

5. Gently tap the nail on the counter to smooth the surface of the coating. Chill for about one minute in the freezer.
6. Insert several short pieces (approximately ½ inch) of licorice laces, in an appropriate color, or uncooked spaghetti as stamens into

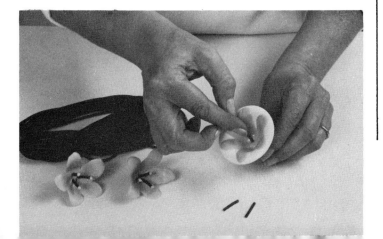

the center of the flower. They will topple over unless the coating is partially set.
7. Chill the flower until absolutely cold—about five minutes.
8. Rotate the nail on its side, gently tapping it on the counter in various places. The flower will pop out easily. If it doesn't, chill it a little longer and try again. The tips of the "stamen" may be dotted with coating, if desired.

Fresh Leaf Flowers

This technique for chocolate flower making hit me like a lightning bolt one day! By varying the procedure for making chocolate leaves a little, fresh leaves can be used as patterns to pipe chocolate flower petals. The petals made this way are thin and natural looking, and their size and shape can be adapted to meet your particular needs. I especially like the gardenia leaf for this work because it is the ideal size and shape.

Method I:

1. Wash and thoroughly dry several gardenia leaves. For easier handling a tiny bit of stem should still be attached to them.
2. Using a chocolate-filled parchment bag cut to the size of a #4 tube opening, outline the shape of the desired flower petal on the *top* side of the leaf. You do not have to use the entire surface of the leaf for this. Be sure to center your petal on the leaf, however.
3. Immediately flood the area with chocolate.
4. Holding the leaf by the stem, tap it lightly on the counter top once or twice. The ripples in the chocolate will flatten. Define the point with an artists' brush, if necessary.
5. Chill the petal on a curved surface, if desired, until it is firm—about three minutes—and then carefully peel away the leaf.
6. Repeat this procedure for the remainder of the necessary petals for each flower.

Method II

1. Use an artists' brush dipped in chocolate to paint the petal on the leaf's surface. Try not to paint too thinly. Another small, clean brush may be used to define the edges of the petal, if necessary.
2. Tap the leaf on the counter top to flatten

the ripples in the chocolate as in step 4 on page 85.

3. Chill briefly and carefully peel away the leaf.

Petal Assembly

These petals are assembled in much the same way as the nonspecific flowers already described.

Calla Lily

The exotic calla lily is a sensational way to dramatize your most sumptuous chocolate dessert. It will be necessary this time to twist the base of a large lemon leaf into the trumpet shape that distinguishes this unique flower. For an amazingly realistic look, use white coating.

1. Wash and thoroughly dry a lemon leaf.
2. Holding the leaf face side up, twist its base just above the stem into a cone about two inches high and secure it well with cellophane tape.
3. Use a small spoon or a parchment bag to partially fill the cone with the coating.

4. Fill the entire interior of the cone, adding more coating if necessary. Continue to coat the whole face of the leaf. I sometimes use an infant-size spoon to do this. Examine the leaf to be sure that it is covered sufficiently with coating. Touch up any thin areas with more of the coating. Use your fingertips to clean the edges of the leaf of excess coating.

5. Tap the back of the leaf on the counter to smooth the coating's surface.
6. Chill for approximately five minutes or until set.
7. Slit the tape and carefully peel away the leaf.

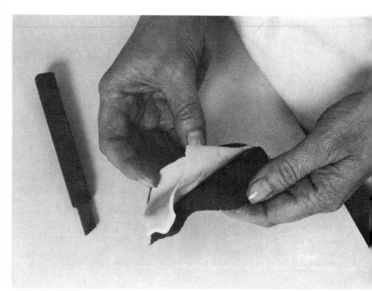

Stamens

Select one of these stamens to complete the calla lily.

Compound Coating Clay Stamens (see the end of this chapter)

1. Roll a small piece of yellow clay between your palms to shape the stamen (approximately 1¾ inches long).
2. Immediately roll it in yellow granulated sugar and set it aside to dry briefly. To color granulated sugar, add a few specks of yellow food coloring to a small jarful of sugar, cover it, and shake it vigorously.

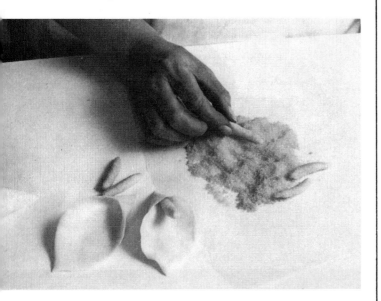

3. Attach the dry stamen to the calla lily with a little white coating.

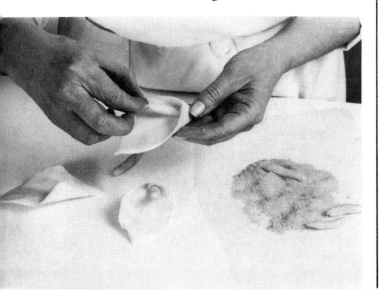

Licorice Stick Stamens

1. Dip a 1¾-inch-long piece of cherry licorice stick into some melted yellow coating. Smooth the coating neatly with an artist's brush.
2. Place the coated stick on a piece of wax paper and sprinkle it generously with yellow granulated sugar. Chill.
3. Attach the stamen to the flower with coating.

CHOCOLATE CONES

Every once in awhile I get a brainstorm, and making chocolate cones with freezer paper is the result of one of them. For years, as I searched for the best way to form shiny, smooth, chocolate cones, I fumbled with wax paper and aluminum foil. It finally occurred to me that freezer paper was not only shiny and smooth on one side, but stiff and capable of holding its shape even when filled with chocolate. These cones are not only incredibly chic but incredibly simple to make as well—a fact that should remain our little secret.

1. Cut several six-inch squares of freezer paper. Smaller or larger cones can be made by enlarging or reducing the size of the squares. Cut each square into two triangles.
2. Shape each triangle, shiny side in, into a cone according to the instructions for making parchment cones on pages 38–39.) It is important, as always, to make the cone with no more than a pinpoint in the narrow end. Secure the paper cone with cellophane tape. The points on the back of

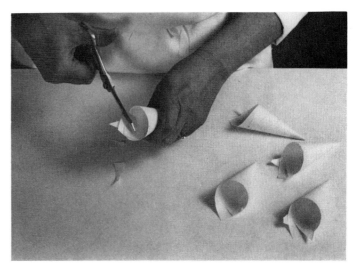

the cone may be cut off completely, if you want the traditional look of a straight-edged cone. Otherwise, trim them so that there is only one point visible for an unusual peaked version.

3. Use a small spoon or a parchment bag to fill the bottom of the cone with approximately two teaspoons of chocolate. Use a medium-sized artists' brush to coat the entire interior of the cone well with it. Add more chocolate as needed.

4. Lay the filled cones on a small cookie sheet or plate and chill them only until the chocolate sets. Overchilling will cause them to crack because they are so thin.

5. Slit the tape with the point of a sharp knife, and the paper will peel away easily. Handle the cones as little as possible, touching them on the inside rather than the outside.

6. The cones may be decorated or left unadorned.

7. Store them covered in a cool place. They may be made weeks in advance.

Note: Make a few extra cones to allow for breakage.

CHOCOLATE FIGURE PIPING

True figure piping done in chocolate or coating has its limitations because, in its melted state, the substance lacks the density of a heavy icing. Obviously, many figures require a stiff medium capable of holding a three-dimensional shape without collapsing. Though a thickened form of chocolate (discussed later in this chapter) can be used for such decorating projects, Royal Icing is still considered the best medium for achieving realistic results in that kind of figure piping.

What melted chocolate may lack in density it makes up for in the magic of its fluidity. It is incredibly adaptable to the pressures exerted on the bag to flow freely, stand firmly, flatten, or swell. It is, above all else, the key to freedom from mold dependency—the crutch on which so many unenlightened chocolate decorators rest their artistic laurels.

It is important to review a few of the chocolate characteristics already covered in previous sections in order to understand the limits to which chocolate can be piped.

1. In general, the warmer the chocolate, the more fluid it is. Therefore, for piping that requires rigidity and dimension, use cool chocolate.

2. Skimming the surface of piped chocolate with the tip of the bag will flatten the ripples. So, if you don't want to lose the dimension of a piped form, don't touch it until it has set.

3. It has a fine adhesive quality. So, if you want to attach a free-form figure to a molded piece, make a good, solid contact and then don't touch it until it sets.

Piping Balls and Dots

1. Half-fill a parchment bag with chocolate and cut an opening in its tip to make it the equivalent of a #4 decorating tube.

2. Hold the bag at a 90-degree angle to the piping surface, slightly elevated, and gently squeeze the bag. Dots are piped at a 45-degree angle. Continue squeezing until the desired size ball or dot is achieved.
3. Relax pressure, giving the tip of the bag several counterclockwise turns as you pull away.
4. Gently tap the bottom of the piping surface to smooth the top of the ball, if necessary.
5. Chill briefly or set aside at room temperature until the chocolate is firm to the touch.

Piping Faces

Faces that are figure-piped in coating, besides being as charming as the Royal Icing ones, are quick to make, ready to use in minutes, taste good, and are usually more adaptable to the multifaceted needs of the decorator. Faces that require some extra detailing with food coloring and an artists' brush for blush, freckles, wrinkles, etc., are, however, better piped in Royal Icing.

These coating, figure-piped faces may be piped directly onto the chocolate surface or mass-produced on wax paper. Extras may be stored, covered, at room temperature for several months under proper storage conditions.

1. Prepare a flesh shade of coating using a combination of pink and yellow coloring toned with brown or use flesh paste food coloring. Place a minimal amount of this flesh-colored coating into a small, uncut parchment bag to be used later for piping the nose and ears onto each face. Set it aside on a warm surface until needed.
2. Place the remainder of the flesh-colored coating in another parchment bag. Cut an opening about the size of a #6 decorating tube in its tip.
3. Position the bag at a 90-degree angle to the piping surface and squeeze the bag to form an oval, round, or semiround face. The coating will flatten to a somewhat larger diameter once piped, so allow for that. Tap the piping surface to eliminate ripples in the coating.
4. Allow the faces to set completely before using the other bag to pipe the nose and ears, as described next.

Left to right: Sequence for piping faces with coating.

Facial Features

1. Pipe two dots in the center of the set face— either of Royal Icing or of white coating.
2. Halfway between the eyes and the bottom of the ball, pipe a smile line using red Royal Icing and a #1 decorating tube or red coating in a bag with an equally small opening.
3. Pipe a nose between the eyes and mouth with the reserved bag of flesh-colored coating cut to a #2 tube size opening. Add ears, hair, etc.

Figure-Piped Extensions of a Molded Chocolate Piece

This technique is a sentimental favorite of mine. It elicited an enormous amount of excitement the night I introduced it to a group of students in a chocolate class, and it resulted in the most satisfying teaching experience of my career. The room was absolutely charged with electricity as we all—teacher and students alike—exploded with enthusiasm and an infectious outpouring of ideas, suggestions for variations and camaraderie.

What we discovered was that the shape of any flat, molded piece of chocolate could be altered by affixing freehand, piped forms—ears, hair, beards, hats, scallops, etc.—to its edge by using the following figure-piping technique.

1. Cover an inverted cookie sheet with wax paper.
2. Place a plain, round, flesh-colored lollipop on the paper. It must lie perfectly flat. Trim any rough spots off the back with a knife, if necessary. If the lollipop stick prohibits it from lying flat, use another lollipop.
3. To pipe ears: Half-fill a parchment bag with

the same flesh-colored coating used to mold the lollipop. Cut the opening to a #4 tube size.

4. Beginning on the side edge of the lollipop in the center, outline an earlobe. Immediately fill it in by applying firm pressure on the bag and directing the flow of coating toward the molded edge to assure a direct contact. The coating buildup should be even with the height of the molded piece at the point of contact, tapering down gradually toward the outside edge of the ear.

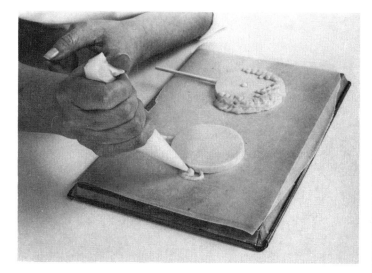

5. Lightly skim the surface of the coating with the tip of the bag, shaping the ear as you do and extending a little of the coating just barely onto the face of the molded piece.
6. Repeat the procedure on the other side for the other ear. Try not to move the lollipop so as not to dislodge the piped coating.
7. Chill the molded piece until the ears are firm.

Piping the Hair

1. Prepare a parchment bag half-filled with dark chocolate. If chocolate coating is used, it should be cool. Cut the bag to a #2 tube opening.
2. With the lollipop still in position on the wax paper, begin piping strands of hair, beginning at the edge of the lollipop that rests on the paper but always staying in direct contact with the molded piece. Continue to build up layers of chocolate strands of hair, eventually extending them onto the face of the piece.

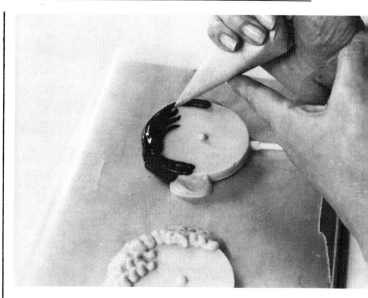

3. Chill the lollipop again until the chocolate hair is firm.
4. Peel the lollipop off the paper.
5. Optional step: Whenever necessary, overpipe the figure-piped forms on the back side, using the appropriate colors. Extend a little of the chocolate onto the back of the lollipop itself.

Piping the Face

1. Pipe two ovals of white coating for the eyes. When at least partially set, dot them with dark chocolate eyeballs.
2. Pipe a flesh-colored ball of coating for the nose or attach a candy nose with coating.
3. Pipe a smile with red coating in a parchment bag cut to a #2 tube size opening.

TECHNIQUES USED TO THICKEN CHOCOLATE

All of the previously mentioned techniques are accomplished with chocolate in its natural, fluid state—melted and tempered. Chocolate in this condition cannot be used to pipe stars, rosettes, shells, roses, or other decorations that require a firm, heavy medium unless it is thickened in some way.

There is a paradoxical, love-hate relationship between liquid and chocolate. On the one hand, a drop of liquid can ruin a pot of chocolate; yet several drops gradually and cautiously added to melted chocolate can turn it into a thick enough medium to be piped with the fanciest of decorating tubes. Here are two methods for converting the fluid consistency of melted chocolate into a thickened form.

Method I

1. Melt and temper the chocolate according to the directions in Chapter 1. Compound coating may be thickened once melted.
2. Add a few drops of liquid (water, vanilla, cognac, liqueur, glycerin) to ¼ cup of melted chocolate. Blend well.

3. Continue to add drops cautiously until the chocolate thickens to the proper piping consistency.
4. Fill a decorating bag (fitted with a coupler and decorating tube) with the mixture and use it promptly.

Note: If the chocolate thickens excessively and tightens to a dry, grainy lump, adding some melted and tempered chocolate to it sparingly will usually salvage it.

Method II

This method of thickening chocolate, Ganache, requires the addition of heavy cream, butter, and some flavoring. It produces a chocolate mixture that can be piped into many different fancy shapes or simply used as a trufflelike filling for candies. Its flavor may be varied by substituting a liqueur for the cognac. The roses piped in Ganache are ideally suited for decorating cakes and small pastries, but they may be served as individual candies in fluted paper cups as well.

Ganache

> ½ **pound** semisweet chocolate, finely chopped
> ⅓ **cup** heavy cream
> ½ **tablespoon** unsalted butter
> **1 teaspoon** cognac (or vanilla or liqueur)

Heat the chocolate and the cream in a small saucepan over very low heat, stirring constantly, until the chocolate melts and is well blended with the cream.

Remove the mixture from the heat and add the butter and cognac, mixing well.

Transfer the mixture to a large bowl and refrigerate until cold (about 1¼ hours). Stir it occasionally as it chills to keep it uniform in temperature.

Beat the cold mixture only until it lightens in color and thickens to the consistency of creamy, chocolate, buttercream icing.

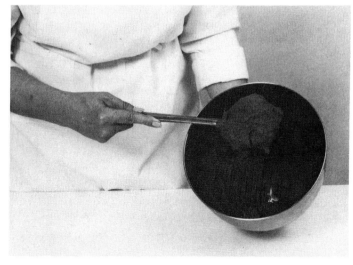

Note: If the Ganache does not thicken when beaten, continue to chill it and try again. If it gets too cold to beat, place the bowl in a warm water bath only briefly. Stir, and then beat. Avoid overbeating the Ganache—it will turn grainy. If it does, reheat, chill, etc.

Piping Roses

Immediately half-fill a polyester bag fitted with a #97 rose tube (or #101s-104) with the mixture and pipe roses on wax paper squares according to the directions on pages 70-73. Keep them refrigerated until needed.

-*Note:* As the mixture warms in the bag, it will darken and soften considerably. Remove the coupler ring and tube and empty the contents into the bowl. Replenish the bag with fresh Ganache and continue piping roses. I use a fresh bag each time. The leftover Ganache in the bowl and in the bags may be remelted over low heat as in step 1 and the whole procedure of chilling, beating, etc., repeated. It may be kept refrigerated for several weeks.

Chocolate Clay

For years the nimble fingers of fine pastry chefs and chocolatiers have astounded us with their extraordinary feats of chocolate artistry. We have stood in awe (and rightly so) as they poured it, curled it, piped it, carved it, molded it, and even sculpted it. Thanks to their generosity, many of their trade secrets are now being shared with today's students of the culinary arts.

The following chocolate recipe is an adaptation of the professional chocolate modeling compound that they use to shape flowers and a variety of other decorative pieces. At least one famous cake is even wrapped in it. A reminder of childhood modeling projects, this is indeed the ultimate adult modeling clay (and a great way to keep a kid happy on a rainy day, too)!

> **10 ounces** chocolate or compound coating
> ⅓ **cup** light corn syrup

Melt the chocolate or compound coating. Add the corn syrup and mix well.

Shape the mixture into a six-inch square on a sheet of wax paper and allow it to set at room temperature for one hour.

Wrap it well, and store it at room temperature until needed. The clay handles best if allowed to ripen overnight.

Note: The clay will keep for at least one week, if well sealed. To restore its original texture, knead a small portion of it at a time.

Coloring Compound Coating Clay

1. Use a toothpick to dot the clay with paste food coloring in several places.

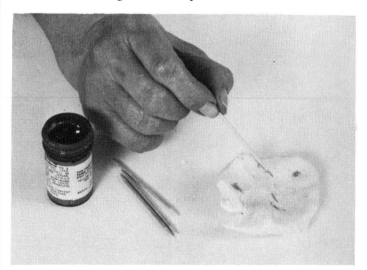

2. Kneading it will result in total or multi-shaded blends of the coloring.

Chocolate Clay Roses

1. Prepare the chocolate or compound coating clay as described above.

2. Work a walnut-sized piece of it between your fingers, kneading it on the counter until it is smooth and pliable. Pinch off small pieces of it and roll them into pea-sized balls.

3. Place about four of these diminutive balls in a row along the bottom edge of a plastic sandwich bag, leaving about ½ inch of space between them. Several rows of balls may be positioned above the first row, if desired. Fold over the opposite side of the bag so that the balls are completely covered.

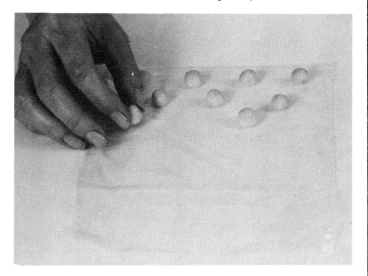

4. Use the tip of your index finger to flatten the "peas," pushing your finger forward as you do to form flat, thin petals about one inch in diameter. The bottom edge of each petal should be thicker than the top.

6. Attach a second and third petal to the first by pressing them against each other. They will adhere easily. Curl the side edges of the petals slightly, if desired.

7. Continue to add rows of petals, arranging them as naturally as possible. The outer petals should open slightly for realism.

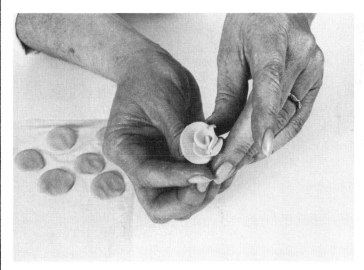

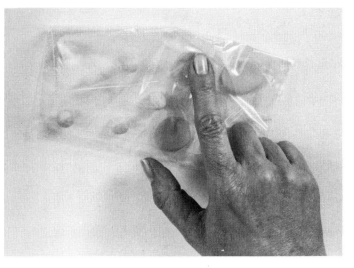

5. Carefully uncover the flattened balls and roll the first petal between your thumb and index finger to form a bud.

8. To remove the excess accumulation of clay at the base of the rose, roll it back and forth between your extended index fingers. The rope-shaped piece of clay that results can be easily snipped off.

9. Set the rose aside to air dry for several hours before handling.

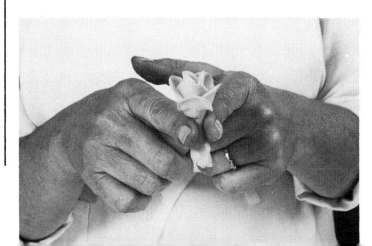

6
Chocolate Lollipops

This chapter is dedicated to the spirit of youth in all of us that delights in the giving as well as the receiving of chocolate lollipops—especially those that have been designed and executed by hand. Lollipop makers will find in these pages a portfolio of some of my happiest inspirations.

The popularity of lollipops is understandable considering how functional they are. They make marvelous stocking stuffers, basket fillers, package trims, party favors, and placecards. The potential for personalization and originality is enormous—so much so that it is possible to depict nearly anything on them. The addition of the recipient's name to the lollipop, whether inscribed on the chocolate itself or on a tag attached to the bow, is a personal touch that adds a great deal to the enjoyment of the gift.

Any of the designs and messages presented in one section can easily be adapted to meet the needs of another by replacing a birthday hat with Santa's, exchanging an Easter basket for a candy cane, or using a personalized message instead of a generic one. Designs found in other chapters of the book also may be used on lollipops.

Unless specified, the lollipops may be decorated in chocolate (thickened, in some instances) or Royal Icing. Wherever appropriate, a

recommendation will be provided. Writing is done with a #1 or #2 tube (I prefer the #1) or a comparable-sized opening in a parchment bag.

I am proud to say that my favorite lollipop mold today is the first mold that I ever bought—a flat sheet of six, plain, round, lollipop cavities (each with a one-ounce chocolate capacity) made by Tomric Plastics, Inc. (#G-63). Similar molds are now available, but I continue to be sentimentally attached to the original one because it was the mold that fired my imagination in the early days and encouraged me to express myself creatively in chocolate. With all due respect to the zillions of detailed lollipop molds on the market today, there is something very exciting about being able to take a plain surface and create a design on it that is original and suitable for any occasion that might arise. Besides finding it challenging and rewarding, you will also enjoy the marvelous artistic stimulation that it provides.

CONVERTING MOLDED CHOCOLATE PIECES INTO LOLLIPOPS

Having a bona fide lollipop mold (complete with stick insert) is not a prerequisite for any of the decorating techniques described in this chapter. Chocolate pieces molded in cookie cutters, cake pans, or conventional molds may be converted into lollipops by following these easy directions.

Method I

1. Allow the unmolded pieces to return to room temperature. Trim any rough edges from their back sides with a knife, if necessary.
2. Position them face down on a wax-paper-covered counter top.
3. Dip one end of a lollipop stick into the melted chocolate to coat approximately one inch of it. Immediately place the dipped

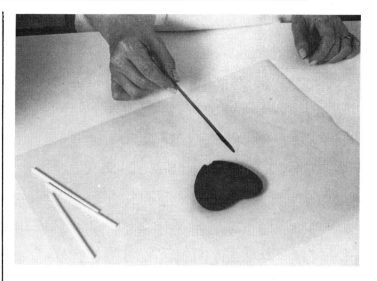

stick into position on the back of the chocolate piece, pressing down firmly on the stick and adding a bit more chocolate, if you think it needs it.
4. Allow the attached stick to set completely before handling it.

Method II

1. See Method I.
2. See Method I.
3. Heat the end of a heavy metal skewer (a shish kebab skewer works well) for several seconds over an open flame.
4. Press the hot skewer gently on the lower portion of the molded piece. The chocolate will melt quickly where it is touched with the skewer, leaving a narrow indentation approximately one inch long. If you work

quickly, you may be able to prepare indentations in several chocolate pieces at a time.
5. Dip the lollipop stick into the chocolate as above and place it in the indentation. Do not handle the lollipop until the chocolate is completely set.
6. Wipe the skewer clean and repeat the procedure on the remaining lollipops.
Note: Be sure to remove all traces of chocolate from the skewer before reheating it over the flame; any adhering chocolate will scorch and make cleaning the skewer more difficult the next time.

Three-dimensional pieces molded in closed-bottom molds may be skewered similarly by inserting the hot skewer directly into their flat bottoms and pushing it in firmly. It may be necessary to repeat this step more than once.

DECORATING ALL-OCCASION LOLLIPOPS

The following designs can be used to express a variety of feelings. Determine the necessary space required for the written message before piping any further decorations.

Floral Lollipops

1. Pipe an arrangement of stems with a #2 tube.
2. Add rosebuds or sweet peas and/or dot flowers according to the directions in chapters 4 and 5.

3. Finish off the arrangement with several miniature leaves piped with a #349 or #65s leaf tube.

4. Add the appropriate message.

1. Follow the instructions at the end of Chapter 5 for making chocolate clay roses.

2. Shape four of the tiniest petals possible into a rosebud. Set the flower aside until it hardens slightly before handling it.

3. Pipe the stems and attach the clay bud in the proper position with a dot of chocolate. Add three sepals to the base of the flower, if desired, with a #2 tube and green icing or coating.

4. Add the appropriate message.

Rainbow Lollipop

This design is probably my most popular one because it is appropriate for almost every occasion. Though it is simpler to pipe the rainbow in colored coating, I usually do mine in softened Royal Icing using a modified run sugar technique.

1. Dye approximately ½ cup of Royal Icing red before softening it with several drops of water. Mix well. Continue to add water only until the icing softens and loses its peaks. It should not be runny.

2. Add the softened icing to a prepared parchment bag. Snip off the point of the bag to leave an opening about 1/16 inch wide. Test the flow by piping a line onto your practice board. If the line of icing flattens to

a width greater than ¼ inch, the icing is too soft. Remove it from the bag and thicken it with firm icing (adjust the color, if necessary) before continuing. If the line is narrower than ¼ inch, enlarge the bag's opening.

3. Pipe an arch of red icing across the top half of the lollipop, working from left to right. Repeat this step on all of the lollipops to be decorated before beginning with the next color.

4. Repeat steps 1–3 with each color of icing (orange, yellow, green, blue) until the rainbow is complete.

5. Write the desired message on the bottom half of the lollipop or personalize it with a name. Dry overnight before wrapping.

Note: The same rainbow design may be piped in pastel shades instead of the traditional vivid colors.

Here are some suggestions for other expressions that may be used on any of these all-occasion lollipops:

You're Special
Thank You
(We) Miss You
Bon Voyage
Get Well Soon
Thinking of You
Good Luck
Congratulations (Cheers, Mazel Tov, Well Done, Congrats!)
Good-bye (Arrivederci, Adiós, Auf Wiedersehen, Au Revoir)

Left to right: Smiley face, smiley face with candy trim, figure-piped faces (including ski cap, Mrs. Claus, and clown).

Juvenile Lollipops

Smiley Face

1. Use a standard Smiley Face mold (complete with indentations for the eyes, mouth) or a plain round shape to mold the chocolate piece (Apollo Mold Co. #668).
2. Once molded, use a parchment bag to fill the indentations with chocolate or, for a special treat, attach appropriately shaped pieces of commercial candy to the face with dots of chocolate for the eyes, nose, cheeks, and mouth.

Figure-Piped Faces

1. Follow the instructions for figure piping flesh-colored lollipops described on pages 89 and 90.
2. Hairstyles, facial expressions, etc., should be piped as desired.

To add a ski cap:

1. Position a parchment bag filled with colored coating and cut to a ¼-inch opening on the top edge of the piped hair.
2. Squeeze the bag firmly, directing the flow of coating 1 ½ inches beyond the molded piece to shape the cap. Some of the coating *must* overlap a portion of the piped hair to assure a good hold.
3. Use a contrasting-colored coating to pipe a zigzag border where the cap and hair meet and a pom-pom at its point.
4. When the cap is completely set, turn the lollipop over and overpipe the back of the cap with the same color coating. Allow some of the coating to overlap the piped hair as above.

Clown

1. Mold a flesh-colored lollipop. Pipe ears (see pages 89-90).
2. Beginning about one inch above each ear, barely touching the face of the lollipop, pipe red coating in a back-and-forth movement to form the clown's hair. Chill briefly.
3. Outline the large eyes with medium-consistency Royal Icing and a #2 tube. Immediately flood them with softened Royal Icing using the run sugar technique. The eyes must dry several hours before being painted with a dampened #00 brush and red and black food colorings.
4. Attach a large red jawbreaker or similar candy to the clown's face with a dot of flesh-colored coating for the nose.
5. Pipe the mouth with red coating or icing and flood it with the soft icing used for the eyes. Once dry, a name may be written in the mouth, if desired.

Note: The color of the clown's hair and his facial expressions may be altered.

Left to right: Baseball, golf ball, basketball, and ski lollipops.

Sports Themes

These lollipops are perfectly suited for party favors as well as year-round gift giving. They may be modified by adding a seasonal touch or a logo and personalized as desired.

Baseball Lollipop

1. Pipe a red curved line going from the 1:00 to the 5:00 position. Pipe an identical curved line, going from 11:00 to 7:00, on the opposite side of the lollipop.
2. Pipe short, horizontal "stitchmarks" at intervals of ⅛ inch along each of the curved lines with the same red used to pipe the curved lines.
3. Personalize as desired.

Golf Ball Lollipop

1. Mold half of a two-piece golf ball in white coating.
2. Attach it to the center of a molded lollipop with a little chocolate and allow it to set before handling it.
3. Messages may be written along the upper periphery of the flat lollipop. The golf ball's surface is perfect for the placement of a simple club logo, a table number, or a name.

Basketball Lollipop

1. In advance of a need for them, pipe a series of copper-colored Royal Icing basketballs with a #12 tube on a wax-paper-covered board using the ball-piping technique found on pages 56–57. Dry overnight. (The basketballs may be piped directly onto the lollipop, if desired.)
2. Attach the dried balls to the center of the lollipop with a dab of chocolate.
3. Pipe the basketball rim with a #4 tube.
4. To pipe the net, use a #2 tube to outline the sides of the net first. Beginning at the left side of the rim, pipe thin lines at a sharp angle, stroking downward from left to right and progressing down the left side of the outlined net. Reverse the procedure just described, stroking downward from right to left along the right side to complete the net.
5. Use a dampered #00 brush to paint the black lines on the dried basketball.
6. If the lollipop is to be used for table assignments, write the guest's name above the ball and the table number on the ball; otherwise, write an appropriate message above the ball.

Ski Lollipops

1. Using a #2 tube and white Royal Icing, pipe repeated vertical strokes to simulate snow-covered ground.
2. Use the #81 chrysanthemum tube and brown icing to pipe the skis, beginning in the snow and moving upward, angling out slightly.
3. The poles are piped with a #2 tube.
4. Add dots of falling snow, if desired, with a #2 tube.

Left to right: Very special birthday year, birthday cake, birthday child, Sweet 16 cone, Sweet 16 record, and vintage bottle lollipops.

DECORATING MILESTONE LOLLIPOPS

Lollipops are ideally suited to commemorate the special events in a person's lifetime. They are not, as some might believe, intended to brighten only childhood festivities. They can also be the delicious records of all kinds of adult achievements.

Birthday Cake Lollipop

1. Pipe a horizontal oval of white coating in the center of a lollipop.
2. With a contrasting-colored coating outline the sides and bottom edge of the cake, flooding it immediately with the same mixture. Allow the coating to set before proceeding.
3. Use a third color and a small opening in the parchment bag to pipe three swags on the side of the cake and several candles on its top.
4. The zigzag borders at the top and bottom of the cake are done with white coating and a very small opening in the bag.
5. Use the bulb technique and yellow coating to add flames to the candles. Touching the tips of the flames with red coating is an optional touch you may wish to add.

Birthday Child Lollipop

1. Follow the instructions given on pages 57–58 for piping confectionery or coating faces. Position the faces in the lower half of the lollipop.
2. Use the same medium used to pipe the face and hair and a #4 tube (or its equivalent) to pipe a birthday hat, diminishing pressure gradually as you move upward to form a point.
3. Streamers, polka dots, and a zigzag border may be added with a #1 tube.

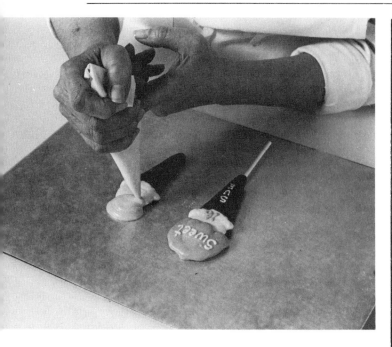

Sweet 16 Ice Cream Cone Lollipop

1. Use an artists' brush or a parchment bag filled with white coating to fill in the ice cream dip section of a flat ice cream cone mold (Chocolate Cornucopia # K-1). Allow it to partially set up at a cool room temperature.

2. Fill the bottom of the cavity with milk chocolate (lightened with a compatible white coating, if desired) and chill the entire cone until firm enough to unmold.

3. Lay the completed ice cream cones on a wax-paper-lined board, leaving several inches of space between them.

4. Fill a parchment bag with a pink coating and cut a large opening in its tip. Pipe a second dip on top of the first using firm pressure on the bag. Coax the coating to drizzle down naturally onto the vanilla dip. Use the tip of the parchment bag to lightly touch the surface of the dip, smoothing out the wrinkles as you do. Chill.

5. Use Method I on page 95 to attach a lollipop stick dipped in milk chocolate to the back of the cone. Set it aside until the chocolate is firm to the touch.

6. Decorate the cone with the words *Sweet 16* and the honoree's or guest's name or as desired.

Sweet 16 Record Lollipop

The lollipops best suited for this procedure are made of dark chocolate and have sticks positioned below the center mark of the lollipop.

1. Use a sharp, pointed skewer to puncture the center of the lollipop, twisting it as you do.

2. Use a toothpick and a round cutter (one inch in diameter) or a comparable circle template or pattern to define the area to be designated as the record label. Brush away the chocolate debris.

3. Outline that circle and the hole in the center with Royal Icing and a #2 tube.

4. Immediately flood the area with softened icing using the run sugar technique. Set it aside to dry for several hours.

5. Use an artists' brush dipped in food coloring to add a border and/or any other details to the label. Writing may be done with Confectioner's Ink (see Chapter 3) or Royal Icing.

Very Special Birthday Years: (18, 21, 39, 40, 50)

1. This is a rainbow variation. See page 96 for complete directions for piping rainbows.

2. The bag opening must be smaller in diameter than previously required for this procedure. Pipe the red stripe beginning at the 8:00 position and extending it almost to the 2:00 position. Diminish pressure on the bag as you finish each stripe so that the rainbow is significantly narrower at the end than it is at the beginning.

3. Pipe the birthday year—18, 21, etc.—with a #2 tube at the end of the rainbow.

4. The piping of the Happy Birthday message completes the design.

Vintage Bottle Lollipop

This mold (Tomric Plastics, Inc. #h-394, four inches high, ¾ ounce capacity) is not readily available but is worth the effort to locate it. When ordering from them (wholesale only), request an open-bottom mold.

1. Assemble the two-piece mold and fill it as described on pages 32-33. Insert a lollipop stick into each cavity before refrigerating the mold.

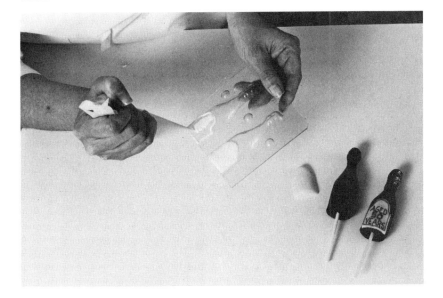

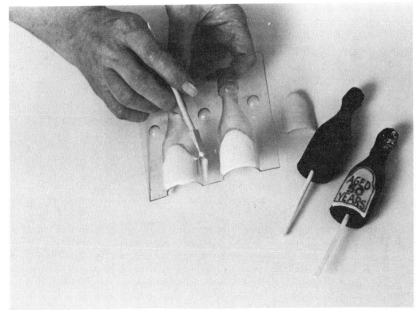

2. Once the lollipops have been released from the mold, clean the mold's exterior and set it aside.

3. Use a parchment bag filled with white coating to pipe the outline of a label in its proper position on the exterior of the bottle mold, and then fill it in. Tap the mold gently to smooth the ripples. Now it will be necessary to redefine the label's borders. I use Maid of Scandinavia's "Dipco" stick (catalog #19747) for this, but a manicure stick may be a suitable substitute.

4. Chill the label in the freezer until the coating is quite cold.

5. Invert the mold and the label should fall away easily. If it does not, continue to chill it until it does.

6. Attach the wine label to the molded bottle with a few dabs of white coating.

7. Use a parchment bag filled with dark chocolate and a tiny opening to outline the entire label.

8. Decorate the label as desired, using tiny openings in the parchment bags being used.

9. Wrap the top of the bottle with confectioners' foil, if desired.

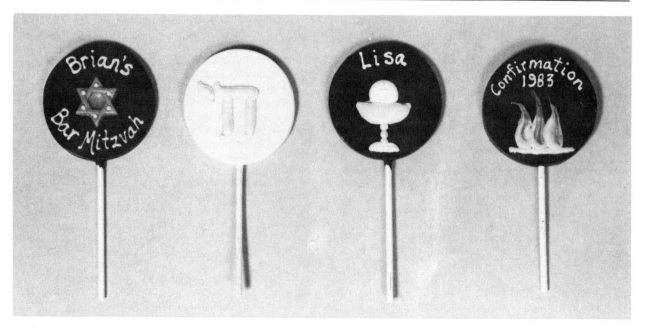

Religious milestone lollipops: Star of David, Chai, First Communion, and Confirmation.

JEWISH RELIGIOUS MILESTONES

BAR MITZVAH AND BAT MITZVAH LOLLIPOPS

These lollipops have challenged me throughout the years to pursue a never-ending search for originality and appropriateness of design. Because the themes for the parties that follow these deeply religious rituals are not necessarily religious in tone, many of the lollipops found throughout this chapter may be used as a favor for these affairs. I am including in this section lollipops with religious symbols often associated with Jewish ritual.

Star of David

1. Use the widely available petite Star of David mold to mold the stars in the color or flavor of your choice. Pipe a dot in the center of each of the six tiny triangles and set them aside.
2. Attach the star to the center of the lollipop with a dab of chocolate.
3. Write an appropriate message or the guest's name above and below the star.

Chai

The Chai is a symbol of Life in Hebrew. Its simple lines are aesthetically beautiful, a pleasure to pipe, and so appropriate to use as a remembrance of this important ceremony.

1. Use a parchment bag with a small opening to outline the two symbols in chocolate directly on the lollipop's surface or use your own pattern and pipe them on wax paper. Immediately flood the areas with more chocolate.
2. The lollipop may be personalized or left without further adornment, as I prefer to use it. The greeting or name may be written on an attached tag (see the end of this chapter).

CHRISTIAN RELIGIOUS MILESTONES

First Communion

1. Use a bag fitted with a #2 tube to pipe a ½-inch circle of white icing or coating, positioning it so that its bottom edge is in the center of the lollipop. Flood its center with soft icing or coating.

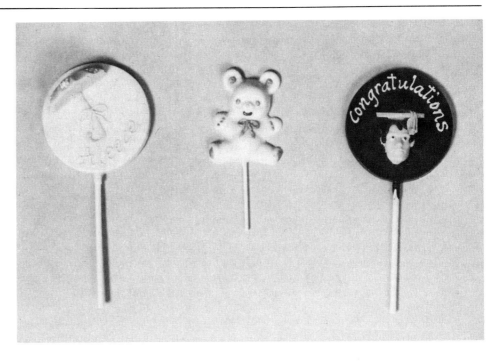

Other milestone lollipops: Bridal shower umbrella, baby shower teddy bear, and graduation.

2. Use a #2 tube and yellow icing or coating to pipe the rim of the chalice. Outline the cup and flood it immediately.
3. Pipe three dots for the handle of the chalice and a base.
4. Affix a cross to the communion host with a #1 tube.
5. The first communicant's name may be added to complete the design.

Confirmation

The Tongues of Fire, symbols of the Holy Spirit, are often used to commemorate this important Christian ceremony.
1. Using a parchment bag filled with yellow coating, squeeze firmly to pipe the bottom of the center flame, diminishing the pressure as you draw the flame to a gracefully curved point.
2. Pipe each of the other two flames as above, varying their height below that of the center flame.
3. Immediately submerge the tip of a parchment bag filled with red coating into each of the flames at midpoint. Squeeze gently as you draw the bag upward to the tip to highlight the flame with a touch of red.
4. Pipe the greeting on the lollipop to complete the design.

OTHER MILESTONE LOLLIPOPS

Bridal Shower

1. Mold umbrellas using Apollo mold #74107.
2. When they have returned to room temperature, slice each of them in half.
3. Attach half of an umbrella to the upper left-hand corner of a round lollipop with a little chocolate. Use the same chocolate and a small opening in the parchment bag to pipe the handle directly onto the surface of the lollipop.
4. Pipe several dot flowers in contrasting colors along the brim of the umbrella and a figure-eight bow on the handle.
5. Add the name of the bride or the name of each guest.

Baby Shower

These teddy bear lollipops are favorites of mine not only for baby showers but for birth announcements as well. Tag them with the questions "It's a Boy? It's a Girl? or with the newborn's vital statistics.

1. Use Linnea's mold #E-045 to mold miniature teddy bears.

2. Use a parchment bag with a small opening and blue coating to fill in the ear lobes and to color the soles of his feet.
3. Pipe dots for his eyes and paws and a figure-eight bow under his chin.
4. Use pink coating to dot his nose and red coating to pipe a smile line.

Note: For baby showers, decorate half of the bears with pink trim following the instructions just given.

Graduation

Wilton Enterprises' people molds, made to be used with gum paste, are perfect for molding chocolate as well. Four figures are included in the set, so choose the face that is most appropriate for this lollipop.

1. Prepare flesh-colored coating (less than 1 teaspoon is required per face).
2. Use a medium-sized artists' brush to apply the first bit of coating to the face portion of the mold to assure a flawless, smooth surface. A little more coating may be added with a small spoon, but it is not necessary to fill the entire cavity. Simply fill it about half-full. Chill until quite cold, invert the mold, and the face will release easily.
3. Attach the face to a lollipop with a dab of chocolate. Depending on the hairstyle, you may wish to add ears. To do so, use a parchment bag with a small opening to pipe

a *c* with flesh-colored coating on the left side and an inverted *c* on the right.
4. Pipe chocolate hair with a very small opening in the bag.
5. A white dot of Royal Icing may be piped into each eye socket. Once dry, paint in the eyeball with food coloring and a #00 brush.
6. Lightly blush the cheeks and lips with a brush barely dipped in pink, powdered food coloring. Do this conservatively. Use another brush to remove excess color from the face, if necessary.
7. Use an offset metal spatula to spread some melted chocolate thinly and evenly on a wax-paper-covered, inverted cookie sheet. Chill only until set.
8. To form the graduation cap, cut the thin sheet of chocolate into one-inch squares. Cut each square into two triangles. The chocolate must be at room temperature to do this.
9. Attach a triangle of chocolate to the graduate's head with a dab of chocolate. Pipe the tassel in place using a bag fitted with a #2 tube.

DECORATING SEASONAL LOLLIPOPS

There is no better time than the holidays—all of them—to put your decorating skills with

Seasonal lollipops: New Year's, "My Funny Valentine," "I'm Yours—All Yours," "You're Better Than Chocolate," St. Patrick's Day.

chocolate to work. Building a repertoire of lollipop designs for each of them will challenge your creativity and may test your stamina, but it will reward you with such an enormous sense of pride as to make all of your efforts worthwhile.

Begin today to compile an idea file for each of the holidays. Keep a record of your favorite designs as well as potential ones that you will want to try next year. The lollipops that follow have been drawn from my own personal file—a sampling of some of my most popular designs.

New Year

1. Use a toothpick and a circle template, a cookie cutter, or a pattern to trace a 1½-inch circle on the lollipop's surface.
2. Outline the circle with yellow Royal Icing and a #4 tube. Complete the remainder of the watch's design.
3. Flood the circle's interior with softened white icing using the run sugar technique and set it aside until dry. Overpipe the yellow outline.
4. Use black Confectioners' Ink to write the Roman numerals on the face of the watch. Icing and a #1 tube may be used to pipe them, if desired, along with the hands of the watch.
5. Use multicolored dots piped with a #2 tube to enliven the background of the lollipop and add the greeting of your choice.

Valentine's Day

The lollipops described in this section are molded in Wilton Enterprises' Heart Minicake Pan (catalog #2105-K-11044). The six cavities are nicely shaped with rounded edges and generously sized. Fill each cavity no more than half-full. See page 95 for stick-attaching instructions. A heart-shaped cookie cutter or a standard heart lollipop mold may be used instead.

My Funny Valentine

1. Center a flesh-colored face in the lower half of a heart-shaped lollipop.
2. For the eyes, position two white balls side by side at the very top of the face using a #4 tube.
3. Pipe a long, oval-shaped nose and two ears with the #4 tube and flesh-colored icing or coating.

4. Use a #2 tube to pipe several zigzag strands of wispy hairs jutting out from the top of the head.
5. Cross the eyes humorously with an artists' brush and food coloring.
6. Paint a smile line with a #00 brush or pipe it on with a #1 tube.
7. A few #1 tube bead-technique hearts and a message may be added, if desired.

Note: Here are some other suitable expressions for this lollipop:

You're a wild and crazy guy
I find you very exciting
Wanna fool around?
Sexpot
You make me smile

I'm Yours—All Yours

1. Position two faces close to each other, one slightly higher than the other, in the lower right-hand section of the lollipop.
2. Pipe flesh-colored noses on each of them, ears on the man, and ball-shaped eyes at the top of his nose. Style their hair with a #2 tube.
3. Paint a demure look on the girl's face with a #00 brush and a smile on the boy's face.
4. Outline a conversation bubble with a #2 tube and flood it with a softened icing as in run sugar. Dry thoroughly.
5. Add a few bead-technique hearts in pink and red in various sizes.
6. Write the greeting with confectioners' ink in the conversation bubble, if desired. Use an artists' brush dipped in yellow coloring to outline the bubble.

You're Better Than Chocolate

1. Mold a large cookie-cutter heart in chocolate.
2. Choose one of the border designs found in Chapter 5 to use on the edge of the chocolate piece. Pipe it using a parchment bag with a very small opening.
3. Use a dab of chocolate to attach a small cluster of chocolate clay rosebuds and leaves to the upper corners of the heart.
4. Write an appropriate greeting in the center of the molded piece.

St. Patrick's Day

1. Use a large shamrock mold (Tomric's #G-53) or a large, open-ended shamrock cookie cutter to mold the lollipop. Attach the stick if necessary.
2. Pipe a flesh-colored face in the center of the shamrock. With a #2 tube, add pointed ears and a tiny dot for the nose.
3. Pipe strings of orange hair and a beard with a #2 tube.
4. Outline the top hat with a #2 tube. To fill it in, use a side-to-side movement with the bag. Add the brim with the same tube. A yellow buckle may be added as well.
5. Complete the facial details, including two rosy cheeks painted on with an artists' brush. Masochists may choose to dot the dried cheeks with freckles using confectioners' ink and a sketching nib.

Easter

Compound coating, tinted in delicate pastel colors, is not only a popular medium for molding Easter lollipops but is also the perfect medium for family participation. Select an Easter lollipop mold from the enormous variety of bunnies and eggs that exist and introduce your child to the wonders of candy molding. He will treasure the memory of it.

Bunny with Easter Basket

1. Use a #6 tube and Royal Icing to pipe the bunny's head. To do so, pipe an elongated shape about ½ inch long. Keeping the tip of the tube submerged in the icing, squeeze firmly as you move first to the left and then to the right to shape the bunny's cheeks. Some puffiness is desired. Pipe ears at a 90-degree angle.
2. Use very light pressure on the bag to pipe his neck.
3. Firm pressure on the bag, held at a 45-degree angle, is required to pipe his body. Use a palette knife, if necessary, to smooth the surface. A lighter pressure on the bag must be used to pipe his relaxed left arm and the right arm that is bent at the elbow.
4. Use a #2 tube and yellow icing to pipe the handle of the basket and to outline the rest of it. Fill in the area with several up-and-down strokes.
5. Pipe several ovals (eggs) in different colors in the basket and a few strands of Easter grass using a #1 tube.
6. Pipe a pink nose and a bow around his neck.
7. Facial details and color highlights on the ears and stomach are painted on with a brush and food coloring once the figure is dry.

Easter lollipops: Bunny with Easter basket, girl with Easter egg, bunnies in the park.

Girl with Easter Egg

1. Pipe a small face in the middle of the lollipop. Use a #4 tube to pipe her neck and a #2 for her hair.
2. Use a #6 tube to pipe the girl's torso, puffing her chest, if desired. Pipe two balls at the shoulder line for her sleeves. Firmly press a jelly bean into her stomach.
3. Use a #4 tube and flesh-colored icing to pipe her arms, beginning at the sleeves. Bend the arms at the elbow and extend the hands partially onto the jelly bean as if to grasp it.
4. Complete the facial details as previously described.
5. Decorate the jelly bean with a dot flower in a contrasting color.

Bunnies in the Park

1. For the heads, pipe two white balls side by side using a #4 tube.
2. Hold the tube almost perpendicular to the lollipop to pipe the ears (this will flatten them). The two center ears may touch and even overlap slightly.
3. Complete their bodies by squeezing firmly on the bag to pipe elongated shapes about ¾ inch long. Use a #2 tube to pipe their arms.
4. Add facial details, with small tubes and/or artists' brushes.
5. Pipe several curved stems on either side of the bunnies with a #2 tube, finishing them off with several multicolored #2 tube dot

flowers and #349 leaves. Pipe an Easter basket next to one of the bunnies, if desired.
6. Add a pink bow to the neck of the girl bunny, a blue bow tie on the boy, and a short message.

Mother's Day

1. Mold a star-shaped piece of chocolate. I use Tomric Plastics' #G-179, but any shape piece may be used. Attach a stick.
2. Pipe a face in the center of the lollipop, decorating it as previously described.
3. Outline the shape of a pointed crown on the top of the head using a #2 tube and yellow icing. Fill it in with up-and-down strokes. Smooth the surface with a palette knife or a damp brush.
4. Write an appropriate inscription.

Father's Day

1. Mold a flesh-colored lollipop, attaching figure-piped ears. Add a flesh-colored nose at the same time.
2. Pipe Dad's hair with chocolate, styling it as desired.
3. Add white coating eyes, overpiped with chocolate eyeballs. and a red smile line. Add a mustache (optional).

Patriotic

1. Pipe a birthday cake in our national colors.
2. Add the message "Happy Birthday, America!"

Mother's Day, Father's Day, and patriotic lollipops.

Skeleton, cornstalk with ghost, "Hang in There," witch, girl pilgrim, boy pilgrim, and Rudy the reindeer lollipops.

Halloween

Treating tricksters to your own chocolate ghouls and goblins will endear you to them forever—and make your house the most popular one on the block. To make Halloween a really special celebration, enlist the tricksters themselves to mold some of the monstrous concoctions. There are plenty of easy-to-use molds available in shapes that are uncomplicated (pumpkins, bats, ghosts) and that require minimal color detailing.

The not-so-scary designs that follow may be personalized with the recipient's name, adding immensely to the enjoyment of the gift.

Skeleton

1. Pipe with a #1 tube, using heavy pressure to build up the volume required for the skull. Move the tip of the bag from side to side, if necessary.
2. In one, long, curlicued movement, pipe the neck and spine down to the pelvis.
3. Pipe a series of attached, flattened circles to shape the rib cage.
4. Note the knobs at the joints of each limb. Pipe the arms and legs by squeezing hard for the knob, diminishing pressure for the bone and increasing pressure again for the knob.

5. Paint the skull's sockets with black food coloring or pipe them with black icing or dark chocolate.

Cornstalk with Ghost

1. Pipe the grass with a #2 tube, moving the tip horizontally across the base of the lollipop.
2. Use a #2 tube to outline the triangular shape of the cornstalk. Fill it in with repeated upward and downward strokes. Hold the tube at a 90-degree angle to the surface to pipe the top of the stalk, smashing the sheaths of hay as you do.
3. Pipe the ghost with a #2 tube and fluctuating pressure on the bag. Use heavy pressure for the head, light for the neck, heavy for the body, and light for the arm. Apply facial features with a brush and food coloring.
4. Pipe a small pumpkin with a #1 tube.

Hang in There

1. Mold the lollipop in a large, round cookie cutter or in the large lollipop mold available from Maid of Scandinavia #46302. Use Maid of Scandinavia's #72893 large lollipop sticks with this mold.
2. Pipe several horizontal strokes along the bottom of the lollipop with a #2 tube for the grass.
3. The tree is piped with a similar-sized tube using vertical strokes. Extend the tree's roots over the grass in several places. Gracefully pull the branches across the top of the lollipop, adding auxiliary branches where feasible.
4. Turn the lollipop upside down. Using black icing and a #1 tube, pipe a ball for the bat's head (with ears) about ⅛ inch from the branch. Pipe his claws clinging to the branch itself.
5. Replace the #1 tube with a #101s rose tube. Holding the tube with the wide end down and beginning under the bat's head, zigzag it to the right to shape the wing. Repeat on the other side.
6. Pipe the eyes and mouth with a #1 tube.
7. Add leaves made with a #349 tube, if desired.

Witch

1. Pipe a flesh-colored face on the lower half of the lollipop.
2. Use a #4 tube to pipe a long, crooked nose in the center of the face.
3. Position two white balls for the eyes above the nose, painting in the crossed black eyeballs later. Paint on a crooked smile line.
4. Pipe the scraggly orange hair with a #2 tube.
5. The hat is piped with a #4 tube and firm pressure, beginning at the top of the head, diminishing pressure as you bend the hat and bringing it to a point.

Thanksgiving

Girl Pilgrim

1. Pipe a face on the lower half of the lollipop. Apply the facial features and hair as previously described.
2. Use a #2 tube and a 90-degree angle to pipe the back of the bonnet—a flattened zigzag. The brim is piped with a #101 rose tube held with the wide end toward the lollipop. Begin at the left side of the head and move across the top and over to the right side of the head without releasing pressure on the bag.
3. Pipe a flesh-colored neck with a #2 tube.
4. Outline the collar with a medium-consistency icing and flood it with a softened icing as in run sugar. Dry thoroughly.
5. Pipe a figure-eight bow in the center of the collar with a #2 tube.

Boy Pilgrim

1. See Girl Pilgrim. Add ears and sideburns.
2. Use a bagful of black icing and a #4 tube to pipe the outline of a top hat using a back-and-forth movement to fill it in. Smooth the ripples with a palette knife or a dampened artists' brush.
3. Pipe the brim with a #101 rose tube held with the wide end against the lollipop as described in step 2 under "Girl Pilgrim."
4. Pipe the collar as in step 4 under "Girl Pilgrim." Add a yellow tie with a #2 tube.
5. Add a conversational bubble or personalize as desired.

WINTER HOLIDAYS

Christmas

No sugarplum dream would be complete without a chocolate lollipop or two to add to the wonder of the season. For many years now I have taken a quiet moment on Christmas morning to contemplate the joy that I know my handiwork is bringing to those children who are discovering my chocolate lollipops in their Christmas stockings and I smile—a long, deliciously satisfied smile. It's a secret moment that Santa and I share.

Rudy the Reindeer

1. The top half of Rudy's face is piped using the bulb technique, a #6 tube, and beige medium-consistency Royal Icing.
2. The #6 tube and brown icing are used to pipe the bottom of his face. Position the tube just below the center of the partially piped face. With one firm squeeze of the bag, pipe two continuous bulbs—one angled to the left and the other to the right. Smooth the center surface as desired.
3. Working from the top of the head outward, at a 90-degree angle, pipe two flattened, bead-like ears using the beige icing and a #2 tube.
4. Pipe the long, narrow eyes with a #2 tube and white icing, painting in the eyeballs with black food coloring when the white has dried.
5. Pipe the antlers with a #2 tube and the brown icing used for the bottom of the face.
6. Pipe a big red ball for the nose and a smile line for the mouth. The bow under his chin is piped with a #2 tube.
7. Use pink paste food coloring to paint a pink accent in the center of each ear.

Snowman

1. Outline the snowman with a #2 tube and medium-consistency icing, beginning with a circle for the head and including the bottom edge of the figure.
2. Flood the outlined area with thinned icing (run sugar).
3. Pipe a candy cane with a #2 tube and firm icing, allowing it to dry slightly before painting the stripes on with a brush and red paste food coloring.
4. To pipe the hat, use a #2 tube and green icing of medium consistency. Outline the shape of the hat and fill it in with back-and-forth strokes. (Run sugar may be used here.) Pipe the brim with the same tube. Trim the hat with three holly balls using a #2 tube and red icing.

Winter holiday lollipops: Snowman, candy cane, angel with wreath, and menorah.

5. The scarf is piped with red icing and a #4 tube. Firmly squeeze the bag to pipe the ends of the scarf.
6. Pipe brown (or black) dots for the eyes and buttons. The nose dot may be replaced with an orange "carrot." To pipe a "carrot," begin to pipe a dot. Pull the string of icing outward, diminishing pressure on the bag as you do so.

Candy Cane

1. Use medium icing and a #4 tube to pipe a white candy cane. When dry, paint red stripes on it with paste food coloring.
2. The evergreen boughs are piped with a #1 tube, beginning with the center stem and then adding the short needles.
3. Add holly balls with a #2 tube and a red bow.

Angel with Wreath

1. Use a #4 tube and firm pressure to pipe the small face. Add a short neck with the same tube and light pressure.
2. For the angel's body, use a #2 tube to outline the gown and elevated sleeves. Flood the area with softened icing (run sugar).
3. Outline the wings with a #2 tube and use a back-and-forth movement to fill in the areas.
4. Pipe a green, flat sphere with a #2 tube above the angel's head. Overpipe it with a zigzag movement.
5. Use a #2 tube and flesh-colored icing to pipe the arms and the hands grasping the wreath. Pipe the hair with a #1 tube.
6. Add dots for holly, eyes, and nose. Use a brush dipped in paste food coloring to position the eyeballs looking upward.

Chanukah

Menorah

The menorah design that follows is an ideal one to use for the Festival of Lights celebrated in the Jewish faith. If you pipe it in coating, it will be ready to give away in minutes.

1. Cut a parchment bag filled with white coating to the equivalent of a #4 tube.
2. Beginning in the center of the lollipop, pipe a vertical stroke down to the bottom of the lollipop.

3. The rest of the arms of the candelabrum are a series of arches piped from left to right, positioned slightly lower than the center arm. There should be a total of nine arms including the center one.
4. Use yellow coating to pipe the flames using a bead technique. Lightly touch the tips of the flames with red coating.
5. Add a line of blue coating at the top of each of the candelabrum's arms for color.

SUPER-SIZE LOLLIPOPS

Large lollipops can be molded in cake pans for special occasions. The larger the pan, the thicker the chocolate must be. Because the extra thickness makes for a very heavy lollipop, substitute a wooden dowel for the lollipop stick. Dowel rods may be purchased in hardware stores in a variety of thicknesses. Cut the length to fit your needs. Use Method II for attaching it to the chocolate.

HOW TO WRAP THE LOLLIPOPS

1. Use a lightweight plastic wrap. I use the commercial 18-inch-wide Reynolds 914 film because it is flexible and sticks to itself.
2. Pull out a 12-inch length and lay three lollipops across its lower edge, leaving at least 1 ½ inches of space between them.
3. Cut the plastic wrap and bring it down over the row of spaced lollipops. The double thickness of plastic wrap should extend about 1 ½ inches onto the lollipop sticks.
4. Cut the plastic wrap between each of the lollipops.
5. Lift the lollipops one at a time and fold the excess plastic wrap behind the lollipop to seal it well.
6. Tie a bow around the lollipop stick (directions to follow), double-knotting it in back. Cut off the excess curling ribbon.

HOW TO SHAPE A LOLLIPOP BOW

1. Cut 10 ½-inch lengths of ½-inch-wide polyester satin ribbon and set aside.
2. Cut 8-inch lengths of curling ribbon, slitting it lengthwise into three very narrow strips.

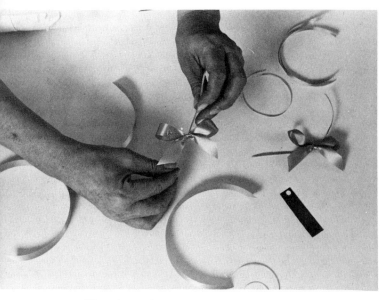

Shaping a lollipop bow.

3. Grasp an end of satin ribbon in each hand, crossing one over the other, leaving tails approximately 1½ inches long.
4. Press the crossed-over flaps against the rest of the ribbon to shape the bow. Grasp firmly, pinching the center together tightly.
5. Place the middle of the narrow curling ribbon on top of the bow's center. Take one of the curling ribbon's ends and wrap it completely around the held bow twice to secure it well.
6. Bring the other end of the curling ribbon to the back and double-knot the two ends.

LOLLIPOP TAGS

Attaching a tag to the lollipop's bow adds further dimension to the lollipop's functionality. The tag may be used in place of a gift enclosure, as a salutation, as an announcement, for table assignment, etc.

1. Cut strips of medium-weight paper (I use a good-quality, unlined index card) approximately 2 ½ inches by ½ inch. The exact size of the tag will depend on the lollipop's size and the space required for writing.
2. Punch a hole in the upper left-hand corner as close to the edge of the paper as possible.
3. To attach the tag to the lollipop, insert one end of the curling ribbon used to tie the bow through the hole. Tie the bow to the stick as previously described.

COACH GREETING CARD

WINE BOTTLE GREETING CARD

WHITE CHOCOLATE MEDICARE CARD

ASSORTED HOLIDAY PLACECARDS

CHOCOLATE PLACECARDS

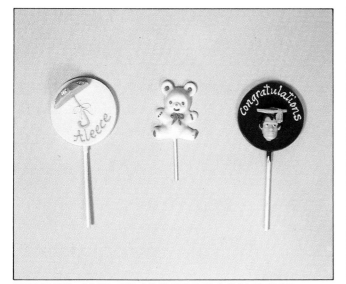

SHOWER AND GRADUATION LOLLIPOPS

EASTER LOLLIPOPS

**OREO DOUBLE-STUF
CHOCOLATE SANDWICH COOKIES**

RELIGIOUS MILESTONE LOLLIPOPS

FLOWER MINIATURES

HOLIDAY PATTIES

FLORAL PATTIES

7
Placecards and Greeting Cards

CHOCOLATE PLACECARDS

Here is another surefire way to dramatize your flair for the unusual and establish yourself as an outstanding chocolate artist. Set your next gala party table with chocolate placecards! It is a knockout idea that is certain to get your festivities off to a great start.

Chocolate placecards can do so much more for your party than simply identify your guests' places at the table. They can complement your centerpiece and theme, be eaten at the end of the evening as an after-dinner mint, and, best of all, make all of your guests feel like Very Important People. That is, after all, what successful entertaining is all about, isn't it—making everybody feel special?

My standard placecard (2 ½ inches by 1 ¾ inches) is molded in a rectangularly-shaped, open-ended cookie cutter with fluted sides. It is manufactured by Creative House Company and is available throughout the country. To date, no mold company makes a shape that I like as well.

If you cannot find this particular cutter, do not despair. I'll show you how to make placecards without it.

Cookie Cutter Method

1. Place the cookie cutters on a shiny scratch-free cookie sheet. The more cutters you have, the faster the molding procedure.
2. Melt the chocolate and flavor it, if you wish.
3. Follow the molding directions on pages 19-21, molding the cards about ¼ inch thick. There is likely to be some chocolate runoff under the cutters. This is normal. Mold more cards than you need since some of them will be used for the backs. Allow them to warm to room temperature before proceeding.

Cutting Backs for the Placecards

1. Select the most perfectly molded pieces for the placecards. Reserve the blemished ones for the backs. Place the latter on a cutting surface.

Cut triangles of chocolate to shape the backs for the placecards.

2. Use a sharp utility-type knife to score them in half widthwise. To score chocolate, merely penetrate the surface about ⅛ inch. If the chocolate is soft, score it several times until the knife penetration is complete. If the chocolate is hard and brittle—as real chocolate is likely to be—score it once and proceed with step 3.
3. Grasp the chocolate with both hands (use clean work gloves if your hands are warm) and snap it to split it into two pieces. Trim any edges that appear ragged.
4. Score each piece in half again, this time lengthwise into rectangles approximately 1¼ inches by ¾ inch.
5. Cut each rectangle into two equal triangles, pairing the matched ones together. You will have four sets per cut-up card—two with fluted sides and two with plain sides.

Alternate Method for Molding Placecards

1. Use a shiny, scratch-free cookie sheet to mold a slab of chocolate approximately ¼ inch thick. Unmold it and place it on a cutting surface. It is important to allow the chocolate to return to room temperature before proceeding.
2. Use a ruler as an edge to score the length of the thinly molded piece into 1¾-inch-wide strips—or any size you choose. Score the

same cut repeatedly, each time penetrating a little deeper into the chocolate until the knife penetration is complete.
3. Use the same technique to cut each strip into 2½-inch lengths and set them aside. It may be necessary to smooth some edges with the knife.

Alternate Method for Cutting Backs for Placecards

1. Follow the directions just given for cutting chocolate.
2. Cut the chocolate into strips one inch wide and then into one-inch squares.
3. Cut each square into two triangles and set them aside.

Attaching the Backs

1. Lay the molded placecards face down on a sheet of wax paper.
2. Dip the slanted side of the triangle lightly into the melted chocolate to coat only its flat edge.
3. Attach that edge to the placecard, positioning it about ½ inch in from the outside edge of the card. Repeat with the second triangle.
4. Immediately stand the placecard, front side facing you. The triangles will slide into their proper position if you push down on

Procedure for attaching the backs to the placecards.

the top of the placecard gently until it is level and does not wobble.

5. Allow the placecards to set undisturbed. Trim the points of the triangles if they are visible.

The approximate weight of each placecard is 1 ounce.

The cards are now ready to be decorated in Royal Icing, chocolate, or coating. All writing and stem work is done with a #1 or #2 tube, depending on the delicacy desired. Many of the designs used for miniature candies and some lollipop designs can be adapted for placecards. Do not underestimate the value of pattern work for these procedures. Many small designs can be mass-produced on wax paper with a pattern and attached to the placecard with a dot of chocolate. Others can be figure-piped in chocolate on wax paper without a pattern and attached in the same way.

Generally speaking, the whole placecard should be decorated in the same medium. That is to say, if the flowers are made of icing, so should the leaves and stems be piped in it. This is not, however, a hard and fast rule; details may be piped in whatever medium is handiest, and chocolate clay flowers combine well with icing or chocolate.

For ease of handling, position the placecards along the perimeter of an elevated turntable. Sitting opposite it, with the placecards nearly at eye level, complete the same procedure for all the cards before beginning the next step. This is a fast and efficient method and the one most likely to produce identically decorated pieces.

All-Occasion Floral Designs

1. Pipe the stem framework for the floral arrangement. It will probably be necessary to turn the placecard upside down to facilitate some of the following decorating maneuvers.
2. Pipe three miniature half roses with a #101s tube in the center of the arrangement.
3. Position two rosebuds, piped with the same tube, on either side of them, extending them out into the spray.
4. Fill in the remainder of the spray with several dot flowers piped with a #1 tube in a contrasting color and tiny leaves piped with a #349 or #65 tube.

Sometimes a dainty floral spray can act as a background for a small decoration that has been molded in chocolate or piped in Royal Icing to coordinate the party's theme.

1. Attach the previously molded or piped

Placecards decorated with floral designs and guests' names.

decoration with a dot of chocolate or pipe it directly onto the placecard. It becomes the focal point of your spray.

2. Pipe several graceful stems emanating from the decoration.

3. Nestle a few tiny buds (rosebuds, sweet peas, dot flowers) around it and others extending outward into the spray.

4. Complete the design with tiny leaves and the guest's name.

I balked the first time that I was asked to put an oversized flower on a small placecard. Well, I was wrong! These placecards have become favorites of everyone—myself included. A dinner table that has as its centerpiece a lovely arrangement of fresh flowers and these placecards, decorated with confectionery reproductions of them, is a party picture that no guest will easily forget.

1. Pipe an assortment of Royal Icing flowers in advance and dry them thoroughly. Apply painted details on those that require them.

2. Pipe some leaves on green floral wire cut into 2½-inch lengths.

3. Gently bend the wire and attach it to the placecards with a dab of chocolate. Attach the flower accordingly. It may be necessary to hold them in place briefly until the chocolate sets.

The paper-thin petals of chocolate clay flowers appear incredibly lifelike when set against the shiny, dark background of a chocolate placecard. Serve a sumptuously rich, glazed chocolate cake for dessert—decorated to match the placecards—to complete the truly beautiful visual effect.

1. See Chapter 5 for the chocolate clay recipe and Chapter 7 for the calla lily directions. The directions for making rosebuds can be found in Chapter 7 also.

2. Shape the flowers and set them aside to dry slightly before handling.

3. Use a dot of chocolate to attach the flowers to the placecard.

4. Pipe the stems and leaves as indicated in the designs, using thickened coating or Royal Icing.

Poinsettia Placecards

These small poinsettia petals may be made over a pattern or piped freehand. Each flower will require six large (½ inch long) and six small (⅜

inch long) petals. Three long green leaves may be added, if desired.

1. Cover the outside of a flower former with your own freezer-paper pattern so that the petals will curve downward.

2. Prepare a parchment bag with red or white coating and cut a small opening in its point.

3. Follow the directions for piping full-bloom flowers on page 83.

4. Assemble the petals as described on pages 83-84, adapting the directions to suit the size of this flower.

5. To complete each flower, pipe a cluster of tiny green Royal Icing or thickened coating dots in the center with a #1 tube. Overpipe them with similar red dots and then touch their tips lightly with a damp brush that has been dipped in yellow coloring.

6. Attach the flower to the placecard with a dab of chocolate.

Other Placecard Shapes and Designs

It is exciting artistically to be able to transform the basic placecard idea into a broader one that encompasses other shapes, sizes, and design modifications. The scope is so broad as to assure that no guest need ever be feted with the same placecard twice.

Stand-Up Number Placecard

1. Mold the necessary rectangularly-shaped placecards but do not attach backs to them. Position them in a row, face side up.

2. Use the popular, small number mold (Apollo Mold Co. #74105) to mold the number 40 in coating or chocolate. Any two of these two-

inch-tall, 1 ½-inch-wide numbers will fit the standard-sized placecard. Slice a tiny bit of chocolate from the bottom edge of each number to enable it to stand without toppling.

3. Attach the numbers about ¼ inch from the back edge of the placecard with a little chocolate. Set it aside until completely set.

4. Center a miniature mum (page 70) or some other small flower at the base of the numbers with a bit of chocolate. Embellish it with a few stems, leaves, and dot flowers piped with #1 and #349 tubes and Royal Icing or thickened coating.

5. Write the guest's name or message on the face of the placecard.

Note: Letters (including Apollo Mold Co.'s smaller Greek and Hebrew alphabet) may be substituted for the numbers in this procedure.

Standing Children Placecards

These figures are molded in a variety of different full-figured cookie cutters, including the gingerbread family cutters. Once molded, the side edges of skirted figures may be trimmed with a knife to convert them to straight-legged ones. The clown and Raggedy Andy figures shown here were altered in that way. Decorate them with multicolored coatings or Royal Icing run sugar (my preference). A #2 tube is used for most procedures.

1. Mold the necessary figures less then ½ inch thick in white or flesh-colored coating, using the technique described on pages 19–21. Some patience is required to release

their narrow arms from the cookie cutter, especially if the coating is cold and brittle. Most breaks can be mended with coating and the repair job concealed by the following decorating procedures.

2. Lay the molded pieces on a flat surface. Pipe the hair and facial features with appropriately colored icing. (The clown's eyes and mouth are outlined and flooded with run sugar.)

3. Outline and then flood one article of clothing at a time.

4. Pipe the zigzag borders, polka dots, suspenders, belts, buttons, etc., only after the flooded areas have dried. Figures decorated in run sugar icing must dry overnight before proceeding with step 5.

5. Cut a thin slice from the figure's feet to enable it to stand without toppling. Attach it to a flat, rectangular placecard with chocolate, personalizing it as desired.

Assorted Holiday Placecards

Holiday table settings can be made all the more festive with chocolate placecards decorated to suit the occasion and personalized to acknowledge each guest's participation in the celebration.

Ghost

1. Duplicate the ghost pattern as often as necessary and tape it to a flat board. Cover the pattern sheet with wax paper and secure it with tape.

Ghost placecard pattern.

2. Fill a parchment bag with white coating and cut an opening in its tip about ⅛ inch wide.
3. It is not necessary to outline this figure before flooding it. Simply use firm pressure on the bag to cover the ghost's shape. The coating will stay where you put it.
4. Chill the ghosts until set, and they will release easily from the paper.
5. Attach the ghost to the upper left-hand corner of the placecard in an in-flight position.
6. Use dark chocolate (or black icing) to pipe in the facial features.

Girl Pilgrim

1. Pipe flesh-colored coating faces on an inverted cookie sheet covered with wax paper. Chill briefly.
2. Add facial details and blonde-colored coating hair.
3. Use a small opening in a parchment bag filled with white coating to outline and then flood the bonnets and collars. Smooth the surface of the coating with the tip of the tube, if necessary. Chill.
4. Peel the faces from the paper and attach them to the upper left-hand corner of the placecard with a dot of chocolate.

Boy Pilgrim

1. See Girl Pilgrim.
2. See Girl Pilgrim.
3. Use a bag with a small opening to outline and then flood a chocolate top hat. Allow it to set.
4. Pipe a yellow buckle on the hat with the same bag and coating used to pipe the hair. Add a chocolate brim.
5. Outline and then flood the collar with white coating. Chill and proceed as described for the Girl Pilgrim.

Santa Claus

1. Pipe a row of flesh-colored coating faces on a wax-paper-covered flat board. Chill briefly.
2. Use cool white coating and a parchment bag with a small opening in its tip to pipe Santa's curly sideburns and beard. To do so, simply pipe a continuous series of *es*. Chill briefly.

3. Pipe ½ of his mustache by pressing firmly and diminishing pressure quickly as you pull away with a flourish. Repeat for the other half. Add a pink nose and white coating eyes overpiped with chocolate eyeballs when the white has set.
4. To pipe the hat, cut an opening about ⅛ inch wide in a parchment bag filled with red coating. Squeeze firmly on the bag as you bring the stocking cap end around to the side of his head. Chill briefly.
5. Use the cool white coating to trim his hat with a zigzag border and pipe a ball at the end of it. Add a sprig of holly (three tiny leaves and three red dots) for color.

Mrs. Santa Claus

1. Follow the Santa Claus directions, minus the beard and mustache but with a smile!

Standing Snowman

1. Mold a tiny snowman (Apollo Mold Co. #404) and use the painting procedure described on pages 34-35. Paint his hat and broom with colored coating prior to filling the mold with white coating. Do not insert the lollipop stick.

2. Complete the necessary details—facial features, buttons, the bow at his neck, and the headband—with multicolored coatings and tiny openings in the parchment bags after the piece has been released from the mold.
3. Trim the bottom of the snowman's feet with

a sharp knife to enable him to stand without toppling. Grasp the decorated snowman by the head and dip his feet lightly into some melted white coating. Immediately stand him on top of a flat chocolate placecard, holding him there briefly until the coating sets.
4. Pipe three holly leaves and berries at his feet and personalize as desired.

Standing Bunny

1. Mold a small bunny (Apollo Mold Co. #104) using the same painting procedure used for the "Standing Snowman."
2. Unmold and complete the details with multicolored coatings.
3. Mold a flat placecard—I sometimes use an egg-shaped (oval) cookie cutter for the base.
4. Attach the bunny to it with a bit of chocolate.
5. Add a flower and two leaves at the base of his body and personalize as desired.

CHOCOLATE GREETING CARDS

Chocolate cards can deliver all kinds of greetings in the most delicious ways! Use them not only to convey the obvious holiday wishes for which they are so well suited, but also to acknowledge job promotions, retirements, births, engagements, housewarmings, and more.

The truly unique thing about these greetings—besides the fact that their sentiments can be consumed—is that they can express your thoughtfulness so personally. Depending on your decorating skills and inclination, chocolate greeting cards can be designed to depict even the most detailed pieces of information—names, dates, locations, physical characteristics, etc. Though the novice chocolate artist may choose only to superimpose appropriately-molded chocolate figures to the card, the more experienced decorator will likely use the full scope of the decorating skills, including figure piping and flower making, to pipe the many personal details that accompany some of the greetings.

Greeting cards can be molded in cookie sheets, cake pans, metal trays, metal lids (without lips), and conventional card molds. Many of the latter contain impregnated designs and messages. Use the mold-painting technique to decorate them. Additional decorations may be added to the exterior of the finished pieces with a decorating bag. Cards molded in cookie sheets may be left whole, when super-sized ones are needed, or they should be allowed to warm to room temperature before being cut to the desired size.

When using a card size different from the ones described here, be sure to adjust the design size to fit your card. Those adjustments may indicate larger or smaller tube openings.

To convert greeting cards to stand-up plaques, follow the same directions given for attaching backs to placecards. The triangle size must be adjusted to suit the card size. For the plain card mold (Apollo Mold Co. #550), use a 2½-inch square. Cut it into two triangles and proceed as described on pages 114–115. Large cookie-sheet-size plaques may require three or four tall ½-inch thick triangles for adequate support.

All of the greeting cards found in this section were molded in the plain card mold, in cookie sheets, in a heart-shaped cake pan, and in my toaster oven's broiling pan (it has never been used for that purpose). The broiling pan is a wonderful mold—6 by 9 ½ inches, shiny, and scratch-free, with smooth, rounded corners. Perhaps you have something comparable in your own kitchen.

All-Occasion Greeting Cards

Floral Spray

This floral arrangement is similar to those described previously. Use flowers made of Royal Icing, chocolate, or chocolate clay, arranging them as desired. The card conveys any number of sentiments, including congratulations, bon voyage, happy birthday, happy engagement, happy retirement, thank you for a delightful evening, get well soon, and others.

Housewarming

1. Mold a chocolate slab less than ½ inch thick in a small cookie sheet. Allow it to return to room temperature before proceeding.
2. Place a copy of the pattern shown on page 121 (enlarging it to the dimensions shown) on the slab and mark off the design with a toothpick. Repeatedly score the outline with a sharp knife until the knife's penetration is complete. Extend the cut slightly beyond the outline, if possible. Reserve the remainder of the slab.
3. Cut two additional pieces of chocolate (¾ inch wide by 3¼ inches long) from the reserved slab for the roof or use the Apollo Mold #485 house mold's roof cavity for this.

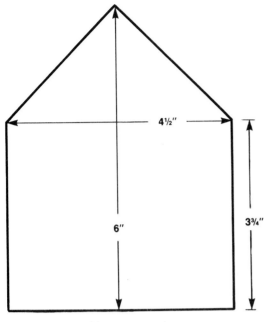

Housewarming
card pattern.

Cut similarly-sized pieces from its two
outside edges.

4. Attach the roof strips to the peaked sides of
   the house front with chocolate.
5. Outline and flood the shape of the door
   directly on the chocolate's surface with red

coating, or pipe it over the pattern on wax
paper. Smooth the surface with the tip of
the bag. Once the coating has set, border
the door with Royal Icing stars piped with a
#18 tube.

6. Use a small gold foil (or paper) candy cup
   to mold a chocolate flowerpot. Peel off the
   foil cup. Cut the molded cup in half to form
   two pots and attach the two pieces to the
   house front with chocolate. Decorate the
   tops of the pots with stems, tiny drop
   flowers, and leaves.
7. Pipe other decorations with coating and/or
   icing as desired. Write the address or the
   names of the recipients above the door.

Birth Announcement

1. Mold a card in the plain card mold or cut
   one to a 6¼-by-4-inch size.
2. Use the run sugar technique to outline and
   then flood the interior of the card, leaving a
   chocolate border about ½ inch wide.

Puncture any air bubbles that appear with a
toothpick and set the card aside to dry for
several hours or overnight.

3. Pipe a plain bulb border around the outlined
   area with medium consistency icing and a #4
   tube. Dry briefly.
4. Use a #102 rose tube to pipe the bow that
   appears at the top of the card. Position the
   tube in the center of the top border, narrow
   end facing you, to pipe the long, flowing
   tail on the right. Repeat the procedure on
   the other side. Pipe a large figure-eight bow

in the center. Two smaller bows appear in each of the bottom corners of the card.

5. Use a #1 tube and white icing to pipe the polka dots on the ribbons.
6. Write the appropriate birth information with confectioners' ink or Royal Icing and a #1 tube.

Anniversary Card

1. Mold a 6¼-by-4 inch chocolate card.
2. Mold two flesh-colored heads in a small, flat egg mold sheet (Apollo Mold #528). Fill the two-inch-long cavity only half-full.

3. Attach the molded pieces to the card with chocolate. Pipe noses and ears on each of them with the same coating in a parchment bag with a small opening.
4. Pipe their hair and facial features with appropriately-colored coatings.
5. Use the bead technique to pipe the hearts that surround the heads and add the desired greeting.

Teacher Card

This card is a favorite class gift to teachers. Each student's name appears on the chalkboard. The design adapts well to a smaller-sized card when it is given as one student's gift to the teacher.

1. Mold a large card approximately 11½ by 7½ inches.
2. Lighten about ½ cup of chocolate with enough compatible white coating to achieve a tan color. Spread this mixture on a wax-paper-lined board so that it is at least 12 inches long. Tap the bottom of the board to

eliminate the ripples in the chocolate. Chill the chocolate only until it sets. Overchilling will cause it to curl up at the ends, making it difficult to cut. Allow it to warm to room temperature.

3. Use a ruler as an edge to cut the thin chocolate into ½-inch-wide strips the length of the molded card. Attach the two lengths to the card with chocolate. Cut two shorter pieces for the remainder of the border and attach them the same way.

4. Write on the "chalkboard" as desired with white coating or Royal Icing. An eraser and a piece of chalk may be added with coating or icing.

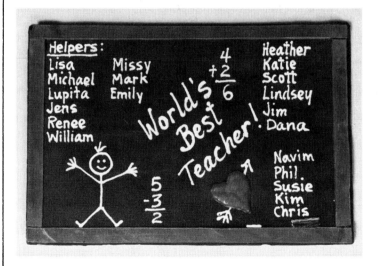

Coach

1. Review the figure-piping techniques that begin on page 56. Pipe the coach using tube #6 for the head; tube #4 for the nose, ears, neck, arms, hands, and belt; and tube #12 for the shirt and trousers. Use a palette knife and warm water to smooth away the ripples in the icing.
2. Use a dampened wooden skewer to open the bottom of the pant legs at the ankles. Insert the #12 tube and pipe the shoes.
3. A #4 tube is used to pipe the bat in his hand and his baseball cap.
4. Each team member's name is inscribed across the background of the card above a baseball piped with a #12 tube and white icing. Paint on the shoe details and the stitch lines on each dry baseball with dampened #00 artists' brush and red paste food coloring.

Birthday Greeting Cards

Piano Keyboard

The keyboard may be piped in semisweet and white coating as well as in black and white icing. If chocolate is used, the white coating keys must be completely set before overpiping them.

1. Pipe a series of one-inch-long white keys along the length of a standard plain card using a #4 tube, firm pressure, and medium-consistency Royal Icing.
2. Overpipe them with the same tube number

and black icing, as they appear on a real keyboard.
3. Outline an opened piece of sheet music and flood it with run sugar icing. Dry thoroughly before writing the musical score for the song "Happy Birthday" on it with confectioners' ink.
4. Figure-pipe a few simple faces peering out from around the sheet music. Some hands, shoulders, and arms may be added as well.
5. Pipe several musical notes on the chocolate background with a #2 tube.

Social Security Card

1. Use a very small opening in the bag and smooth royal blue coating to pipe the outline that borders the entire white coating card. This border should be thicker than all of the others; overpipe it, if necessary.
2. With a real Social Security card in front of you, pipe as many of the lines and words that appear on it as possible.
3. Use black Royal Icing to print the name on one line and to write it in script on the other. Use the person's own Social Security number, if desired.

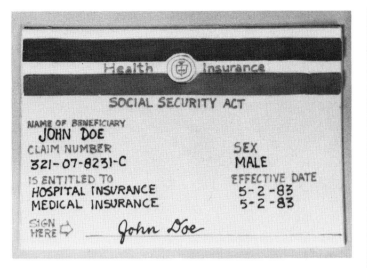

Medicare Card

This is another perfect group gift for someone celebrating a 65th birthday. The card shown is a large (11½-by-7½-inch) one molded in white coating.

1. Spread a narrow width of red coating and another of bright blue coating at least 12 inches long on a wax-paper-lined board. Chill them only until they are set and then allow them to return to room temperature before proceeding.
2. Cut a ¾-inch width of each color and carefully arrange them on the top of the card, leaving a ¼-inch space between them. Use a one-inch round cutter to cut the indentation that appears in the center of the strips. Attach them with white coating. Once set, the ends may be trimmed.
3. Using a real Medicare card as a guide, complete the remainder of the decorating with red and blue coatings in parchment bags with very small openings. Use black icing and a #1 tube to write in the personal information.

Wine Bottle

1. Mold a card approximately 6 by 9 ½ inches.
2. Copy the wine bottle pattern and prepare it for use.
3. Half fill a polyester bag with Royal Icing and fit it with a #12 tube. Hold the bag at a 90-degree angle to the surface as you press firmly to fill in the pattern. Add more height where necessary. Use a palette knife

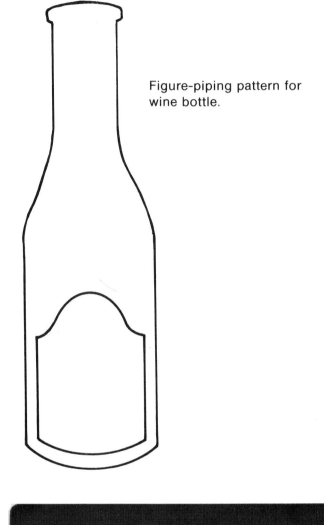

Figure-piping pattern for wine bottle.

dipped in warm water to smooth the surface. Dry several hours.

4. To paint the bottle, tint a small amount of softened Royal Icing a red-violet shade. Use a dampened soft brush to stroke it on. Paint the clear glass area a dark green and the top of the bottle a shade of red. Prepare those

colors the same way as above. Dry
overnight.

5. Outline the label directly on the bottle's
surface with white icing and a #4 tube. Fill
it in using back-and-forth strokes and
smooth the ripples with a very clean soft
damp brush. When dry, decorate with
confectioners' ink or Royal Icing and a #1
tube.

6. Attach the bottle to the card with
chocolate. Decorate the base with an
arrangement of fantasy flowers, stems and
leaves, or as desired.

Assorted Holiday Cards

Valentine Card

1. Use an eight-inch heart-shaped pan to mold
a ½-inch-thick chocolate card.
2. Thicken ¾ cup of chocolate (see pages
91–92). Pipe a stem arrangement in the
upper-right-hand corner of the card with a
#4 tube. Fill it in with chocolate roses,
rosebuds, and leaves using tubes #104 and
#352, respectively.
3. Complete the card with a greeting.

Easter Floral

1. Use yellow coating to pipe the petals and
trumpet of a jonquil. Assemble the flower
directly on the surface of the chocolate
card.
2. Embellish the jonquil with coating stems on
each side and several chocolate daisies
and/or dot flowers and leaves.

Holly Card

1. Outline and flood the interior of a standard
card with run sugar icing, leaving a
chocolate border about ½ inch wide. Set the
card aside to dry overnight.
2. Pipe a #4 tube plain bulb border along the
outlined edge of the icing plaque. Dry at
least partially.
3. Pipe a border of green icing stems covering
the upper left-hand corner of the card and
the lower one opposite it. Fill it in with #2
tube holly berries and #349 leaves.
4. Add an appropriate holiday message.

Dove card pattern.

Shalom

1. Copy the dove pattern sheet and prepare it for use.
2. Use a parchment bag filled with white coating and cut to an opening of ⅛ inch to outline the body of the dove. Immediately flood it and set it aside to set. Pipe the tail.
3. Outline the wing, piping each row of feathers individually. Allow the coating to set before proceeding.
4. Overpipe the rows of feathers beginning with the bottom row. Chill.
5. Carefully peel the dove from the paper and attach it to the card with a few dots of coating.
6. Overpipe the dove's yellow beak with coating or icing and add a chocolate dot eye.
7. Pipe the branches with green coating directly onto the surface of the card. Add the shalom greeting with white coating.

Above:
Sequence for piping dove for Shalom greeting card.

8
Miniature
Chocolates

What every aspiring chocolatier needs is a repertoire of high-quality, exceptionally beautiful miniature chocolates to distinguish himself as a master of this fine art. It is not enough that the candies be aesthetically perfect, however; they must be delectably sublime as well. These chocolates will require time and patience to complete them, so make sure that the quality of their ingredients warrants such an investment. Use real chocolate and ingredients of comparable worth whenever possible.

Included in this chapter are many of my personal favorites as well as some traditional ones that you will want to make often. Most of them can be modified to satisfy your requirements as to color, size, theme, and flavor. Miniature chocolates are an immensely popular way to solve gift-giving problems and the definitive way to commemorate all kinds of special events.

Cashew Baskets

These baskets, similar to those made famous by Eva Myers of Cora Lee Candies, are suitable for almost any celebration, but they seem especially appropriate for engagement parties, weddings, or anniversaries.

> Approximately 30 one-inch-diameter fluted candy cups
> ½–¾ **pound** salted cashews (allowance made for broken, unusable ones)
> **1 pound** white coating
> Decoration: Royal Icing or thickened coating (approximately 5 ounces)

Place a row of 10 candy cups on a flat cookie sheet. Work with no more than 10 cups at a time so that you will have time to position the cashews in them before the coating sets.

Select pairs of equal-sized cashews and set them aside.

Use a small spoon (an iced tea spoon works well) or a parchment bag to fill the cups ¾ full of coating.

Stand the two cashews in the coating, wide ends down so that the narrow ends touch and

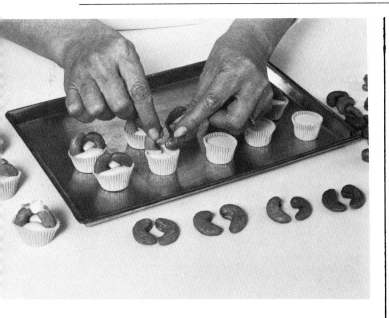

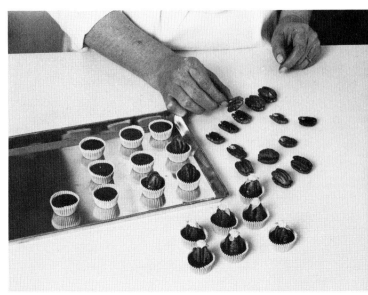

form the handle of the basket. It is not necessary to push them to the bottom of the cup. Allow the coating to set completely before handling them so as not to disrupt the cashews.

Use a decorating bag fitted with a #16 star tube and filled with Royal Icing or approximately five ounces of coating thickened with about 15 drops of water to pipe a small rosette atop the center of each cashew handle.

Use green Royal Icing or thickened coating in a bag fitted with a #349 leaf tube to pull out two small leaves on either side of the rosette.

Pecan Cups

Approximately 30 one-inch-diameter fluted candy cups
½ **pound** pecans (Stewart variety)
1 pound milk chocolate, melted and tempered, or chocolate-flavored compound coating, melted

Select pairs of very large salted (or unsalted) pecans that are equal in size. Sandwich them together with a little chocolate applied with a parchment bag or small spoon and allow the chocolate to set.

Arrange about 10 fluted paper candy cups on a flat cookie sheet. Use a spoon or parchment bag to fill the cups ¾ full with chocolate.

Stand the sandwiched pecans in the cups, straightening any that topple over as the chocolate sets.

Decorate the tops of the pecans with #16 tube thickened chocolate rosettes and #349 leaves as described in the Cashew Baskets.

Foil Cups

These candies are surely among the easiest that you will ever make. The directions that follow use the widely available gold (or red, green, etc.) foil candy cups, but the plain, fluted paper cups may be used as well.

Left:
Cashew baskets,
Right:
Pecan cups.

VARIATION I

Approximately 30 foil cups
1 pound chocolate, melted and tempered, or chocolate-flavored compound coating
Decorations: confectionery sprinkles, chocolate shot, tiny dragées, or other cookie trims, chopped nuts, etc.

Assemble a row of 5-10 foil cups on a flat cookie sheet.

Using a half-filled parchment bag or small spoon, fill each of the cups nearly to the top with chocolate. Tap the cups to settle the chocolate.

Sprinkle the tops of the filled cups with dragées, chocolate shot, or sprinkles, etc. Set aside without handling until the chocolate sets.

VARIATION II

Decorations: Royal Icing or chocolate flowers.
Fill the cups as just described and allow the chocolate to set in them completely.

Pipe a Royal Icing drop flower in the center of the cup or attach a previously made chocolate flower with a dab of chocolate. Use tube #349 or #65 to pipe two Royal Icing or thickened chocolate leaves on either side of the flower.

VARIATION III

Decorations: Thickened chocolate, candy coffee bean, or large gold or silver dragée
Allow the chocolate in the cups to set completely.

Pipe a rosette of thickened chocolate with a #18 tube to cover the entire surface of the cup.

Insert a candy coffee bean or large dragée into the center of the rosette, if desired.

VARIATION IV

Fillings: toasted hazelnut, macadamia nut, caramel ball, piece of glacéed fruit
Half-fill the foil cups with chocolate using a spoon or parchment bag. Swirl the chocolate around to cover the interior sides of the cup or use a brush to do so. Place the coated cups on a flat surface.

Insert a surprise filling from those listed above or from your own imagination. Caramel balls may be fashioned from high-quality commercially made caramels or from your favorite homemade caramel recipe. Fill the remainder of the cup with chocolate.

Tap the cup to settle the chocolate and chill it until the chocolate has set completely.

Decorate the top as desired.

VARIATION V

Filling and decoration: Ganache (see recipe, Chapter 5).

Prepare chocolate-coated cups as described in Variation IV and chill briefly to set the chocolate.

Prepare a recipe of Ganache for piping roses.

Use a decorating bag half-filled with the Ganache mixture and fitted with a #22 star tube to fill the chocolate-coated cups with a large, swirled rosette. Refrigerate the cups until needed.

VARIATION VI: FOIL CUP BASKETS

These are a little challenging but worth it.

Measure the over all width of the handle pattern given to determine if it will fit the diameter of your foil cups. Adjust the pattern size accordingly.

Using the handle pattern as a guide, draw rows of handles on a sheet of paper, leaving at least ½ inch space between them.

Tape this pattern sheet to a flat board or cookie sheet. Cover it with a sheet of wax paper and tape it to the board.

Half-fill a parchment bag with tempered chocolate or chocolate-flavored coating. Cut off an ⅛-inch piece from the tip.

Working close to the surface of the board, pipe handles.

Chill the sheet for about three minutes or until the handles are firm.

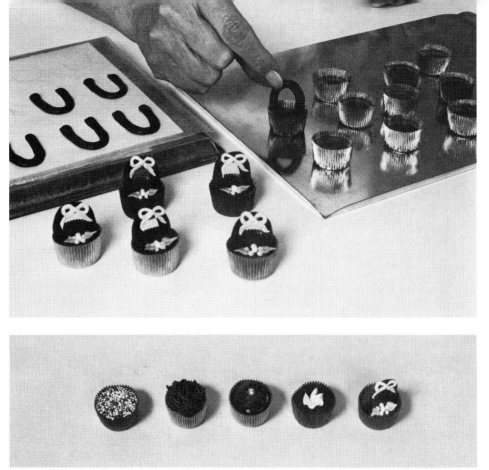

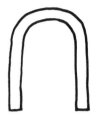

Sequence for making chocolate foil baskets.

Pattern for foil cup chocolate handles.

Five variations of foil cups.

Fill the foil cups about ¾ full with the tempered chocolate or cool coating. Do not attempt to fill more than 5–10 cups at a time.

Peel the handles from the paper as needed and insert them into the still soft, filled cups. If the coating in the cups is too warm, the bottom of the handles will melt.

Straighten any handles that begin to topple over as the chocolate in the cups sets.

Pipe a horizontal, figure-eight bow with two squiggly tails hanging from it in the center of each handle. To do so, use Royal Icing and a #2 tube or thickened colored coating in a parchment bag cut to a comparably-sized opening. Pipe a dot flower or a drop flower directly onto the surface of the filled cup and two leaves on either side.

MOLDED MINIATURES

The hardest thing about molding miniature chocolates may very well be deciding which mold to use! There is indeed a mind-boggling number of them available today for every holiday, hobby, sport, occupation, or milestone. There are the classic-shaped ones that mold the hollow chocolate shells for the filled continental confections—the bonbons, creams, and cordials.

There are also novelty-shaped molds with impregnated designs. When colored-coating details are applied to the empty cavities with a parchment cone or an artists' brush prior to filling them, you eliminate the need for any further decoration.

The candies may be enhanced even more by adding flavoring oil or finely chopped nutmeats, coconut, or candy to the melted chocolate. You will find that half of the enjoyment of chocolate candy making lies in experimenting with a variety of textures, colors, and flavors, so have fun creating your own very special concoctions. Here are a few suggestions to get you started.

Peppermint Patties

These patties may be molded in any shape that you choose or even prepared as a bark candy to be cut into rectangles when completed. They are flavored and texturized simultaneously through the addition of crushed peppermint candy canes or Starlight peppermint candies.

Note: To make bark, spread the chocolate–peppermint candy mixture on a sheet of wax paper to form a thin sheet. When set, cut into bite-size pieces.

Peanut Brittle Candies

These chocolate patties profit from the crunchy addition of peanut brittle—a good, commercial brand or your own butter-rich version.

Almond Brickle Patties

Use "Bits O' Brickle" made by L. S. Heath and Son, Inc., to make a crunchy chocolate treat that is similar to peanut brittle candies. It is available in most supermarkets as well as in candy supply shops across the country.

Krispies

The popular Rice Krispies cereal, when gently crushed and added to chocolate or coating, results in a delicious, textured treat that is sure to please everyone.

Other Additions

Finely chopped coconut, raisins, candied and dried fruits, and nutmeats of all kinds may also be added to the chocolate for some molding procedures. These extracoarse additions, however, are best suited to molding in the large, deep-cavity molds or fluted paper candy cups rather than thin, shallow molds.

Mixing Instructions

1. Melt (and temper) the real chocolate or compound coating.
2. Crush any hard candy addition in a food processor or blender or with a hammer to the desired degree of coarseness. Other kinds of additions may be chopped with a knife.
3. Gradually add the desired mixture to the chocolate, mixing it well. Use approximately ¼-½ cup of addition to every cup of melted chocolate, depending on the degree of coarseness desired.
4. When molding with coarsely textured chocolate, it may be necessary to prepare a shell molded of smooth chocolate first. Once firm, the shell may be filled with the coarse mixture; otherwise, the surface of the molded pieces may be rough and uneven, making it difficult to decorate. Chill the filled molds again and release them from the molds once the filling has set. Decorate as desired or leave unadorned.

The most versatile miniature candy mold of all is the plain, round, flat one. Its smooth surface is the perfect canvas for piping out original designs. The molding process is an easy one. Just follow the directions on pages 28-29 for molding in a flat mold. Note the suggestion to trim the plastic edge off the mold to facilitate filling the cavities quickly and neatly. You may wish to flavor the chocolate—mint, perhaps, especially if you are using the compound coatings. Flavoring them improves their taste considerably. If you are using white coating, you may wish to tint it a pastel shade as well.

Perhaps my most often requested patty is the personalized one. The standard plain patty mold (Apollo Mold #495) is approximately 1 ¼ inches in diameter—a small area, to be sure. Its size demands that any decorating done on it be done to scale and necessarily with a small-opening tube or parchment bag. Writing can be done with Royal Icing in a bag fitted with a #1 or #2 tube or with chocolate or coating in a parchment bag cut to a comparably sized opening. Any name having more than five letters will require using a #1 tube. You may choose to use a #2 tube for shorter words if you lack the patience required to keep the #1 tube's opening unplugged.

Personalized Patties

1. Mold all the necessary patties and allow them to return to room temperature before decorating them.
2. Assume a comfortable position for writing. Writing on patties can be a tiring, tedious project.
3. Prepare a decorating bag less than half-filled with soft icing or smooth chocolate. Force the chocolate through a fine sieve, if necessary.
4. Depending on the word(s) to be written, write in tall, narrow script rather than full, rounded letters to save space.
5. Set the completed patties aside until dry and then store them, covered, for as long as several weeks under proper storage conditions.

Other Inscribed Patties

Besides writing names on the patties, it is often appropriate to write a number, a date, a simple

Inscribed patties: Personalized, number, date, logo, monogram, Star of David, menorah, and cross.

company logo, a monogram, or a religious symbol. It may be necessary to practice the design several times on a practice board before attempting to pipe it on the chocolate patties. The Star of David is an especially difficult figure to pipe without practice. Here are some examples of several popular designs:

All of the designs were piped with a #1 tube using the standard writing techniques.

Star of David

This tricky design *must* be piped with a #1 tube. The lines of the two piped triangles must be carefully placed to achieve the equal-sized triangles that make up the six points of the star.

Menorah

Pipe the vertical line first, using a #1 tube. Pipe the other arms of the candelabrum, beginning with the center ones. Use the bead technique to pipe the flames.

Cross

The cross is piped with a #1 or #2 tube using the bead technique. Pipe the stems, leaves, and dot flowers with a #1 tube as well.

Floral Designs

Confectionery flowers are as diverse as their natural counterparts. When it comes to selecting them for a 1¼-inch patty, however, the selection narrows. Obviously, you want to use small ones, and, because of the probable need to make so many of them, you do not want to burden yourself with a complicated, multistep flower.

Dot Flower Patties

Here are some variations on the same theme: a dainty, light, feminine look appropriate for baby showers, weddings, engagement parties, birthdays, etc. Use Royal Icing, if you wish, and the smallest plain tube (preferably #1) that you can tolerate. Review the instructions for dot flowers, stems and leaves. The leaves should be piped with the smallest leaf tube possible or a plain tube #1 to maintain the delicate look.

Other Floral Designs

In keeping with the dainty look of the preceding group of patties, here are some examples of other delicately decorated patties in the classic style that require patient attention to detail and an ability and willingness to work with the #1 tube.

Design 1

Pipe the stem framework and leaves with a #1 tube and Royal Icing. Coating may also be used but with less delicate results. The tiny fantasy flowers are piped with a #1 tube using the rosette technique. Complete the fragile bouquet by piping a #1 tube bow at the top of the patty.

Top row, left to right: Design 1, Design 2, Design 3, and Design 4. Bottom row, left to right: Two rosebuds, compound coating rosebud, and calla lily.

Design 2

Pipe the center stem first, moving in a graceful, downward stroke. Pipe the two auxiliary branches and some assorted leaves, all with the #1 tube. The two large leaves at the base of the flowers are piped with slightly increased pressure on the bag. Positioning the bag at a 90-degree angle to the patty will flatten the icing as it flows out of the tube's opening, creating the desired effect. These miniature flowers are piped with the #1 tube using the sweet pea procedure.

Design 3

Follow the same procedure as for Design 2 except for the addition of two dot flowers.

Design 4

Pipe the large thick leaves in the 90-degree-angle position described in Design 2 above. The tiny lilies of the valley are piped using the similar squeeze-pull maneuver used in leaf piping. Pull out one petal on the left and another on the right.

Assorted Made-in-Advance Flowers

Some flowers should be piped first on wax paper, allowed to dry, and then attached to the patty. They may be made up well in advance of a need for them and stored, covered, at room temperature. Review the instructions for confectionery flower making and chocolate flowers. Use a dot of chocolate to attach the completed flowers to the patties. Apply the finishing touches (stems and/or leaves) at that time.

1. Drop Flower

Use the #225 tube or any other small-sized drop flower tube for piping these simple flowers in mass-production style. A #2 tube may be used to pipe the dots for their centers in a complementary color. Drop flowers should be made with Royal Icing or thickened chocolate. Pipe leaves made with the #349 or #65 tubes directly onto the patties.

2. Poinsettia

Review the instructions for confectionery leaves and the use of the flower nail before piping this flower. The poinsettia's petals are actually leaves that have turned red. Use Royal Icing or thickened chocolate and a #349 or #65 tube positioned in the center of a wax-paper-covered #7 flower nail. Pipe a complete circle of eight narrow leaves. Return to the center and pipe another circle of smaller leaves, positioning them between the others wherever possible. Pipe a cluster of green dots with a #2 tube in the center. Overpipe them with red dots. When the dots are dry, touch them lightly with an artists' brush dipped in yellow paste food coloring. Dry the Royal Icing flowers thoroughly (for 24 hours) before handling.

3. Wild Rose

Use Royal Icing or thickened chocolate in a bag fitted with a #101 tube to pipe small wild roses. Dry them on a curved surface (flower formers) if desired. Pipe leaves made with the #349 or #65 tube directly onto the surface of the patties.

Top: Ganache rose. Bottom, left to right: Violet, daffodil, jonquil, wild rose, poinsettia, drop flower.

4. Daffodil

Small daffodils are piped in the same manner as wild roses except that they have six petals. Use a #2 tube to pipe a spiral of icing in the center of the flower, forming its trumpet.

5. Violet

Review violet making. Pipe several violets using a #59° tube on one square of wax paper, using Royal Icing or thickened coating. Dry on a curved surface, if desired. Leaves piped with a #349 or #65 tube may be added when the flowers are attached to the patties.

Rosebud

The classic beauty of the rose is legendary, so it is understandable that the dainty bud would be a natural for a chocolate patty. Once you have mastered the piping procedure you will probably use it more than any other flower for miniature patties because it is quick and uncomplicated. Really!

1. Pipe the bud directly onto the patty using a #101 rose tube and Royal Icing or thickened chocolate or coating.
2. Pipe the stems and leaves with a #1 tube.

Chocolate Clay and Compound Coating Clay Flowers

Miniature patties decorated with chocolate clay flowers are almost too pretty to eat. Their thin, porcelainlike petals take longer to shape by hand than do the piped ones, but they are so beautiful that they always seem worth the extra effort.

Chocolate Clay Rosebuds

1. Prepare the chocolate or compound coating clay.
2. Shape a three-petaled miniature rosebud following the general chocolate clay, rose-making instructions, using the tiniest balls of clay possible.
3. Trim the excess clay from the base of the bud, if necessary.
4. Attach the bud to the previously molded patty with a dot of chocolate. Add two leaves, if desired, with thickened green coating or Royal Icing.

White Compound Coating Clay Calla Lilies

1. Prepare a recipe for compound coating clay.
2. Flatten tiny balls of the firm mixture between the plastic bag flaps, as described on page 93.
3. Pinch the bottom edges of the flattened petal together with your right thumb and forefinger into the trumpet shape that distinguishes this flower and shape the rest of it by pinching the tip gently between the left thumb and forefinger. This will automatically cup the petal.
4. Pipe a yellow coating stamen into the center cone of the lily using a parchment bag cut to a #2 size opening.
5. Attach the calla lily to the previously molded patty as above, adding a long green stem.

Ganache Rose Candies

The roses described on page 92 made of Ganache may be served as individual candies. Place them in fluted paper cups after they have been thoroughly chilled.

Figure-Piped Patties

These designs may challenge you, but do not let them intimidate you. Review the figure-piping instructions beginning on page 56. Practice the figures on wax paper before you do them directly on the patties.

Wedding Bells

1. Prepare a decorating bag half-filled with Royal Icing or thickened chocolate and fitted with a #2 tube.
2. Holding the bag at a 45-degree angle to the patty, pipe out a narrow and then increasingly wider elongated mound. As you conclude the mound, define the circular bottom of the bell by piping a circle.
3. Make another bell in the same way, positioning it alongside the first one.
4. Pipe a dot in each bell to simulate a clapper,

using the same bag and tube or another color.

5. To finish off the bells, pipe a horizontal figure eight at the top of the bells. Pull out two jiggled tails to complete the bow.

The baby patty assortment, which usually includes some patties with the baby's name, has always been my very favorite gift to new parents. Often it is delivered directly to the hospital for the enjoyment of the mother, her visitors, and the hospital staff. New fathers find that sharing these personalized chocolates is a thoughtful way to include non-cigar-smoking friends in the happy celebration.

Diaper Pin

1. Prepare a decorating bag fitted with a #1 tube and filled with Royal Icing or a parchment bag cut to a comparably-sized opening and filled with chocolate or coating.
2. Draw a diaper pin in an open position on the patty.
3. With a contrasting color and a #1 tube, add a bow and several dot flowers or polka dots.

Baby Rattle

1. Prepare two decorating bags filled with different colors and fitted with #1 tubes. Royal Icing or coating may be used for this procedure.
2. Pipe a ball near the outer edge of the patty.
3. Beginning at the base of the ball, pipe the handle of the rattle and half of a circle at the end of it.
4. With a contrasting color, pipe a bow and a little zigzag detail on the ball. The zigzag may be painted on the dried Royal Icing ball with paste food coloring, if desired.
5. Add some dot flowers or polka dots on the surface surrounding the rattle.

Baby Booties

1. Prepare one decorating bag half-filled with Royal Icing or thickened coating and fitted with a #2 tube and another bag fitted with a #1 tube and filled with a contrasting color.
2. Position the bag with the #2 tube at a 45-degree angle to the center of the patty.
3. Pipe an elongated mound for the foot of the bootie, broader at the toe and narrowing down as it approaches the heel.
4. Now place the bag perpendicular to the heel of the bootie and press out a standing mound approximately ⅛ inch high.
5. Define it by piping a circle on top of the mound. Repeat for the other bootie.
6. With the other decorating bag, pipe a bow on the front of the bootie.
7. If you have the patience, zigzag the top of the bootie with a #1 tube to give it a ruffled look.
8. Pipe polka dots with a #1 tube on the surface surrounding the booties.

Holiday Patties

Here is an assortment of patties to use throughout the holidays of the year. Many designs found in other chapters of the book may be used as well, provided that they can be piped to scale, of course.

Holly Leaves and Berries

1. Prepare a parchment bag filled with green coating. Flatten its point and cut it to make it suitable for piping leaves.
2. Position the tip of the bag near the center of the patty and pipe a leaf in the 12:00 position. Pipe two more leaves in the 4:00 and 8:00 positions respectively.
3. Use a #00 artists' brush to lightly pull out points along the edges of the leaves to resemble the holly leaf's points.
4. Pipe three red berries with red coating in the center of the leaves once they have set.

Note: To pipe the same design in Royal Icing, use tube #349 or #65 for the leaves and #2 for the berries and follow the same instructions.

Wreath

1. Draw a circle in the center of a molded patty using Royal Icing or coating and a #2 tube or its parchment bag opening equivalent.
2. Pipe a zigzag (back-and-forth movement) over the previously piped circle.
3. Use a #2 tube and red icing or coating to pipe several clusters of dot berries (see above) and a red bow. (Allow the coating wreath to set completely before adding the berries and bow.)

Noël

Only a masochist would attempt to write Merry Christmas on miniature patties.

Holiday Patties: Holly leaves and berries, wreath, Noël, peppermint candy cane, pumpkin, ghost, shamrock, Easter basket, grapes, cornucopia, trio of hearts, and lips.

Fortunately for the rest of us, there is a shorter version—Noël. Use a #1 tube, if possible, or a comparable opening in a parchment bag to write in Royal Icing or coating.

Peppermint Candy Cane

Here is a fast and festive design that even inexperienced decorators will love.

1. Use a #4 tube in a decorating bag filled with white Royal Icing to pipe the candy cane.
2. Paint the red lines on the dried, piped candy cane with a dampened #00 artists' brush and paste food coloring.
3. To complete the candy cane, pipe a bow around the stick using a #2 tube and green Royal Icing.

Pumpkin

1. Use a #2 tube and Royal Icing to pipe the outline of a pumpkin.
2. The segments of the pumpkin resemble a series of inverted cashews. Begin with firm pressure on the bag, diminishing it as each stroke nears completion. Pipe the center segment last.
3. The stem, leaf, and tendril are piped with a #1 tube as are the eyes, nose, and mouth.

Ghost

1. Use a #2 tube and Royal Icing or coating to pipe the ghost.
2. The ghost's body is formed by increasing and decreasing the pressure on the bag to shape the broad head, narrow neck, broad body, and narrow tail.
3. The #2 tube is used to pipe the *B* that is contoured to the shape of the ghost's body and the rest of the letters.

Cornucopia

1. Use a #2 tube and Royal Icing or thickened coating to draw an arch to guide you as you shape the curve of the cornucopia.
2. Beginning at the narrow end, pipe a spiral of increasingly larger circles.
3. Fill the cornucopia with two or three dot flowers and leaves piped with a #1 tube.

Trio of Hearts

1. Use a #2 tube and Royal Icing or red coating in a parchment bag cut to a comparably sized opening to pipe three hearts across the center of the patty. To pipe the hearts, use the bead technique. Angle the two beads so that they touch, forming a heart shape.
2. Pipe a pink line above and another below the hearts with a #2 tube. Pipe two more lines next to the pink ones in the same way with red icing or coating.

Lips

1. Use a #2 tube and Royal Icing or red coating in a parchment bag cut to a comparably sized opening.
2. Begin at the left side of the upper lip. Fluctuation of pressure on the bag is required to shape the contours.
3. If coating is used, allow the upper lip to set completely before piping the bottom lip. In either case, press firmly in the center of the lip to get it to pout.

Shamrock

1. Royal Icing or coating may be used to shape the shamrock. Follow the heart-piping instructions given under "Trio of Hearts" to pipe the three- or four-leaf clovers. The same #2 tube is used to pipe the stem.
2. Paint the facial features on Royal Icing designs with a dampened #00 artists' brush and paste food coloring once the shamrock has dried.

Easter Basket

1. Use a #2 tube and Royal Icing or coating in a parchment bag cut to a comparably sized opening to outline the basket.
2. Use an up-and-down movement to fill it in.
3. Pipe elongated balls in several colors to resemble eggs.
4. Pipe a #1 tube bow on the handle.

Grapes

1. Use a #2 tube and Royal Icing or thickened chocolate or coating to pipe a long, tapered, plain bulb.
2. Cover it with rows of tiny beads, beginning at the outside edges of the large bulb and finishing on top of it.
3. Pipe the stem, leaves, and tendrils with a #1 tube.

Faces

1. Use a bag fitted with a #4 tube and half-filled with soft, flesh-colored Royal Icing or a parchment bag cut to a comparably sized opening and filled with coating to pipe an elongated face for an adult or a round one for a child on each patty.
2. Facial features may be added to the icing faces with a dampened #00 artists' brush and paste food coloring after the faces have dried. Use colored coating to pipe these features on the set coating faces. Hair, hats, scarves, and other details may be piped on with a #1 tube.

CHOCOLATE-DECORATED PATTIES

These are the most exciting patties to make of all! The designs are traced in chocolate or coating over a previously made pattern (as on page 126). If you are unhappy with any of them, you simply melt them down and try again.

Before you begin, decide how you will keep your bag of chocolate or coating fluid throughout the work session.

Butterflies

1. Trace several rows of miniature butterflies using the patterns provided. Tape this pattern sheet to a flat board and cover it with wax paper. Secure with tape.
2. Half-fill a parchment bag with warm, fluid white coating or tempered chocolate. Cut off the tip of the bag to leave an opening equivalent to a #2 tube.
3. For a filigree butterfly, simply outline the pattern with the coating or chocolate and chill.

Filigree butterfly pattern.

Filled-in butterfly pattern.

4. For a filled-in butterfly, outline the pattern and wait for a few minutes until the coating firms slightly.
5. Flood the top of the wing with yellow coating. The outline will act as a wall to contain the filling.
5. Flood the other section of the wing with white coating. Chill. Once chilled, the butterfly wings will peel off the paper easily. They are best assembled when cold.

Assembly

1. Arrange a row of previously molded patties in a complementary-colored coating or in chocolate.
2. Using the same bags used to pipe the wings of the butterflies, pipe a dot for the head on the surface of the patty, followed by a line about ½ inch long.
3. Stick the two wings in an in-flight position into the line of chocolate. If the wings are cold, they will immediately stand firm; otherwise, hold them in that position until they do.

4. To complete the butterfly, pull out two antennae directly on the surface of the patty, starting at the butterfly's head.
5. Use the tiniest of openings in a parchment bag to dot the upper halves of each wing in a contrasting color (optional).

Swans

1. Prepare a pattern sheet as previously described and cover it with wax paper. Secure it to a flat board.

Swan pattern with wings.

2. Mold some chocolate patties and set them aside.
3. Half-fill a parchment bag with warm, fluid white coating or tempered chocolate. Cut an opening in the bag that is the equivalent of a #4 tube.
4. Beginning at the swan's head, pipe the head and continue to follow the pattern down the neck. When you reach the body of the swan, first outline it and then flood it.
5. Return to the head and with a light, downward movement, pipe a beak.
6. Using a back-and-forth movement with the bag, pipe the wings. Complete the whole sheet of swans in this manner. Chill.
7. Carefully release the swans from the paper, taking care not to break their fragile necks. They will peel off the paper easily if cold.
8. Turn the bodies over and immediately pipe the back side of each swan as you did the front. This will strengthen them and give them depth.
9. When set (it is not necessary to chill them), pipe a dot of white coating or chocolate on the body and attach the appropriate piece of wing. Allow it to set,

turn the body over, and attach the other wing.
10. When the wings are both completely set, trim the bottoms of the swans with a paring knife so that they will stand without toppling.
11. Pipe a dot of white coating or chocolate in the center of the previously molded patty and stand the swan in it.
12. Use Royal Icing or thickened coating and a #2 tube to pipe a dot flower at the base of the swan.
13. With green Royal Icing or thickened coating, pipe out two leaves on either side of the flowers with tube #349 or #65.

Decorate the other side of the swan in the same manner, if desired.

14. Finally, pipe pink or blue eyes on each side of the head with a #2 tube.

SANDWICHED PATTIES

It is always desirable to vary the shapes and flavors in an assortment of chocolates. Sandwiched patties meet that need splendidly by combining dark and light chocolates, perhaps, and a broad range of complementary fillings.

Because of the thickness of these completed candies, try to use a mold that produces thin patties. Maid of Scandinavia sells a thin yellow mold (#53562) that I use for this procedure, but the standard mold may also be used if you fill the cavities sparingly.

1. Arrange a row of patties, positioning them upside down.
2. Select a complementary oil flavoring to use for the chocolate filling and prepare a parchment bag full of it.
3. Pipe a small mound of the filling in the center of each inverted patty with a parchment bag opened to the equivalent of a #6 tube. A spoon may also be used to do this.

4. Top each mound with another molded patty right side up. Gently press down on it to spread the filling evenly. Allow the sandwiched patties to set undisturbed.
5. Decorate the tops as desired.

Sandwiched Heart Patties

These heart patties may be made as single or sandwiched patties. The tedious piped trim on their borders may be omitted in either case.

1. Mold some heart patties (Apollo Mold #204) in chocolate or pastel-colored coating. Try not to overfill the cavities so that the patties will be thin and perfectly flat on the bottom.
2. Position half of them on a wax-paper-covered board, leaving at least one inch of space between them.
3. Half-fill a parchment bag with chocolate, cutting an opening in the bag that is the equivalent of a #4 tube.
4. Pipe a series of tiny plain beads all around

Two sandwiched patties with scroll designs, sandwiched heart patty, layered patty, and chocolate-covered peppermint patty.

the border of each of the hearts, being sure to make direct contact with the heart itself each time one is piped.

5. Chill the patties until their borders have set.
6. Position a row of borderless heart patties upside down on a cookie sheet.
7. Pipe a mound of flavored chocolate or coating in a contrasting color on each of them. Attach a bordered patty to each of them, pressing down gently to flatten the filling as you do.
8. Set them aside until the filling has set before handling them.
9. Decorate as desired.

LAYERED PATTIES

Delicious combinations of color and flavor can be achieved by layering two or more kinds of melted chocolate or coating in the same mold. Not only are there innumerable flavor and color possibilities, but the range of mold selection is so broad as to make this technique a really exciting test of your originality.

Have you seen the fluted cup mold (Maid of Scandinavia #93734) that produces candy that resembles the popular, commercially made peanut-butter cups? It is ideal for this type of molding, but fluted paper candy cups may also be used. The paper cups will be removed at the completion of the molding procedure. Unfortunately, the chocolate that is molded in them will not shine.

1. Spoon about one teaspoon of peanut-butter-flavored or pastel-colored coating into the bottom of the mold or cup. A filled parchment bag cut to a #10 tube equivalent does an excellent job of filling the cups neatly and accurately. Tap the mold gently.
2. Allow that layer to firm up either at room temperature or in the refrigerator, but do not let it get too cold.
3. Use a spoon or parchment bag to layer about one teaspoon of milk chocolate-flavored coating over the firmed-up layer. Tap the mold gently.
4. Chill the mold briefly and unmold. The

layer molded in the bottom of the cavity becomes the face of the finished piece.

5. The patties may be decorated as desired. They are always attractive when decorated with a simple scroll design in chocolate.

CHOCOLATE-COVERED PEPPERMINT PATTIES

Here is a quick and convenient way to use a commercially made candy in a unique way. Purchase a box of chocolate-covered peppermint patties. You will recognize them as being the ones often wrapped individually in foil.

1. Mold some plain white or pastel coating patties in the small patty mold or make some freehand as described below.
2. Assemble a line of unwrapped peppermint patties.
3. Attach the tiny patties to the peppermint ones with a little chocolate. Allow them to set completely before handling them.
4. Decorate each one with a miniature rose or as desired.

Piping Freehand Patties

1. Draw several rows of 1⅛-inch circles on a sheet of paper, leaving at least ½ inch of space between them. Attach the paper to a flat board and cover it with wax paper. Secure it with tape.
2. Half-fill a parchment bag with melted chocolate or coating. Cut an opening in its tip to make it the equivalent of a #5 tube (approximately ⅛ inch).
3. Position the tip of the bag, slightly elevated, in the center of the circle. Using a circular movement, fill in the pattern almost to the outline. Gently tap the board after filling in four or five circles. The chocolate will flatten and spread to a slightly wider circumference than what was piped
4. Briefly chill the board of piped patties and release them from the paper.

Note: The board (or cookie sheet) used for this procedure must be at room temperature.

9
Chocolate Gifts

Part of the joy of working with chocolate is sharing the results of such delectable endeavors with others. This sharing of your creative talents is not only a natural response, but a very valuable one, as well. The flurry of year-round gift giving will keep you motivated and challenge you to update your repertoire constantly.

The gifts described here call for both conventional and kitchen cabinet molds and utilize many of the molding procedures found in Chapter 2. If you are unable to locate a particular mold, you must learn to substitute one for another. Learning to improvise in these instances is an important lesson that will reward you a hundredfold. Remember that all of these instructions are intended to whet your creative appetite and in doing so awaken the artist in you. Every new idea is introduced to you as a seed, not as an end unto itself. Take each idea and run with it!

ALL-OCCASION GIFTS

Chocolate Flowerpots

Timbales are used in the culinary world to prepare small, savory custards made of pureed vegetables, fish, or meat. I use them to mold chocolate! The tin molds come in an assortment of sizes, so be content with whichever size you find. Mine have 2¼-inch openings at the top and are 2¼ inches tall. Each one holds about three ounces of chocolate. Look for them in well-stocked gourmet-cookware shops and in some gourmet catalogs.

These chocolate flowerpots can be used as special gifts or party favors all year long by varying the flowers each season. They make marvelous teacher and get-well gifts and are perfect presents for Mother's Day, Secretary's Day, and just about every other holiday. I often use them as favors for fancy luncheons, matching their flowers to those in the centerpiece.

1. Follow the directions for molding a solid tart shell on pages 22–23.
2. Prepare an assortment of icing flowers, calyxes, and wired stems (see Chapter 4). Attach the calyxes to the flowers and dry them for several hours.
3. Cut the wires to the desired lengths and insert them into the center of the flowerpot. Use two or three flowers and at least as many wired leaves per pot.
4. Attach a ½-inch-wide satin ribbon around the top of the pot, securing it with

Chocolate flower pot,
tennis racquet,
and cigar.

chocolate. Once set, attach a matching bow in the center of it in the same way.

Note: For variety, use Method II for molding hollow tart shells on page 24, first molding a semisweet shell and then immediately filling it with a milk chocolate center.

Chocolate Cigars

Even a confirmed cigar smoker will appreciate a chocolate one now and then. These are molded in the Fischer Mold Co. #68 flat mold and may be decorated in chocolate or in a not-too-thin run sugar icing pages 74–75. Chocolate cigars can add a festive touch to any celebration—Father's Day, a baby's birth, a job promotion, housewarmings, etc.

1. Use Method II described on pages 33–34 for molding a three-dimensional figure in a flat mold. Set the cigars aside.
2. Fill a parchment bag with white coating and cut the opening no larger than $\frac{1}{16}$ inch wide. Use it to outline the shape of the front of the cigar band. I pipe a decorative circle in the center of the band.
3. Using the same color or a contrasting one, immediately flood the area, working from the center outward. Do not use any more coating than necessary to cover the surface. Smooth the ripples with the tip of the bag or tap the back of the cigar on your palm several times.

4. Set it aside until the piped band is firm. Turn the cigar over and complete the back of the band.
5. Personalize the cigar, if desired.

Approximate weight: 1 ounce.

Tennis Racquet

1. Use a chocolate-filled parchment bag with an $\frac{1}{8}$-inch opening to fill in the frame of the racquet's face (Maid of Scandinavia #70211) and to fill the handle and grip partially. Do not allow the chocolate to overflow onto the face of the racquet.
2. Use another parchment bag filled with white coating to cover the racquet's face. Chill only until the chocolate loses its wet look.
3. Fill in the remainder of the racquet's frame, handle, and grip with chocolate. Add more white coating to the center, if necessary to level the surface. Chill to complete the molding procedure.
4. Combine ¼ cup of milk chocolate with enough compatible white coating to lighten it in color. Fill a parchment bag cut to an $\frac{1}{8}$-inch opening to pipe the trim on the surface of the frame of the racquet's head. It is not necessary to outline this narrow area; merely press firmly on the bag and the coating will cover the surface without spilling over the sides.

5. Once the coating trim sets, use a bag with a small opening and a contrasting-colored coating to pipe a few accent lines and a greeting on the racquet's face. Pipe a series of diagonal lines on the grip following the molded design.

Assorted Molded Items

Most standard, novelty-shaped chocolate pieces suffer from a lack of character, personality, and pizzazz. What they need is something to emphasize their identity or designate their purpose. Even a not-so-skilled-hand is capable of decorating most of the molded pieces that follow, using chocolate or coatings in parchment bags with small openings.

Chocolate Wine Bottles

The wine bottles, nine and eleven inches tall, available through George H. Hake, Inc., are two of my favorite molds. Being able to reproduce edible wine labels will enable you to personalize them in many interesting ways. Here are some examples: Château Chocolate, Aged 50 (21, 25, 40) Years, Château John Smith—Vintage 1935, Holiday Spirits—Vintage 1983.

1. Mold a solid or hollow bottle according to the directions on pages 30–33.
2. Make a copy of one of the wine-label patterns shown here and trace it on the back of a 3½- or 4-inch square piece of freezer paper (for the small and large bottles respectively). The pattern must be visible on the shiny side of the paper.
3. Tape the pattern to the outside of the bottle mold, shiny side up, positioning it in its proper position on the mold.
4. Use a white-coating-filled parchment bag with an ⅛-inch opening to outline and flood the curved top and then the whole center of the label with a side-to-side movement of the bag. Gently tap the bottle on the counter to flatten the ripples and coax the coating to flow toward the edges of the label, adding more coating wherever

CHOCOLATE WINE BOTTLES

TENNIS RACKET

CHOCOLATE BASKET

SANDWICHED PATTIES

CHOCOLATE-DECORATED PATTIES

MOTHER'S DAY, FATHER'S DAY, AND PATRIOTIC LOLLIPOPS

HEART-SHAPED WISHES

FLOWER BASKET CENTERPIECE

ASSORTED HOLIDAY GIFTS

Patterns for wine bottle labels.

HOLIDAY
SPIRITS

CHÂTEAU
CHOCOLATE

1984

Patterns for additional bottle trims.

necessary. Expect some distortion of your outlined pattern.

5. To redefine the outline, use Maid of Scandinavia's Dipco stick or a small artists' brush with firm bristles. Draw it straight across each edge to remove the excess chocolate. Wipe the brush and repeat this procedure as often as necessary until the edges of the entire label conform to that of your outline. Any additional bottle trims may be piped, freehand, directly onto the surface of the mold. They will release easily when cold.

6. Chill the mold until the label is quite cold. Peel it off the paper, pipe several lines of white coating on its back, and attach it to the face of the molded bottle.

7. Use a very small opening in the bag to pipe a thin line of dark chocolate around the edges of the label and for all of the writing. To pipe a grape cluster onto the label, see page 137.

8. Wrap the top of the bottle with confectioners' foil, if desired.

Approximate weight: large bottle, 2 ½ pounds; small bottle, 1 pound

Small wine bottle and large wine bottle in champagne bucket.

Champagne Bucket

The champagne bucket is molded in a tin container (5½-inch-wide opening, 4⅞ inches tall) normally used to shape brioche mousseline. It is not easy to find unless you have access to a very fine gourmet-cookware store. Substitute a plastic freezer container, a metal bucket, etc.

1. Add 1½ cups of chocolate to the mold, swirling it around to coat its bottom and sides completely. Add more, if necessary. Invert the mold over the bowl of chocolate to eliminate some of the excess chocolate. Tap the sides of the mold with your hand to settle the chocolate. Clean the rim of the mold with a spatula and chill it only until the chocolate loses its wet look—approximately five minutes.
2. Use the back of a large spoon or a metal spatula to spread another layer of chocolate on the sides only. Tap the mold as before and some of the chocolate will flow to the bottom of the mold. Chill briefly again—approximately four or five minutes.
3. Add a final layer of chocolate to the entire interior of the mold as in step 1. Spread the chocolate on the sides of the mold with a metal spatula as smoothly as possible. Chill until completely set—approximately 15 minutes.
4. Grasp the inside and outside edges of the mold with one hand and give the chocolate a gentle ¼-inch twist. If it has set enough, it will release effortlessly. If not, continue to chill it until it does.

The Handles

1. Use a parchment bag to fill the very shallow crevices of the #1906-2120 shape in Wilton Enterprises' set of Baroque Gum Paste Molds #1906-K-1299. Fill all parts of it except for the two side swirls.
2. Chill the filled mold briefly and then overpipe it with more chocolate to make it less fragile.
3. Chill it again for three or four minutes. Slap the inverted mold into your palm to release the chocolate. Continue to chill it if it does not loosen easily. Expect some frustration. The thin brittle pieces break easily, but most can be repaired with chocolate. Pipe a second handle.

4. Attach the handles to the sides of the bucket with chocolate.

Presentation

1. Fill the bottom of the bucket with crushed, clear, food-safe cellophane paper.
2. Insert a plastic-wrapped, 11-inch chocolate wine bottle and surround it with pieces of rock candy to simulate ice cubes.
3. Wrap the entire thing in wide plastic wrap and tie it with a bow.

Approximate weight of bucket only: 1½ pounds

Box of Dominoes

Dominoes

1. Mold a set of dark or white coating dominoes in the flat mold made by George H. Hake, Inc.
2. Pipe a contrasting-colored chocolate dot over each hole in the molded pieces.

Domino Box

1. Mold a ¼-inch slab of chocolate in a small cookie sheet.
2. Cut the following pieces from the slab:

   Bottom—6⅞ inches by 2 inches (cut one)
   Ends—1¼ inches by 1⅞ inches (cut two)
   Sides—6⅞ inches by 1½ inches (cut two)

3. Lay the bottom piece on a wax-paper-lined board.
4. Pipe a line of chocolate onto one of the long outside edges. Stand one of the side pieces on the wax paper, face side out, and butt it up against the piped line, pressing it firmly in that position for a few seconds.
5. Pipe lines of chocolate on the surface of both ends of the bottom piece and up both

sides of the attached long side piece to position the end pieces, face sides out. Press firmly. Trim the exposed outside edge of the bottom piece, if necessary, before proceeding.

6. To attach the final wall, pipe lines of chocolate onto the outside edge of both end pieces and along the outside length of the bottom piece. Rest the side piece on the wax paper, face side out, and butt it up against the piped lines. Hold it there briefly.

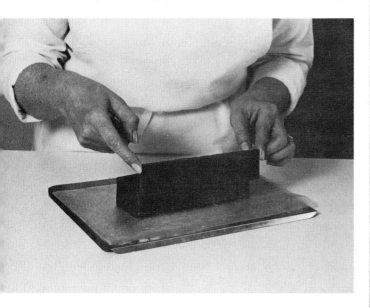

7. Any poorly butted seams may be reinforced on the inside of the box with more piped lines of chocolate. Set aside until completely set.
8. Position the box at eye level to pipe one of the ornamental borders found on page 79. I use border #B.
9. Fill the box with dominoes, separating each layer with a narrow sheet of paper.

Chocolate Baskets

Chocolate baskets are so exceptionally well suited to gift giving that they almost warrant a chapter of their own. Method I, described on page 23 for molding hollow tart shells may be used to mold baskets, though some modifications of those procedures are necessary when molding large ones.

Use conventional two-piece open-bottom molds (my favorite is Tomric Plastics, Inc. #h-489) or unconventional ones (fluted gelatin molds, brioche pans, turban molds, and deep tart and muffin tins). Fill the baskets with fabulous surprises—mushroom meringue cookies, dipped strawberries, dipped dried fruit (see Chapter 13), or your favorite cookies or candies. You will think of many other exciting ways to fill them. See Chapter 10 for ways to utilize baskets as centerpieces.

Molding Procedure

Basket molds do not have flat bottoms. Refer to page 32 (Solid Molding with an Open-Bottom Mold) for ways to support them in a standing position.

1. Follow steps 1-4 on page 23 to mold the basket. The amount of chocolate required will, of course, depend on the size of the mold. For small baskets, omit the following step and proceed with the handle attachment (below).
2. For large baskets (Tomric's is 9 inches long × 5¾ inch wide, by 4½ inches tall), coat the interior of the mold a third time.

Handle Attachment

1. Position the basket in a well-supported position on the counter.
2. Bend an 18-inch piece of plastic-coated conduit wire to fit the width of the interior

of the basket. Dip the ends into the chocolate and place them in their proper position in the freshly coated basket. Hold the handle there until it is stable and then carefully transfer the whole basket to the refrigerator to complete the chilling. Readjust the handle, if necessary.
3. Remove the clips and release the molded piece. If the mold does not come away easily, continue to chill it until it does.
4. Grasp the basket (use a cloth or gloves so as not to smudge the surface) and hold the

wire over the open pot of chocolate. Spoon the chocolate over the wire to cover one side and then the other. Allow the excess chocolate to drip back into the pot.
Approximate weight: 1¾ pounds

ASSORTED HOLIDAY GIFTS

Teddy Bears

Here is a good example of a plastic gelatin mold, purchased in a department store, serving as a perfect chocolate mold. Substitute any similar mold for this one—be it conventional or otherwise. (Tomric Plastics' #G248 has the identical mold.) Included are directions for two different ways to decorate Teddy. You will probably think of many more.

Valentine Teddy

1. Use the directions on pages 28-29 for flat molding, filling the cavity no more than half-full, if it is a deep mold as mine is. Chill and unmold.
2. Fill a parchment bag with red coating and cut an opening in its tip about ⅛ inch wide. Outline the shape of a large heart on his stomach and immediately fill it in with the same coating and firm pressure on the bag. Smooth the ripples with the tip of the bag.
3. Write an appropriate inscription (To My Teddy, Be My Teddy, You're My Teddy,

Assorted holiday gifts: Christmas teddy, molded chocolate box, decorated Easter egg, dog biscuits, Valentine teddy, and bunny with basket.

etc.) above the heart or personalize the heart itself.

Christmas Teddy

1. Mold the bear just described.
2. Mold a small round disc (Maid of Scandinavia #71668).
3. Slice small slivers of chocolate from the bottoms of the bear's feet to enable him to stand without toppling.
4. Pipe his facial features with appropriately colored coatings, using parchment bags with small openings.
5. Cut off any uneven spots from the back of the molded bear and lay him on a wax-paper-covered board.
6. Use a parchment bag filled with red coating, an opening ⅛ inch wide in its tip, and firm pressure to pipe a Santa's hat over one ear. Be sure that the coating actually overlaps the molded ear to assure a solid adherence. Chill briefly before adding a zigzag border and ball with white chocolate.

7. Attach the bear to the molded base with chocolate. Wrap some square and rectangular pieces of chocolate with bright-colored confectioners' foil to resemble presents and attach them with chocolate to the base as well. Pipe bows on the packages with white coating using a parchment bag with a small opening.

Note: For baby showers, the teddy bear may be molded in white coating and decorated in pastel-colored coatings to accompany the miniature bear lollipops on pages 103–104.

Decorated Easter Egg

The Italian custom of inserting a surprise gift inside a hollow chocolate Easter egg is a tradition worth keeping. It is a charming way to add a surprise bonus to what is already a beautiful Easter gift. The standing decorated egg is a classic example of the best of confectionery artistry.

1. Follow the basic instructions (Method II for molding hollow tart shells) and use one of

the numerous egg molds that are available to mold the hollow Easter egg. For a standing egg, use only the round top half of the conventional mold to mold the front and back of the egg.

2. Modify step 2 in the aforementioned instructions to comply with the size of the egg being molded. Extra large eggs should be chilled longer to achieve an exterior thickness of ¼–½ inch.

3. Decorate the top of the egg as desired with Royal Icing, thickened chocolate, Ganache, or clay flowers.

4. Insert the surprise into the bottom half of the egg, pipe a line of chocolate onto its peripheral border, and attach the top half to it. Brace the egg as it sets to prevent it from rolling. Use gloves or a cloth to handle it so as not to blemish its shiny surface.

5. Use a small spoon to shape a thick circle of chocolate on a wax-paper-lined board. Immediately stand the egg, broad side down, into the chocolate. Support it in that position, without fingering its face, until it can stand unsupported.

6. Thicken ½ cup of chocolate and, starting at the top, pipe tube #18 shells down the seam line on one side of the egg. Return to the top and pipe the other side. The bottom shell on each side is difficult to pipe. Wait until the others have set, if desired, and then tilt the egg to make it easier to pipe them. Pipe a shell border around the base of the egg to complete the procedure.

Bunny with Basket

Often two separate molded pieces can be combined to double the enjoyment of the chocolate gift. The bunny-basket combination should inspire you to combine other molds in the future. There is great potential for originality here.

1. Mold the front side of the popular flop-eared, smiling bunny (#E-042, Linnea's molds).

2. Pipe the facial features as previously described. Add a blue bow tie or a pink bow under the bunny's chin and a long-stemmed dot flower in his hand.

3. Mold a small, straight-sided basket (#E-027, Linnea's molds) using the directions for molding a hollow tart shell. If your mold is

closed on top, cut away the plastic with a sharp pair of scissors to leave a standard-shaped, open-ended hollow mold.

4. Pipe some chocolate an inch or so from the bottom of the bunny's base. Immediately press the basket in place and hold it there firmly until the chocolate begins to set.

5. Fill the basket with jelly beans or as desired. Personalize the front of the bunny.

Dog Biscuits

A decorated dog biscuit may seem an inappropriate selection for a gift item in a book on chocolate art. It is, in fact, one of the most popular items that I make. The biscuits are used as gifts, as stocking stuffers, and as a special treat for the pampered pet on Valentine's Day.

1. Personalize large or small (large are more fun) biscuits with colored coating in a parchment bag with a small opening. Royal Icing will not stick to the biscuits.

2. Wrap the large ones individually in plastic wrap, tied with a bow and a sprig of artificial holly. Several small ones may be wrapped together and tied as above.

Molded Chocolate Box

2-2 ½ pounds semisweet chocolate or semisweet compound coating
1 shiny, scratch-free, straight-sided eight-inch round cake pan
½ pound red or white coating
Approximately **2 ounces** green coating

1. Spoon about two cups of melted chocolate into the center of the cake pan. Swirl the chocolate around the sides and bottom of the pan, adding more as needed to coat the entire surface well. Allow most of the excess to run off into the pot of chocolate. Free the top rim of the pan of clinging chocolate with a knife or metal spatula.
2. Refrigerate the coated pan only until the chocolate on the sides of the pan loses its wet look—about five minutes. Do not overchill the pan or the very thin coating will crack. If it does, remove it and start again.
3. Use a metal spatula to coat the sides only with chocolate to add a second layer to the thin shell. Smooth the coated sides with the spatula, clean the rim of the pan, and refrigerate briefly again.
4. Add the third layer as above.
5. To complete the shell of the box, coat the sides again. Then spoon enough chocolate into the bottom of the shell to coat it as well. It will swirl sluggishly over the cold bottom layers. Use an offset spatula or spoon to spread it, if necessary. Clean the rim and refrigerate until the chocolate is thoroughly chilled—about eight minutes.
6. Grasp the outside of the cold pan for a minute. The warmth of your hands will usually cause the chocolate to contract from the sides of the pan.
7. Take hold of the chocolate wall with your fingers, palm grasping the pan's exterior, and give the shell a gentle twist. If it is ready, you will feel it pull away from the pan. If not, chill it a few minutes more and try again.

Note: Anticipate some anxious moments when unmolding the shell. The straight sides of the pan may prohibit its easy release. Be patient and gentle with it.

Molding the Lid

1. Spoon approximately ¾ pound of chocolate into the bottom of the same pan used to mold the shell. Be sure it is clean of all residue and buffed to a nice shine.
2. Chill, unmold, and set aside.

Poinsettia

The poinsettia is the perfect flower to utilize the fresh-leaf-flower technique. Follow Method I on page 85, modifying the procedure by piping the petals on the back side of lemon leaves. Select leaves with slight curves, if possible. It will be necessary to pipe a total of six large petals and six small ones (with several extra in case of breakage).

Piping the Petals

1. Use a parchment bag filled with red or white coating to pipe the outlines of the large petals on the backs of the lemon leaves. Gauge the suggested size by the large leaf pattern shown here. The leaves may be

Poinsettia petal patterns.

painted on the leaf, if preferred. Use an artists' brush to define the edges and points, if necessary. Chill the petals briefly and peel them off the leaves.
2. Repeat the piping procedure, using the small petal pattern as a gauge to shape six more petals.
3. Pipe three green leaves the same size as the large petal pattern. Chill, peel off, and set aside.

Assembly

1. Pipe a thick one-inch circle of red coating in the center of the chocolate lid.

2. Attach the base of a green leaf to the piped line, adding more coating as needed.

3. Attach three large poinsettia petals in the same way, positioning them as gracefully and naturally as possible. Prop a petal up with a cotton ball here and there to add realism to the arrangement.

4. Add another green leaf as above, followed by two more red petals, a green leaf, and the last red petal.

5. The petals of the second row are positioned between those of row 1. To do so, pipe a little coating on the back of each small petal and set them in place.

6. Pipe a cluster of green dots with coating or Royal Icing in the center of the flower. (I prefer the icing for this.) Overpipe them with red dots. When dry, touch the red dots lightly with a damp artists' brush dipped in yellow paste food coloring.

Ornamental Borders for Box (Optional)

1. Select a border from those shown on page 79.

2. Use thickened chocolate and a parchment bag with a tiny opening to pipe it along the top and bottom of the molded box.

The Finishing Touches

1. Attach a nine-inch paper doily to a nine-inch cardboard round with a little chocolate.

2. Secure the box to the doily in the same way.

3. Fill the box with something absolutely smashing, something that will make it a really dramatic presentation: sinfully intoxicating truffles, perhaps, or giant, long-stemmed strawberries dipped in the very best chocolate that you can get your hands on.

10
Chocolate Centerpieces

One of the best ways to showcase your skill as a chocolatier is to create a chocolate centerpiece. It is a fine way to coordinate a party theme and table decoration with your culinary talents. Whether it is used to provide the ambience for a beautifully appointed dinner table, to glorify a lavish sweets table, or to add a festive touch to a tray of miniature delicacies, a custom-made chocolate centerpiece is sure to impress your guests and establish your reputation as an outstanding chocolate artist.

That reputation will not come easily, however. Constructing some centerpieces can be tedious, time consuming, and very frustrating. It will be less so if you design each one carefully and complete as many of the nonaesthetic steps as possible before you begin the chocolate procedures.

Determine the purpose of the centerpiece first. Besides using it decoratively to reiterate the party's theme, a centerpiece can be used as a receptacle for chocolate favors, to handle the distribution of chocolate table assignments, or to add a unique chocolate focal point to a buffet table.

The design of the centerpiece is greatly determined by the size required to achieve its designated purpose. If it is to be used as a decorative touch on a dinner table, it should be sized so as not to inhibit cross-table conversation or crowd the table settings. It must, however, be large enough in proportion to the table size to make an impact; otherwise, it is not worth the time and effort. If it is to be used to distribute table assignments, it must be large enough to accommodate all of the guest's names. Two may be required for very large parties. For buffet tables, a chocolate centerpiece is most often used to fill a need for additional height and bulk. Its presence there can add that and more.

The shape of a centerpiece often corresponds to the shape of the table on which it is placed. Round or oval ones, generally viewed from all sides, must be designed with that in mind. Rectangularly shaped centerpieces, when positioned with their backs to the wall, require less decoration.

Regardless of the size or shape of the centerpiece, most of them need to be elevated in some way. Styrofoam discs and sheets are extremely useful for this purpose. They may be cut and stacked to suit your needs.

PREPARING STYROFOAM FOR CENTERPIECES

How to Cut Styrofoam

1. Use a ruler, a yardstick, or another similar object as a straight edge for cutting the Styrofoam.
2. Hold it in place securely as you score the Styrofoam with a sharp knife, penetrating it approximately ⅓ inch. It is not necessary to cut through to the bottom.
3. Position the Styrofoam so that the scored edge rests on the edge of the counter top. Grasp both sides of the cut. Push down on the extended portion to break it off.

How to Assemble the Styrofoam Base

1. Use an all-purpose glue or Royal Icing to secure one piece of Styrofoam to the surface of another.
2. When stacking several layers, it may be helpful to skewer them together with a hibachi stick. Dry thoroughly.

How to Paint Styrofoam

1. Prepare a recipe of Royal Icing. The quantity needed will vary according to the size of the centerpiece. Dye the icing, if necessary, in its thickened form.
2. Soften the icing as if for run sugar. Adjust the texture of the icing as often as necessary until the consistency is soft but not runny.
3. Cover the work area with wax paper and position the Styrofoam there. The next step is messy.
4. Use a spatula or a pastry brush to spread the "paint" smoothly over the surface of the Styrofoam. Further icing adjustments may be necessary if it does not spread smoothly. Add fresh icing to it if it appears runny or transparent. Dry overnight.

BASKET CENTERPIECES

Large chocolate baskets make not only sensational gifts but superbly versatile centerpieces as well. Set a chocolate basket on a silver pedestal, fill it with dipped strawberries, dipped dried fruit, or with your richest chocolate mousse and see how it livens up your next sweets

table. Or fill it with personalized chocolate marshmallow eggs for each guest at the Easter dinner table and place it in the center of your prettiest platter. Surround the basket with cellophane grass and extra decorated eggs to complete a centerpiece that is not only meaningful to all those present but beautiful—and easy.

Several years ago, I made the following basket centerpiece (more than 20 of them, actually) for a young girl's Bat Mitzvah reception. The guests received a bouquet of wired confectionery mums and leaves, tagged with their names and table numbers, as they entered the room. This basket, filled with similarly wired mums and leaves, adorned each table and served as a receptacle for the guests' personalized lollipops. The centerpiece remains a favorite of mine.

The Styrofoam Base

1. Glue two twelve-inch beveled Styrofoam rings together back to back. A two-inch by twelve inch round disc may be substituted. Attach a one-inch by eight-inch round Styrofoam disc over the opening of the Styrofoam ring.
2. Dye the icing to match the ivory color of white coating. To do so, use a toothpick to conservatively add a touch of yellow and brown to half of the Royal Icing recipe. You will need to adjust the color several times, I'm sure. Add more white icing to lighten the color, if necessary. Soften the icing as previously described.
3. Paint the base and dry thoroughly.
4. When dry, add a border of #6 tube bulbs at the base of the eight-inch disc and along the center line of the joined Styrofoam rings. (Omit if the two-inch by twelve-inch disc is used.)
5. Pin or glue a ½-inch-wide piece of brown ribbon around the exterior of the eight-inch disc for color.

The Basket

1. Mold a large, white coating basket using the Tomric mold #h-489 or a comparably large basket mold. Do not attach a handle to it.
2. Line the interior of the basket with plastic wrap. Now fill the cavity with two one-inch-thick pieces of Styrofoam trimmed to fit snugly in the cavity. Skewer an extra

piece, about two inches square, in the center with a lollipop stick.

The Flowers and Leaves

1. Make at least 25 standard-sized mums and 10 miniature ones in assorted fall colors (orange, egg yellow, and copper). Dry overnight.
2. Use 20-gauge floral wire, cut into five- to ten-inch lengths, to make at least 25 calyxes and approximately 15 wired leaves. Dry.
3. Assemble the large mums and reinforce the backs of the leaves.

The Lollipops

1. Mold the necessary plain chocolate lollipops. The Tomric basket can accommodate 10 of them.
2. Pipe a stem arrangement with a #2 tube. Attach a miniature mum with a dab of icing or chocolate. Use another #2 tube and the same fall colors to pipe several dot flowers and each guest's name on the lollipops. A #349 tube is used for the leaves. Dry thoroughly.
3. Wrap the lollipops in plastic wrap and tie them with dark green bows. The bows will add fullness to the basket.

Assembling the Basket Centerpiece

1. Extend the length of each lollipop stick by attaching another stick to it with green floral tape.
2. Position two lollipops, back to back, in the elevated two-inch square of Styrofoam in the center of the basket.
3. Position two more sets of back-to-back lollipops to the left and right of the elevated ones. They should stand slightly lower than the first set. Trim the extended lollipop sticks with wire clippers, if necessary.
4. Begin adding wired mums and leaves, trimming the wires as needed to add a variety of heights to the arrangement.
5. Place two more lollipops, side by side, in the center of the basket, lower than the rest. Repeat on the other side.
6. Continue to add more flowers and leaves until the basket is evenly filled. I use 10-12 leaves and 22-24 flowers per basket.

Note: The centerpiece may be assembled many weeks in advance.

CHOCOLATE RECORD CENTERPIECE

There are few teenage themes more popular than this one. The record centerpiece is as attractive on a sweets table as it is positioned at the entrance to the party room where it is often placed when used to designate table assignments.

The Styrofoam Base

The size of the base depends on need. The one that follows will accommodate 50 individual lollipops. Sometimes, for larger parties, one centerpiece may be used for boys and another for girls.

1. Purchase two sheets of Styrofoam and cut the following pieces from them:

   12 by 24 inches
   9½ by 19½ inches
   6 by 16 inches
   3 by 10 inches

2. Center the 9½-by-19½-inch piece along the back edge of the 12-by-24-inch piece and glue it there. Continue in that manner until all of the pieces are glued together. The completed base will have four staggered levels and a four-inch-high, straight-sided back.

3. Cover the exposed edge of each Styrofoam sheet with a one-inch-wide piece of color-coordinated ribbon. Glue it in place.

The Large Record

Method I: George H. Hake Inc. #33⅓ RPM Record mold

Approximate weight: 1 pound
1. Fill the cavity with dark chocolate.
2. Position two eight-inch-long wooden dowel rods onto the surface of the melted chocolate. Allow three inches of the rod to extend beyond the edge of the record. Cover the exposed surface of the embedded dowel rods with more chocolate. Chill only until set. Unmold and set aside.

Method II: Cake Pan

1. Fill a shiny, scratch-free, twelve-inch round cake pan with 1–1½ pounds of chocolate to mold a ridgeless record.

2. Unmold and warm to room temperature before continuing. Use a hot skewer to make the characteristic hole in the record's center.

The Record Label

1. Use the pattern provided here to trace the label onto the cake pan record's surface. The label may be piped onto wax paper, if preferred. Once dry, it can be decorated and then attached to the record with chocolate. The shape of the commercial mold's label is discernible on the surface of the molded piece.

2. To pipe the label onto either of the molded records, follow the directions given on page 100 for the Sweet 16 Record lollipop.

3. Designs may be painted on the dry label's surface with food coloring, if desired. Messages are written in confectioners' ink or Royal Icing.

The Lollipops

1. Again, follow the directions on page 100 for making record lollipops.

2. Match their labels to the large one only in so far as you are able. Tag them, if necessary, to supply any extra information.

Assembling the Centerpiece

1. Measure the distance between the two dowel rods attached to the large record.

2. Make two appropriately spaced holes, four inches deep, in the center of the top Styrofoam piece with a similarly sized dowel rod.

3. The record, once inserted, should rest on the Styrofoam with no parts of the sticks visible.

4. Position the lollipops on the rest of the base so as not to obstruct the view of the large record.

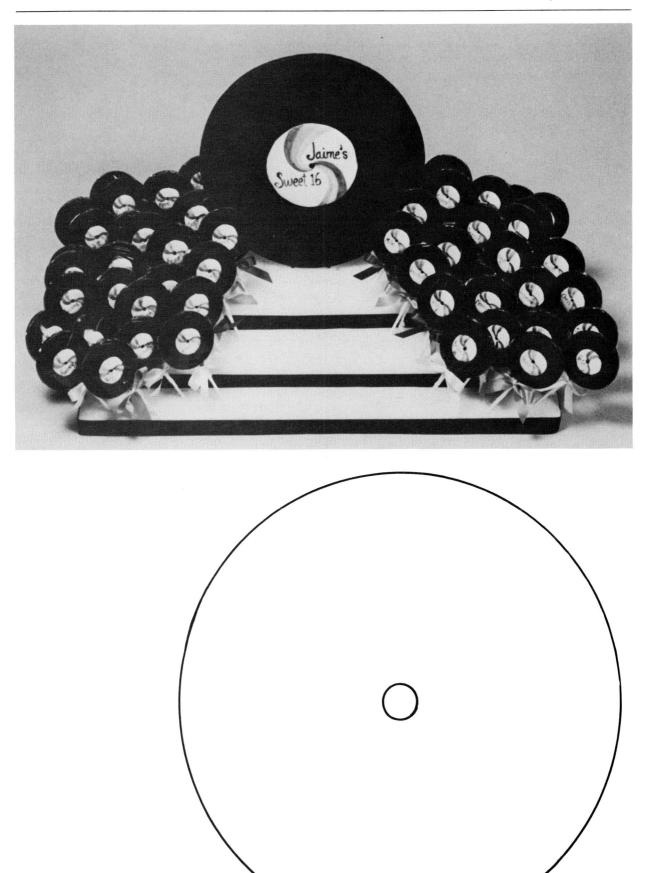

A twelve-inch
record label pattern.

Chocolate Strawberry Tree

Here is an outstanding addition to any sweets table—a tree full of chocolate-coated strawberries. Select fresh, firm berries and dip them in real chocolate, if possible, for a taste combination that is really divine.

Purists do not wash the strawberries before dipping them, but I do. It is important, however, to dry them thoroughly so as not to introduce moisture into the dipping chocolate. Whether the berries are washed or not, some moisture contamination of the chocolate is inevitable, so plan to eat the leftover chocolate rather than use it for future melting purposes.

> **4-5 pints** fresh strawberries
> **2 pounds** milk, semisweet, bittersweet chocolate or white coating
> **12-inch** Styrofoam cone
> Several lemon leaves (optional)

Rinse the strawberries in cool water early in the day. Do not soak them or remove their hulls. Drain the berries on several thicknesses of paper towels and air dry them for several hours, turning them over occasionally.

Arrange the dry strawberries by size on a large, paper-towel-lined cookie sheet.

Cover the Styrofoam cone with wax paper and secure it with tape.

Set the cone on a wax-paper-lined flat board.

Prepare the chocolate for dipping (see Chapter 1).

The placement of strawberries begins at the base of the cone. Select large ones for the bottom rows and increasingly smaller ones as you reach the top. Grasp a large berry by its hull and submerge it halfway into the melted chocolate. Immediately position it up against the cone with

its pointed end down. Continue in that manner all around the base of the cone.

Position the strawberries in subsequent rows in between those of the previous rows wherever possible. It is not usually necessary to chill the cone as you work, but if the dipped strawberries become unmanageable (the room may be too warm), chill the cone briefly and then continue.

Once completely covered with dipped berries, remove the cone from its work surface and position it in its place of honor on a flat serving dish. Surround it with approximately 30 chocolate leaves made on the backs of lemon leaves, if desired. The tree may be stored in a cool place (preferably not in the refrigerator) for several hours until needed.

Note: Though the chocolate pulls away easily from the wax-paper covered cone, a small knife is sometimes required to separate the occasionally stuck-together strawberries.

CUPID CENTERPIECE

My creative spirit soared the first time that I realized the potential for using Wilton Enterprises' People Molds #1906-A-5154 (designated for gum-paste work) to mold chocolate figures. Each of the four figures in the set are composed of three plastic molds—the head and upper torso, the lower torso and legs, and the arms. The resultant molded pieces are three-dimensional and can be joined easily with coating.

Cupid is molded in the five-inch child mold using flesh-colored coating. He is trimmed with Royal Icing hair and eyes and wears a compound coating clay sash. Use him to decorate the tops of wedding cakes, Valentine's Day cakes, or as a miniature centerpiece on a tray of very special personalized heart candies.

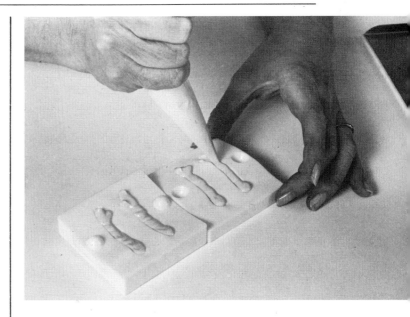

Molding Procedure

1. Dye about ½ pound of white coating flesh color.
2. Fill a parchment bag with the mixture and cut the opening about ⅛ inch wide. Open all three molds to expose their cavities. Squeeze a small amount of the coating into the face cavity and use a small brush to coax it into each of the tiny facial crevices.
3. Fill the remainder of the mold ¾-full and fill the other half the same way. Close the mold and secure the two halves with a tight rubber band.
4. Stand the closed mold on the counter top with the open end up. Continue to fill it until the coating is level with the opening of the mold. Rap the mold on the counter several times to settle the coating. Chill it for approximately 10 minutes or until the two pieces of the mold come apart easily. Unmold. Use a parchment bag filled with the same flesh-colored coating and a very small opening to pipe two ears.
5. Fill both halves of the arm mold with coating. Be sure that the cavities are not underfilled. Close the mold as before and secure it with a rubber band. Chill about five minutes.
6. The lower torso mold is more challenging than the others because it is open at both ends. Have ready a small, flat, wax-paper-covered board. Fill the legs of both halves generously with coating. Extend some of the coating into the torso areas and onto the upper parts of the feet. Close the mold and immediately stand it, feet down, on the flat, prepared board. Secure the mold as before with a tight rubber band. Lift the board on which the mold stands and rap it on the counter several times to force the coating down into the feet cavities. Insert a lollipop stick in and out of each leg cavity to rid it of air pockets. Add enough coating to bring its level even with the top of the mold. Chill for approximately 10 minutes.
7. Remove the rubber band and open the mold. If it does not open easily, chill it for a while longer.

Assembling the Figure

1. Allow the pieces to return to room temperature before removing the excess coating from them with a sharp knife.
2. Use a knife to slit the lower torso in half vertically so as to separate the legs. Reattach the two halves with a little flesh-colored coating, positioning them so that one foot is a step ahead of the other. Once the coating has set, trim the uneven top of the torso to make it flat.
3. Attach the upper torso to the lower one with coating.
4. Mold a chocolate disc (Maid of Scandinavia #71668) and attach the feet of the armless

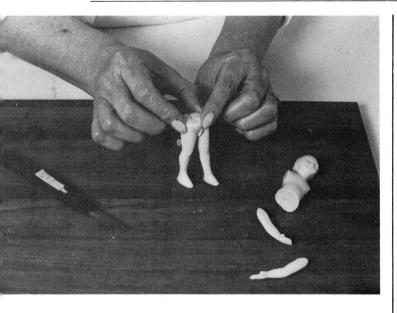

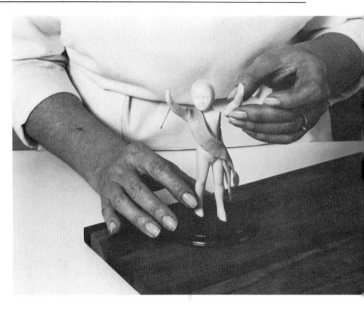

figure to it with flesh-colored coating. Allow the figure to set undisturbed before handling.

Dressing the Figure

1. Dye a walnut-sized ball of white compound coating clay a soft shade of blue. Place it on a cutting board and roll it to a thickness of ¹⁄₁₆ inch with a rolling pin. If the clay sticks to the surface as you roll it, dust the board with a light coating of confectioners' sugar and try it again. Brush the excess sugar from the clay before using it.

Note: A pasta machine may also be used to roll out the clay. Use #2 and #3 settings.

2. Cut the rolled piece into a ½-inch-by-8-inch-long strip. Use a diagonal cut for the ends.

3. Position the strip across Cupid's right shoulder and gather both pieces together at his left hip. The sash should hang rather loosely so as to conceal the figure's seams. Trim the ends, if necessary.

4. Personalize the sash as desired with Royal Icing and a #1 tube.

5. Attach the arms with coating in an outstretched position.

6. Use a #1 tube and brown Royal Icing to pipe a head full of tiny ringlets (a series of *e*s).

7. Pipe the whites of his eyes with a #1 tube and Royal Icing. When dry, paint in blue eyeballs with food coloring.

8. Dye about ¼ teaspoon of soft white icing a shade of flesh slightly deeper than Cupid's skin color. Apply a very light amount of it to his cheeks and lips with a brush. Buff it with a soft brush before it dries.

9. Surround his feet with compound coating clay rosebuds, stems, and coating leaves.

10. *Optional:* See the wing pattern provided. Pipe two of them on wax paper and chill. Turn them over and pipe their back sides. Chill again briefly and attach them to Cupid's back with a little white coating.

11. Position the centerpiece in the middle of a large, doily-covered tray. Arrange your most beautiful, heart-shaped, personalized chocolate patties all around the base of the centerpiece and accept the applause graciously.

Wing pattern for Cupid.

SWEET 16 FIGURE

One of the loveliest ways to commemorate a girl's 16th birthday is to mold a miniature chocolate likeness of her. It is a centerpiece that she is sure to treasure.

The porcelainlike figure that follows is molded in the 8¼-inch woman's mold that is part of the People Mold Set previously mentioned. She is dressed for the occasion in the perfect medium for this procedure—compound coating clay. A florist's touch could easily transform this delicate centerpiece into a larger, more elegant one.

Molding Procedure

1. Dye about ¾ pound of white coating flesh color.
2. Follow the same directions given on page 159 for molding the Cupid figure.

Assembling the Figure

1. Assemble the girl figure as previously described for the Cupid Centerpiece, omitting step 2 on page 159.
2. Attach her feet with coating to the larger, rectangularly fluted mold that is found on the same flat sheet mold used for Cupid's base.

Dressing the Figure

1. Dye approximately four ounces of compound coating clay the desired color. For best results, use clay that is at least 24 hours old. Place it on a cutting board and roll it to a thickness of ¹⁄₁₆ inch with a rolling pin. Lift it off the board frequently as you roll it to keep it from sticking. The surface may be dusted lightly with confectioners' sugar, if desired.
2. Prepare a dress pattern using the one given on page 163 or one of your own design. Lay it on the thin sheet of clay and cut around it with a sharp knife.
3. Lift the cut piece with two hands and gently position it on the front of the figure. No adhesive is required. Shape it to the contours of her upper torso by pressing it gently, particularly at the shoulder line and waist.
4. Use your sharp utility knife to cut out the scoop neck carefully. Be careful. Too deep a knife penetration will mar her "flesh."
5. Encourage the folds of the skirt to fall gracefully in the front and on the sides of the figure. The piece will not cover the back. Trim the length, if necessary.

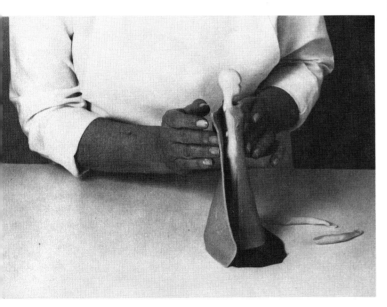

6. Knead the remainder of the clay and roll it out again. Use the same pattern to cut the back of the dress. Reserve the rest of it for the sleeves. Secure the cutout piece to the figure with a few dots of coating placed on the shoulder blades and waistline.

7. Shape the clay as before, pressing gently to conceal the seams, if possible.

8. Use the knife to trim away the excess clay from the armholes and to shape the scoop-necked back.

9. Arrange the folds of the long train so that they fall naturally. Stretch the piece, if necessary, so that the train rests casually on the chocolate base.

10. Use some of the reserved rolled-out clay scraps to cut two small triangles to use for the sleeves. Attach them to the figure with a dot of coating. Use your fingertips to smooth them into place and a knife to trim away the excess.

11. Pipe tiny dots of Royal Icing with a #1 tube all over the bodice, the sleeves, and the entire train. Add a border of piped beads with the same tube along the bottom edge of the front of the dress.

12. Style the figure's hair with a #1 tube and Royal Icing. Overpipe it as necessary to add fullness.

13. Pipe the eyes as previously described. Use pink-toned, soft icing to blush the cheeks and color the lips. Do not use red.

14. Attach compound coating clay rosebuds, stems, and coating leaves to the base to complete the centerpiece.

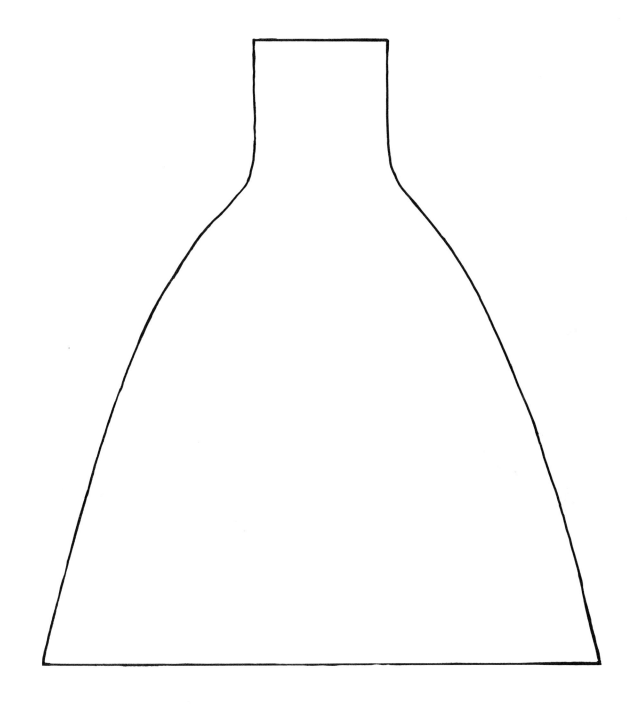

Pattern for Sweet 16
figure's dress. Make two.

11
Architectural Designs in Chocolate: Chocolate Houses

Chocolate artistry inevitably leads to experimentation with architectural designs. The experiences derived from these activities are certain to deepen your appreciation of this wondrous medium and broaden your awareness of its potential as an art form.

The construction of most chocolate architectural pieces can be likened to the procedures used to create gingerbread or gum paste extravaganzas. They all require considerable time and patience, but they provide an enormous opportunity for creative expression as well.

Be sure to read the lengthy directions thoroughly before you begin to work in order to familiarize yourself with what lies ahead. Assemble all the necessary equipment and then allocate enough time to devote to the project; rushing through it will turn what should be an enjoyable experience into a potential nightmare.

Fortunately, one does not need a background in architectural studies to design a chocolate house. Begin your apprenticeship with proven blueprints such as those provided here or use one of any number of gingerbread house plans that can be found in cake-decorating books and holiday

magazine issues. Soon, as your experience and confidence build, you will be able to modify these plans or design more elaborate ones of your own.

GENERAL INSTRUCTIONS
Foundation

The construction work should begin with the foundation. The base on which you build your house must be strong enough to support its weight and large enough to accommodate some confectionery landscaping. Use pieces of wood, Styrofoam, or something comparable measuring at least 12 inches square. To make these materials food-safe, seal them with a thick coating of Royal Icing and allow them to dry thoroughly before using.

House Patterns

It is necessary to prepare four heavyweight paper patterns for outlining the shapes of the six chocolate pieces that make up the standard house. (I like the weight of vanilla folders for making patterns.) The front and back of the house are

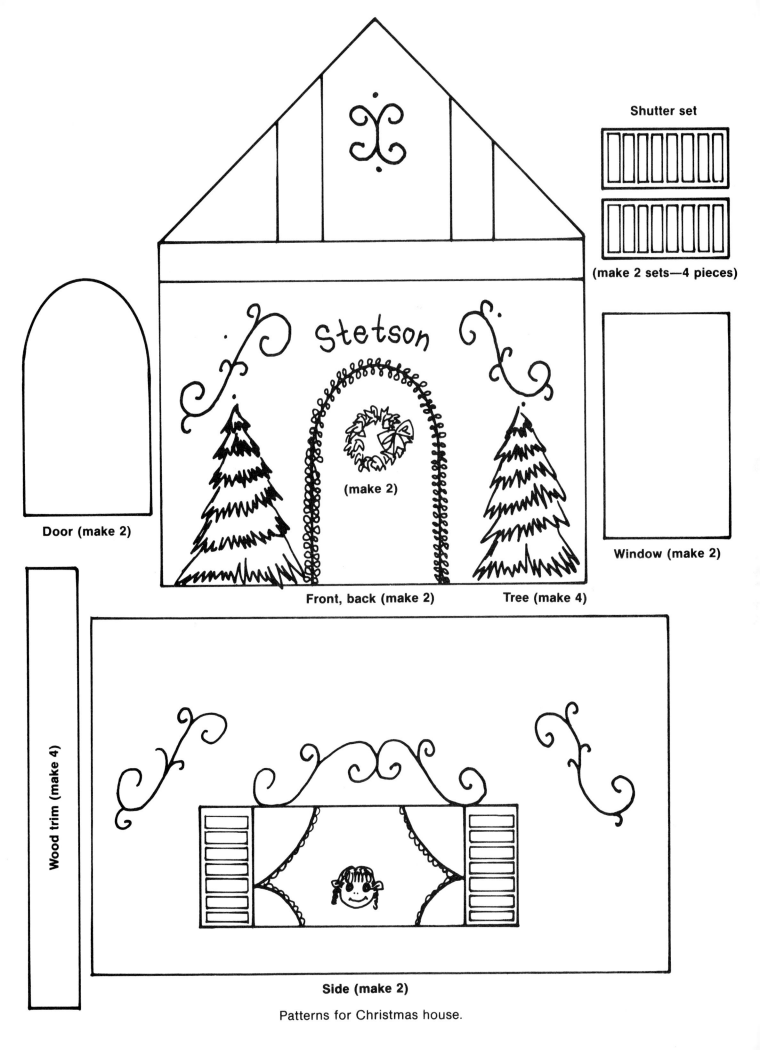

Shutter set

(make 2 sets—4 pieces)

Door (make 2)

Stetson

(make 2)

Front, back (make 2)

Tree (make 4)

Window (make 2)

Wood trim (make 4)

Side (make 2)

Patterns for Christmas house.

Top

Smaller roof section

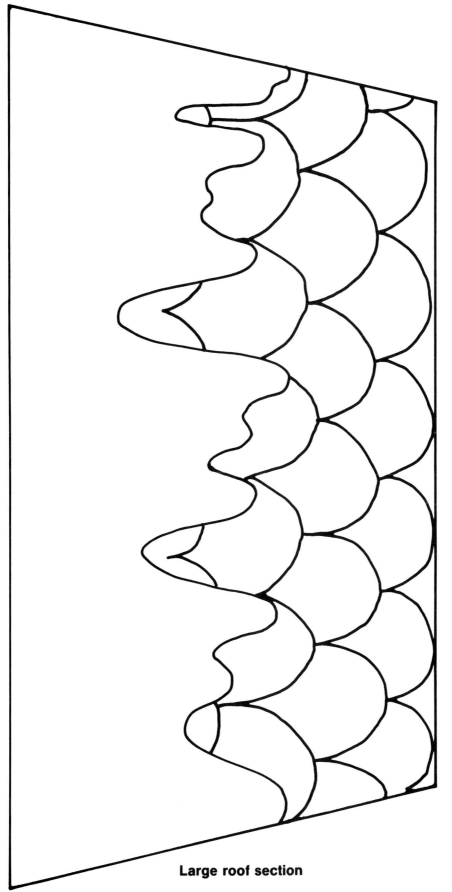

Top

Large roof section

shaped with one pattern and the two sides with another. The two roof patterns are not equal in size; the smaller roof section is designed to abut the other from below.

Molding the Slab

Chocolate houses may, of course, be molded of real chocolate or compound coating. If the piece is to be used solely for decoration (many of them are), then by all means use compound coating. It is easier, faster, and less expensive. Under proper storage conditions these houses may be stored for several years.

1. Melt 2½ pounds of chocolate. Use approximately 2¼ pounds of it and a 12-by-18-inch cookie sheet to mold one slab. See pages 25–26 for complete directions.
2. Remember to allow it to return to room temperature before proceeding.

Outlining the Patterns on Chocolate

Each pattern should be positioned on the slab according to the plan that follows. The proper placement not only utilizes the chocolate surface efficiently, but facilitates the subsequent cutting procedure by eliminating unnecessary cuts.

1. Place the slab, face up, on a cutting surface. Handle it as little as possible; use gloves or a cloth to touch it as you work.
2. If necessary, use your sharp utility knife to trim away (conservatively) the rounded edges of the slab.
3. Position the house front pattern in the lower left corner of the slab so that it is even with the bottom edge of the chocolate. Hold the pattern in place firmly as you define its shape on the chocolate's surface with a sharp point. Accuracy is essential throughout the outlining and cutting procedures.
4. Reposition the same pattern, aligning it as before so that it touches the side of the previously outlined one; define its peaked top and right edge.
5. Align the house side pattern vertically on the slab so that its left edge touches that of the previously outlined shape. Outline it as before.
6. Repeat step 5 for the second side piece.
7. Position the large roof pattern, wide end down, above the outlined house sides so that

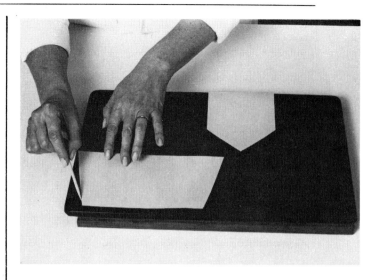

it rests on their top edges. There is no room to spare, so be sure to position it correctly. Outline it on three sides.

8. Align the other roof pattern so that it abuts the diagonal edge of the previously outlined roof section. Outline its remaining three sides.
9. Use a soft-bristle brush to lightly clear away the chocolate debris caused by the outlining.

Cutting the Outlined Chocolate Pieces

1. Use gloves and a sharp utility knife to score, slowly and precisely, the bottom edges of both roof sections, extending the cut the full length of the slab. Repeat this maneuver at least two more times, penetrating the chocolate deeper each time until the knife cuts through completely and the slab is split

in half lengthwise. Set aside the roof half of the slab.

2. Use the same restrained cutting technique to separate the house sides and the front and back pieces. Trim all of their remaining edges and set them aside.

3. Repeatedly score the roof sections along the diagonal edge that they share to separate them. Trim away the remaining edges.

4. Reserve the scrap pieces of chocolate; they will be remelted and used as assembly adhesive later.

Piping the Decorations: Christmas House

The patterns shown on page 165 may be used under wax paper (see directions that follow) or for outlining the shapes directly on the chocolate's surface (see pages 74–75). The latter method will necessitate the use of compatible media: compound coating decorations on compound coating house sections and cocoa butter coating decorations on real chocolate.

1. Trace the following patterns, in the quantities indicated, in preparation for the upcoming outlining and flooding techniques:

> two doors
> two windows
> two shutter sets
> four wood trim strips
> four Christmas trees
> two wreaths

2. Secure all the patterns to the work board and cover with wax paper.

3. Prepare parchment bags, each filled with approximately two ounces of each of the following melted, colored coatings: white, flesh, red, yellow, and green.

4. Doors: Use a #4 tube size opening to outline them with red coating; flood with the same. Flatten the ripples (page 79).

5. Wood trim strips: Draw the bag of red coating back and forth across the paper. Flatten the ripples.

6. Windows: Outline in white coating, then flood. When set, use a #4 tube size opening to outline the curtains with yellow coating and then flood them. When set, add a zigzag border along the edges of the curtains. Add a Christmas tree in one of

the windows and a child's face in the other.

7. Shutters: Use the equivalent of a #4 tube opening to pipe a series of continuous horizontal lines working from the top of the shutter pattern to the bottom. Once set, add a sprig of holly and three red berries on each shutter (page 136).

8. Christmas tree: Use a small opening in the bag of green coating to outline the shape of the tree first. Pipe a vertical zigzag, moving from left to right across the bottom of the tree to form row 1. Repeat for three more slightly overlapping rows. When set, trim with assorted-colored dots.

9. Wreath: See page 136. Add holly berries and bows.

10. Chill the piped decorations only until set.

Attaching the Decorations

1. Once set, release the individual pieces from the paper with a spatula. Most of the pieces are now ready to be affixed to the house sections with chocolate or coating. Consult the pattern illustrations for placement guidance.

2. Trim the butting edges of the windows and shutters to assure neat joints. Cut the wood trim strips so that their ends are straight and attach as shown.

3. Set aside all the decorated house sections until they are firmly set before assembling them.

4. Fill a parchment bag with red coating and cut an opening in it equivalent to a #2 tube opening. Beginning along the bottom (narrow) edge of each roof piece, pipe a row of scallops. Continue piping more rows of scallops until half of each side is covered with them. The remainder of the roof will be covered with icing snow.

Royal Icing Touches

1. Use a #18 tube to pipe a border of stars (pages 51–52) around the frame of both doors.
2. Pipe scrolls as shown on page 165 with a #2 tube. A family name, address, or special greeting placed over the front door will add a special personalized touch. Dry thoroughly before handling.

House Assembly

Readiness List

- Prepared base; pencil.
- 12-inch decorating bag filled with white Royal Icing and fitted with an open coupler; metal spatula.
- Four decorated house sections and two roof halves.
- Soft toweling.
- Parchment bag filled with tempered chocolate or melted coating.
- Several tall cans or jars for propping sides—one should be approximately 2¾ inches tall to support the roof.

1. Draw a 4½-by-6¾-inch rectangle (denoting the house size) on the prepared base, positioning it as desired. Pipe thick lines of

icing on the 4½-inch-wide back and the longer side lines.

2. Lay the back section of the house, decorated side down, on a bed of soft toweling as you pipe a line of chocolate along both of its straight sides.
3. Immediately stand it in the back line of icing, temporarily propping it there with cans, if necessary. Position the two side pieces into the other lines of icing, butting them firmly against the chocolate adhesive on the back piece.

4. Use a metal spatula to smooth the excess icing up against the inside base lines of the positioned pieces for added support. Smooth the icing on the outside base lines to simulate slightly drifted snow.
5. Pipe another thick line of icing where the front piece belongs. Repeat step 2 using the front of the house. Stand it in this line and press it firmly against the edges of the side pieces.
6. Examine all the joints to be sure that none of the pieces has shifted. Make adjustments and add more chocolate adhesive as needed. Allow the frame of the house to firm up completely; trim away the excess chocolate from the exterior seams.
7. Pipe lines of chocolate along all of the top edges of the right half of the house. Position the small half of the roof, narrow end down, wide edge even with the top of the peak. Support it from below with a 2¾ inch can until it is firmly set.

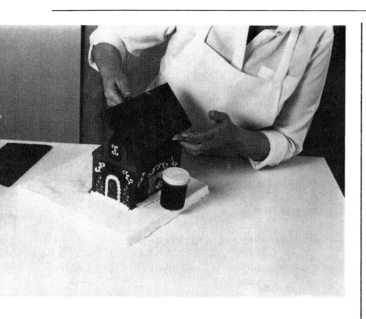

8. Pipe lines of chocolate along the top edges of the rest of the house and along the top edge of the attached roof section. Position the remaining roof piece there, holding and supporting it from below with the 2¾-inch can until firmly set.

FINAL DECORATIONS

Readiness List

- White Royal Icing, tubes #12, #18.
- Crystallized sugar, optional (Maid of Scandinavia #30406).
- M&Ms.
- Sugar ice cream cones.
- Green Royal Icing, plus other assorted bright colors; tubes #75, #2–#4.
- Scrap pieces of chocolate; confectioners' foil.
- One-inch-wide velveteen ribbon, approximately 50 inches long.

1. Use a bag of creamy Royal Icing fitted with a #12 tube to pipe the snow on the roof. It may be applied with a spatula, if preferred. Sprinkle it with crystallized sugar.
2. Use a #18 star tube to pipe a shell border over the seams at each of the four corners of the house.
3. Spread a fresh layer of snow icing over the entire base; sprinkle it with crystallized sugar. Implant several rows of colorful M&Ms into the soft icing for a curved front walk.
4. To landscape the house with trees and shrubs, use sugar ice cream cones. Cover them with rows of tube #75 leaves made of Royal Icing. Start at the base of the tree and move upward. To make larger trees, stack several cones and then decorate them. Break off a portion of the sugar cone's base to make small trees and bushes. Trim at least one large tree for Christmas with cookie trims, balls of icing dyed in bright colors, and piped-on white candy canes. Once dry, paint on the peppermint stripes as on page 137.
Note: To facilitate this whole procedure, pipe the trees and bushes ahead of time by positioning the cones on the necks of bottles for easy handling. Dry thoroughly before transferring them to the house base. Attach with Royal Icing.
5. Wrap pieces of chocolate in foil, decorate with an icing bow, and affix to the base with icing. The packages may be personalized for each family member, if desired.
6. Glue the velveteen ribbon onto the exposed edges of the base (if Styrofoam is used) with Royal Icing. Use straight pins to hold it in place until the icing adhesive dries.

SANTA CLAUS (optional)

Figure-piping a shape this large requires freshly made, very stiff Royal Icing. Santa may be piped in place or on wax paper long in advance of a need for him. Dry thoroughly before handling, in either case.

1. Prepare Santa's head. My first choice for this is a marble-sized ball of flesh-colored compound coating clay. A miniature marshmallow—skewered with a toothpick, dipped in flesh-colored coating, and allowed to set—is an acceptable substitute. Discard the toothpick before assembling.

2. Use a #12 tube and firm red icing to pipe a thick, 1¾-inch-tall cone shape for the upper torso.

3. Use slightly lighter pressure to pipe his legs, extending them to the calves only.

4. The same bag and tube are used with still less pressure to pipe the arms. Brace the torso with your free index finger as you do so. Remember to bend the arms at the elbows.

5. Use a #10 tube and black icing to pipe the top of his boots. Position the tube perpendicular to the surface to pipe the feet. Correct minor shaping flaws with a dampened artists' brush, if necessary.

6. Affix the head to the body with icing. Use a #2 tube and white icing to pipe his curly sideburns, extending them into the beard. Pipe the long curly hair.

7. The stocking cap is piped with the originally used bag of red icing. Squeeze hard to attach it well to the head and then diminish pressure as you pull it down to the side.

8. Pipe two eyes and a nose on his face. Complete the face with a moustache piped in two parts.

9. Use white or flesh-colored icing to shape his mittens.

10. A #4 tube is used to pipe the black belt and a #2 tube for the yellow buckles that adorn his belt and boots.

11. Pipe #2 tube zigzag borders on Santa's cap (pipe a ball at the end of it, too), wrists, and at the top of the boots. An additional border should be added along the hemline of his jacket.

HAUNTED HOUSE

The basic house plan can be modified in many ways to keep it viable all year-round. The haunted house has an added front porch and touches of spooky semi-Victorian decor. It features a real shingled roof, elaborate landscaping, and a larger base to accommodate it all. You will surely want to add some of your own ghoulish ideas.

Preliminary Steps

1. Prepare one recipe of chocolate clay. Allow it to ripen for several hours or overnight before using.
2. Make at least one recipe of Royal Icing. Part of another may be required for extended landscaping work.
3. Use a sheet of Styrofoam approximately 12 by 16 by 1 inch for the base. Coat it with moss green Royal Icing (green tinged with brown). Dry thoroughly.
4. Have on hand the five patterns (same as before plus the porch patterns) required for outlining all of the house sections. Cut out and set aside the patterns for the side and attic windows as well.
5. Trace the remaining patterns and prepare them for the outlining and flooding procedures.
6. Mold a sheet of chocolate as before. Mold an additional thin card-sized piece (Apollo Mold Co. #550) to use for the porch.
7. Outline and then cut out all the chocolate house sections, including the porch roof and floor.
8. Dye 3½ ounces of coconut moss green. To do so, place it in a covered container, a blender, or a food processor. Add specks of creamy paste or liquid food coloring. Cover and shake vigorously or process briefly.

Preparing the Decorations

1. Doors: Using the prepared patterns as a guide, pipe two chocolate doors; flood them immediately. Overpipe the firmed-up doors with chocolate ornamental mouldings as illustrated.
2. Ghosts: Pipe at least eight white coating ghosts in various sizes and stances; pipe on the tiny facial features with chocolate after they have set.
3. Skeleton: Use a very small opening in the bag to pipe two white coating skeletons in case one breaks (see pages 108–109).
4. Tombstone: Outline and then flood one or more tombstones. Once set, overpipe the back for strength and depth. Inscribe it with chocolate, as desired.
5. Ghoul: Mold a ghoulish figure to stand in the yard. I use the Fischer Mold Co. #471 mold without the stick.
6. Bats: Thicken approximately ¼ cup of chocolate with water and pipe several bats. Use a #101 tube with the broad end against the surface to zigzag one wing and then the other. Pipe a #4 ball for the head and pull out two small ears with the same tube.
7. Shovel: Pipe a shovel with the thickened chocolate and a #4 tube.
8. Pumpkins: Use a #4 tube and thickened coating dyed orange to pipe 8–10 pumpkins. Once set, attach pairs of similar ones together with more coating to make three-dimensional pumpkins. Add chocolate or icing stems. For jack-o'-lanterns, add yellow icing or coating facial details.
9. Windows: Use the patterns to cut out four rectangular and two half-circle pieces of edible rice (wafer) paper. Regular paper may also be used. Use tiny scissors to cut several holes in each piece to resemble broken window panes.
10. Shingles: Roll out the chocolate clay and trim it so that the sides are squared; cut it into ¾-inch-wide strips. Press the tines of a fork (I use a three-tined dipping fork) across each strip and then cut it into ¾-

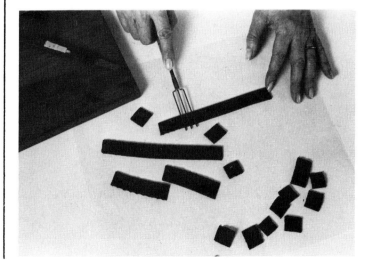

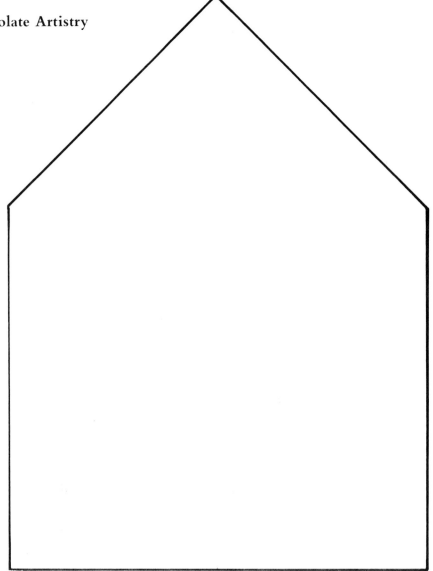

Front, back (make 2)

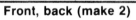

Side (make 2)

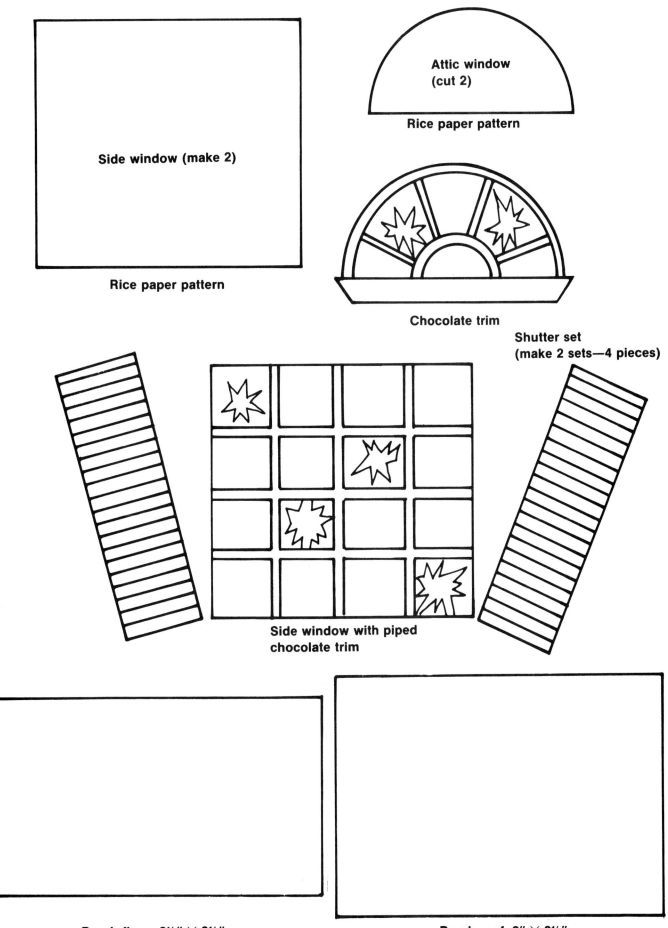

Side window (make 2)

Rice paper pattern

Attic window
(cut 2)

Rice paper pattern

Chocolate trim

Shutter set
(make 2 sets—4 pieces)

Side window with piped
chocolate trim

Porch floor, 2½″ × 3½″
(make 1)

Porch roof, 2″ × 3½″
(make 1)

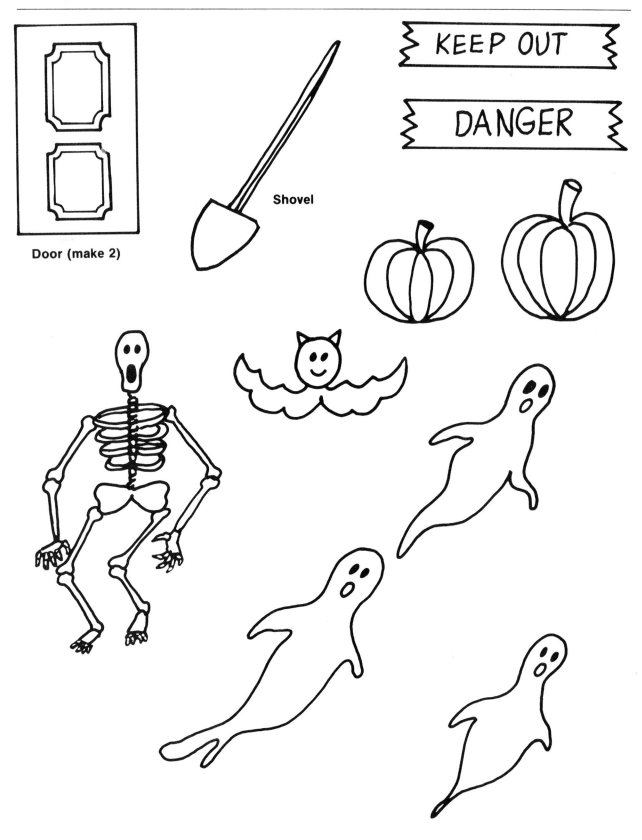

KEEP OUT

DANGER

Shovel

Door (make 2)

Haunted house patterns.

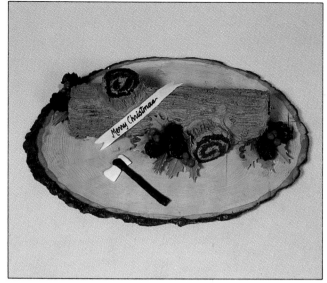

CHOCOLATE YULE LOG

HAUNTED HOUSE

CHOCOLATE HOUSE

**CHOCOLAT'S CHOCOLATE HAZELNUT
CAKE WITH FILIGREE BUTTERFLY**

TORTA MEXICANA

ALMOND TORTE

CHOCOLATE WALNUTS

DIPPED COOKIES AND DRIED FRUITS

DIPPED FORTUNE COOKIES

EASTER NESTS

VIENNESE COOKIES

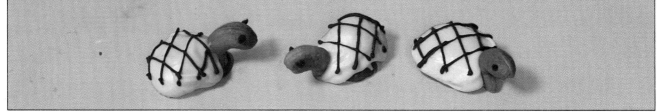

CASHEW TORTUGAS

PERSONALIZED PRETZEL STICKS

inch-wide shingles. Repeat as often as necessary to shape approximately 100 shingles. Air dry them for several hours to facilitate handling.

11. Use the method just described to shape two sets of shutters. Cut each one ¾ inch wide and 2¾ inches long.

Attaching the Decorations

1. Lay the rectangular rice paper windows in a vertical position on each of the house side pieces. Use a chocolate-filled parchment bag with an opening equivalent to a #4 tube to outline the exterior of the window frames.

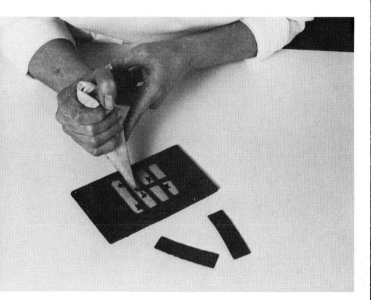

The lines of chocolate must touch not only the papers' edges but the chocolate's surface as well. Complete the remainder of the frames. Repeat this procedure with the attic windows on the front and back sections of the house.

2. Attach a ghost drifting upward, slightly off center, to the bottom of the front and back sections.

3. Affix a row of shingles along the bottom of each roof piece (porch roof included) with chocolate. Position the subsequent rows so that at least the first few shingles in each row are centered between the ones in the previous row. Trim the end shingles to conform to the shape of the roof.

Temporarily leave the uppermost part of both roofs bare. The porch roof may be completely covered prior to assembly.

Assembly

Readiness List

- Prepared base; pencil.
- 12-inch decorating bag filled with green Royal Icing and fitted with an open coupler; metal spatula.
- Two chocolate doors and signs.
- Four decorated house sections, two shingled roofs, porch roof, and floor; two lollipop sticks cut to approximately 2½ inches long.
- Parchment bag filled with tempered chocolate or coating.
- Several tall cans or jars for propping sides—one should be about 2¾ inches tall to support the main roof and another about 2½ inches tall to support the porch roof.

1. Pencil in the shape of the house on the surface of the prepared Styrofoam base, positioning it diagonally.

2. Pipe mounds of green icing as on page 170. Assemble the sections as previously described and check their alignment.

3. Adhere the porch floor to the base directly in front of the house with some of the excess icing. Add more, if necessary.

4. Attach the doors to the front and back sections with chocolate, leaving them slightly ajar. The ghosts should appear to be floating out of them. Affix the signs as desired.

5. Conceal the joints at each of the four corners of the house with a chocolate zigzag border.

6. Use chocolate to attach the roof sections to the assembled house; complete the top rows of shingles. Attach the porch roof with chocolate, supporting it with the 2½-inch jar.

7. Position two lollipop sticks, the ends of which have been dipped in chocolate, under the porch roof for support. Once set, use an artists' brush to paint them with chocolate.

Final Decorations

Readiness List

- Twigs.
- Chocolate clay.
- Green Royal Icing; green coconut.
- Brown sugar.
- Piped bats, ghosts, ghoul, skeleton, shovel, pumpkins.
- 58 inches of one-inch velveteen ribbon.

1. Cut twigs from live bushes or trees in your garden. Wash and dry them thoroughly. Prune them to resemble miniature trees for the haunted house's yard. Insert them into the Styrofoam and cover their bases with a thin layer of chocolate clay to simulate tree bark. Attach a few bats and ghosts to the branches with chocolate, as desired.

2. Position the tombstone in a prominent place, affixing it with icing. Brace it from behind with a mound of icing. Use an open coupler to pipe a mound for the freshly dug grave in front of it. Coat the mound with brown sugar. Plunge the shovel into it.

3. Coat the ground with green icing, sprinkling it liberally with a layer of dyed coconut. Press on it gently to make sure it adheres to the icing.

4. Pipe a few sugar-cone evergreen trees and bushes and position them throughout the yard.

5. Attach pumpkins to the porch floor with chocolate. Position the molded ghoul behind one of the trees in the yard, affixing it there with white coating.

6. Hang the skeleton from one of the branches of the largest tree.

7. Trim the Styrofoam edge with ribbon.

12
Decorating Cakes with Chocolate

To the uninitiated, decorating a cake is a formidable challenge that requires natural artistic ability, a great deal of skill, and an even greater degree of patience. Such an impression is certainly understandable in light of the intricate, highly sophisticated techniques that do indeed exist in the realm of cake decorating. The fact remains, however, that such an impression is grossly exaggerated. As in chocolate artistry, what is needed most is an understanding of several basic skills and a realization that beautiful results are possible with a minimal amount of decorating.

The cakes that follow are variations of the classic ones found in any good baker's repertoire. Some of the recipes require conscientious effort, prior knowledge of rudimentary techniques, and an adventurous spirit. The chocolate designs that adorn them, however, can be created by any willing student and are adaptable to most other cake recipes. The intent here is not to teach baking skills but rather to dramatize the effect that chocolate artistry can have on the presentation of your final product when it is combined with a few sound cake-decorating procedures.

The ultimate criterion for any successfully decorated cake must be the inherent quality of the product itself, not the complexity of the design. There is something amiss if the decoration outshines the taste and quality of the cake. Pledge now never to defraud your guests or sacrifice your time and creative energy by decorating an unworthy cake.

Most people underestimate the importance of the neatly frosted surface on which the final decorations are placed. The buttercream icing, whipped cream, or glaze used to ice cakes is too often applied awkwardly and haphazardly with very little regard to developing good icing techniques. The difficulties experienced by novice decorators are usually due to an apparent lack of knowledge as to how to cope with the different types of icing textures that exist. What a pity, for therein lies the secret to a beautiful cake.

BUTTERCREAM ICING

The most delectable buttercreams are distinguishable by their ivory color—a telltale sign that butter really is present. They are generally quite soft, quite perishable (unless refrigerated), and sometimes quite unmanageable—especially in hot weather. Use all-butter buttercreams mainly to ice and fill cakes and for the simplest of decorating techniques. The inexperienced decorator would be ill advised to attempt to use them for three-dimensional floral or fancy border work. A little white vegetable shortening may be substituted for part of the butter called for in most icing recipes to produce a buttercream better suited for those procedures.

Icing a fragile cake with buttercream that is dry and firm can be a classic lesson in futility. These so-called buttercreams, usually made of all white vegetable shortening with heavy additions of confectioners' sugar, are inferior in taste to the aforementioned icings. They are very white in color, need little or no refrigeration, and hold up well, even in hot weather. Use this type of icing for specialty piping rather than to ice and fill cakes. To thin this firm mixture, gradually add enough milk, cream, or corn syrup to make it spreadable or substitute butter for part of the amount of shortening called for in the recipe.

WHIPPED CREAM

There is something pure and honest about wrapping a genuinely good cake in a coat of whipped cream. It expresses confidence in the merits of your cake and an affirmation of your desire to use nothing but quality ingredients.

Whipped cream is a soft mixture best suited to filling and icing cakes and for simple piping techniques such as rosettes and shell borders. The secret to piping with it is to underfill the bag and replenish it frequently with fresh cream.

PRELIMINARY STEPS TO DECORATING A CAKE

A cake must have flat, even surfaces in order to be suitable for decorating. Use a long knife with a serrated edge and a gentle sawing motion to level uneven tops or trim away rough edges.

To compose a wonderfully rich, multilayered torte, cut each baked layer into two or three horizontal slices with a serrated knife.

Torting the Cake

1. Attach one of the cakes to a similarly sized cake cardboard with a little icing. Position one hand on top of the cake to assist in turning it throughout the torting procedure.
2. Determine the cutting position on the side edge of the cake and begin the sawing motion there. It is important, however, to eventually penetrate the cake to its center, keeping the knife as parallel to the surface as possible.
3. To remove the top layer of the split cake, insert another cake cardboard-round between the layers and lift it off. The cardboard will also facilitate the handling procedure involved in assembling the cake.

Assembling a Layered Cake

1. *For soft, thin fillings:* Fill a pastry bag with the icing that will be used to coat the cake. Remove the coupler ring and pipe a wall of icing around the circumference of the layer's surface. Spread the cake layer with approximately ⅛ inch of the desired filling, extending it to cover the entire contained area. The piped wall of icing will prevent the filling from overflowing onto the sides of the cake. *For firmer fillings:* Omit the piped wall of icing. Use a metal spatula to spread the cake surface to within ⅛ inch of the edge with the desired filling.
2. Hold the cardboard-round-supported top layer over the previously filled one. Coax about one inch of it beyond the cardboard's edge to enable you to position that part of it properly on the filled layer. Slowly remove the cardboard as you guide the layer and it will fall nicely into place.
3. Repeat steps 1 and 2 as often as necessary to complete the layering process. To assure a smooth, crumb-free top surface, place the final layer, top or bottom side up with the raw crumb side down.

Icing a Cake with Buttercream

1. If possible, place the assembled cake on a decorating turntable or use a makeshift one—a revolving spice rack or a lazy Susan.
2. Fill a small bowl with about one cup of soft

icing. Thin it, if necessary. Use a metal spatula to coat the entire surface of the cake with a thin, transparent layer of icing, filling in any gaps between the layers. Smooth the surface to eliminate excess icing. This is only an undercoat.

3. Refrigerate the cake at least 15 minutes to partially set the crumb coat and facilitate the next step.

4. Use a metal spatula to apply a thicker coat of icing to the sides and top of the cake. Use firm pressure and a back-and-forth movement to spread the icing evenly.

5. Rotate the turntable with your free hand as you remove the excess icing from the top and sides of the cake. Clean the spatula and repeat as often as necessary.

6. Dip the spatula into hot water until no trace of icing remains on it. Shake off the excess moisture and draw it across as much of the top surface of the cake as you can in one movement. Repeat only as often as necessary to smooth the whole surface. (The less you fuss with it, the better.)

7. Use the same method to smooth the sides of the cake, dipping and shaking off the excess moisture on the spatula before each smoothing stroke. Smooth away the excess icing that inevitably accumulates on the top edge of the cake.

8. Secure a glassine-coated paper doily to a cardboard round slightly larger than the one under the cake with a little Royal Icing or double-faced tape. Secure the cardboard round under the cake to the doily in the same way.

Covering a Cake with Whipped Cream

1. Brush away any loose crumbs from the cake's surface to prepare it for a single application of whipped cream.

2. Apply a full spatula of whipped cream to the side of the cake. Use a back-and-forth movement to push it forward without allowing the blade of the spatula to touch the cake's bare surface.

3. Each subsequent application of cream should be placed strategically on the edge of the previously coated surface rather than on the bare cake.

4. Pile a heap of cream on top of the cake and flatten it with a large metal spatula as you spread it to cover the surface.

5. Remove the excess cream upon completion by holding the spatula in place as you rotate the turntable.

Cocolat's Chocolate Hazelnut Torte

This elegant, positively scrumptious dessert is one of Alice Medrich's many specialties. She is the charming proprietress of Cocolat, the extraordinary French Pastry and Chocolate Specialty Shops in the San Francisco/Berkeley, California area. The quality of Cocolat's divine pastries and truffles has earned Alice and her talented staff an enviable reputation for excellence that extends across the country.

> **6 ounces** semisweet or bittersweet chocolate
> **6 ounces** sweet (unsalted) butter
> **4 large** egg yolks
> **½ cup** granulated sugar
> **½ cup** ground, toasted hazelnuts*
> **4 tablespoons** sifted flour
> **⅛ teaspoon** almond extract
> **4 large** egg whites
> **⅛ teaspoon** cream of tartar
> Pinch of salt
> **¼ cup** granulated sugar

*Toast the hazelnuts in a 375° F. oven for about 15 minutes. Allow them to cool and then rub off most of their skins between your hands or in a towel. Pulverize them (one handful at a time) in a blender or food processor using an on-off action. Guard against making nut butter.

Preheat the oven to 375° F. Grease and flour an eight-by-three-inch round cake pan or line the bottom of it with parchment paper.

Melt the chocolate and butter in the top of a small double boiler over warm water. Stir occasionally until smooth.

Whisk the egg yolks and ½ cup of sugar in a large bowl until the mixture is pale and forms a ribbon when the rubber spatula is withdrawn from the bowl.

Stir in the warm chocolate mixture, the nuts, flour, and almond extract. Set aside.

Combine the egg whites, tartar, and salt in a

clean, dry mixing bowl and begin mixing at high speed. When soft peaks form, start sprinkling the remaining ¼ cup of sugar over the mixture. Continue to beat them until the meringue is stiff but not dry.

Fold about ⅓ of the meringue thoroughly into the chocolate nut batter to lighten it; then quickly fold in the remaining meringue.

Turn the mixture into the pan and bake at 375° F. for 40-45 minutes. The center of the cake should test definitely wet but not too runny. About one inch from the edges of the pan it will test drier and look as though it is beginning to crumb. Cool the cake in the pan set on a cake rack.

Glaze with Chocolate Cognac Glaze (below).

CHOCOLATE COGNAC GLAZE

> **6 ounces** semisweet or bittersweet chocolate, chopped into small pieces
> **4 ounces** sweet (unsalted) butter, cut into pieces
> **1 tablespoon** light corn syrup
> **2-3 teaspoons** cognac (or water)

Place the chocolate, butter, and corn syrup in the top of a small double boiler over warm water. Stir until smooth and completely melted.

Add the cognac and stir.

Remove from the heat and cool until almost set but still spreadable.

GLAZING THE CAKE

Run a knife around the edges of the cake. The cooled cake will have settled in the center, leaving a higher rim around the edges. Firmly press down on these edges with your fingers to flatten them and level the cake.

Now invert the cake onto a cardboard circle cut exactly to fit it, peeling away the parchment paper, if you have used it. The bottom of the cake has now become the top.

Spread the edges of the cake with just enough cooled glaze to smooth out any imperfections, cracks, or ragged places. Do the same on top of the cake, if necessary. This is just the crumb coat—the preparation for the final glazing.

Gently reheat the remaining glaze over warm water until it is smooth and pourable but not thin and watery. Dry the bottom of the pan and pour

the glaze through a fine strainer. Place the cake on a plate or decorating turntable.

Pour all of the glaze onto the center of the cake. Use a clean, dry, metal spatula to coax the glaze over the edges of the cake. Use as few spatula strokes as possible. Do not work the glaze back and forth more than necessary. Examine the sides of the cake to be sure that they are completely covered.

When the cake is completely glazed, use a metal spatula to remove the excess glaze from the turntable's surface. Lift the cake and place it on a rack to dry. Once dry, position it on its final serving platter, attaching it there with a bit of left-over glaze, and decorate as desired.

Note: To mold a chocolate serving plate (see cover), use an appropriately sized metal tray and one pound of semisweet chocolate. My tray is actually 12 inches in diameter, including a 1-inch lip, but I only fill its 10-inch cavity.

CHOCOLATE DECORATIONS

The shiny, dark surface of this cake is the perfect foil for either of these two touches of drama.

Calla Lilies

1. See page 86 for directions for making white coating calla lilies. Make two or three of them (depending on the size of the lemon leaves).
2. Dye about ½ cup of white coating a natural shade of green (green toned with brown) and pipe three medium-sized leaves on the backs of lemon leaves.
3. Attach the flowers and leaves to the dry cake, with a few dabs of chocolate or coating.

Filigree Butterfly

1. Use a felt-tip pen to trace the butterfly wing patterns given on page 184. Place the patterns on a flat board, cover them with wax paper, and secure with tape.
2. Fill a parchment bag with chocolate and cut a very small opening in its tip. The smaller the opening, the more delicate and beautiful (and fragile!) the butterfly. Your skill and patience should determine the size of the opening.
3. Outline the wing with a fine string of chocolate and proceed with the interior lines, following the pattern only as far as you are able. The more lines that touch each other, the stronger the wing.
4. Repeat the procedure for the other wing. Chill only until the chocolate dries. Prolonged chilling will cause the wings to curl on the edges and ultimately to crack. Use a metal spatula to release them from the paper. Carefully turn them over.
5. Overpipe their back sides with chocolate for additional reinforcement. It is not necessary to pipe over every line. Chill briefly.
6. Cut two pieces of chocolate-flavored shoestring licorice into 1½-inch lengths. Other flavors may be painted with chocolate. Set them on wax paper to dry.
7. To assemble the butterfly: Pipe a ½-inch ball of chocolate on the wax paper surface and immediately insert the ends of the licorice for the antennae. Continue to pipe the butterfly's body by piping a gradually tapering column of chocolate that is three inches long and ½ inch wide.
8. As with the miniature butterflies described on pages 138–139, insert the chilled wings into the soft body in an in-flight position. They must be propped for support throughout the setting period.

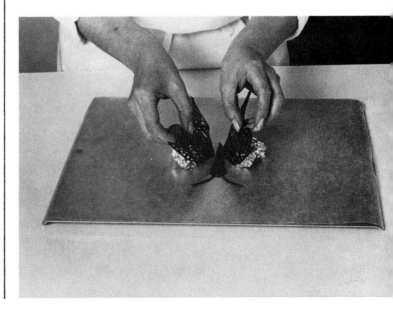

Butterfly pattern for
filigree chocolate work.

9. Use a few dots of chocolate to attach the butterfly to the glazed cake.

Chocolate Yule Log

The Yule Log is traditionally served on a long, narrow French bread board. I present mine on a ¾-inch-thick piece of tree trunk, complete with bark, that I purchased in a craft shop. It adds a good deal of charm to an already delightful cake and affords me extra width for chocolate decorations.

CHOCOLATE SPONGE CAKE

¼ **cup** granulated sugar

⅛ **cup** all-purpose flour, sifted

⅛ **cup** cornstarch, sifted

¼ **cup** unsweetened, Dutch-process cocoa, sifted

5 **large** eggs, separated

⅛ **teaspoon** salt

1 **teaspoon** vanilla

Preheat the oven to 350°F. Grease and flour a jelly-roll pan (15½ inches by 10½ inches by 1 inch) and line it with parchment or wax paper. Grease and flour the paper.

Sift the sugar, flour, cornstarch, and cocoa together several times and set them aside.

In a small bowl, beat the yolks until they are very thick and lemon colored.

Place the egg whites in a large, grease-free bowl. Add the salt and beat the mixture until it is quite stiff but not dry. Transfer it to a large, shallow bowl to facilitate the next step.

Use a rubber spatula to lightly fold the thickly beaten yolks into the whites. Fold the dry ingredients into the mixture in about four additions. Fold in the vanilla last.

Pour the mixture into the prepared pan and smooth its surface evenly with an offset metal spatula, if you have one.

Bake for 12–15 minutes or until the cake tests done. (It will spring back when touched in the center.) Do not overbake. Allow it to cool in the pan for about five minutes before removing.

Loosen the sides of the cake with a sharp knife. Invert the cake onto a wax-paper-covered cake rack and continue to cool it. Remove the baking paper and replace it with a sheet of aluminum foil. Invert the cake again (top side facing up) and once cool, spread with the following filling.

CHOCOLATE WHIPPED CREAM

½ **cup** confectioners' sugar, sifted
5 **tablespoons** unsweetened, Dutch-process cocoa powder, sifted
2 **cups** cold whipping cream
2 **teaspoons** rum

Sift the sugar and cocoa together several times. Place all of the ingredients in a large, deep, cold mixing bowl. Stir them until well blended.

Beat at low speed until the mixture begins to thicken. Increase the speed and continue beating until the cream is quite thick.

ASSEMBLING THE LOG

1. Cut a strip of cake cardboard about 2½ by 11¾ inches. Other heavy cardboard may be used for this, provided it is covered with aluminum foil.
2. Spread the entire surface of the cake with about ¼ inch of the chocolate whipped cream.

3. Use the aluminum foil under the cake to help roll the long edge into a tight roll about 2½ inches wide.
4. Cut and reserve a 1½-inch vertical piece of cake from each end of the roll.
5. Carefully lift the log with two hands and place it on the prepared cardboard seam side down. The board should not be visible. Trim it, if it is.
6. Place the roll on its final serving tray. You may wish to slip some narrow sheets of wax paper under it on all sides to protect the tray from drips during the icing procedure. Ice the roll with a roughly applied coating of whipped cream. Leave the ends bare.
7. Slice off and discard a small wedge from the flat outside edge of each of the reserved cut pieces. Attach one piece—wedge side in—to the side of the log to simulate a pruned limb. Attach the other piece—wedge side down—to the top. Cover all but their exposed ends with cream, concealing the joints.
8. Pass the tines of a dinner fork back and forth across the surface of the log and up the stumps to simulate the rough look of bark.

Note: The bare ends may be protected with small rounds of wax paper to retard drying. Remove prior to serving.

CHOCOLATE DECORATIONS

Holly Leaves

1. Make a variety of 15–20 holly leaves in different sizes on the backs of several lemon

leaves using bright green coating. Draw out the points that distinguish this leaf with an artists' brush. Chill the piped leaves briefly; then peel them off the leaves.

2. Pipe a line of green coating on the backs of some of them and attach a two-inch piece of floral wire. Apply more coating to cover the top of the wire. Allow it to set undisturbed.

Holly Berries

1. Pinch off tiny bits of white compound coating clay, dyed bright red, and roll them into balls (berries) of various sizes. You will need at least 15.
2. Attach them to the clusters of holly leaves with a little coating, now or at assembly time.

Pinecones

1. Shape about eight or ten one-inch-high cones out of chocolate clay and spear them with cocktail stirrers. (Thickened chocolate may be used to pipe these cones, if desired.) Stand them on a small scrap piece of Styrofoam. (Review the full rose lesson that begins on page 70.)
2. Follow the instructions for thickening chocolate on page 91. Thicken about ½ cup of chocolate at a time and fill a vinyl bag fitted with a #102 rose tube with the mixture.
3. Beginning at the top of the cone, pipe one petal standing straight up, followed by two on either side of it.
4. To shape the remainder of the cone's petals, use the rose technique with these modifications:
   a. Make the petals long and narrow (about ¾ inch long and ½ inch wide).
   b. Begin each row lower on the cone than for roses to allow for the petals' length. Pipe at least five rows.
   c. Keep the angle of the tube at a constant 45-degree angle to the cone for all of the rows.

Ax

1. Prepare a pattern for the ax given here. Attach it to a flat board, cover it with wax paper, and secure it with tape.

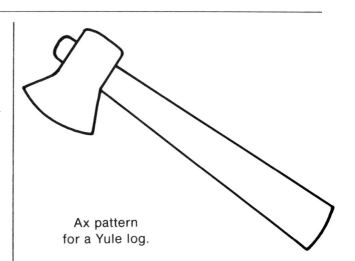

Ax pattern
for a Yule log.

2. Use parchment bags filled with white coating and chocolate to outline and then fill in the blade and handle of the ax. Chill until set, turn over, and overpipe the back for strength.

Scroll

1. Roll out an eight-inch-long, narrow piece of white compound coating clay. Use a sharp knife to cut a strip six or seven inches long by ¾ inch wide from it, cutting a *V* shape at each end, if desired.

Decorating Procedures

1. It is not necessary to attach clusters of leaves and berries to each other until you place them on the log. Some of them can be pressed into the whipped cream without any further adhesive. Wired leaves can be inserted into the cake to create interesting effects. Caution! If wires are used, you must assume the responsibility for the potential danger that they present. Remove them once the cake is cut.
2. Position clusters of leaves into the corners created by the stumps. Tuck a few pinecones in among the berries. If you angle them so that they point downward, they will look more like pinecones and less like roses.
3. Lay the scroll across the log, pressing gently on it so that it does not slide off.
4. Place the ax in front of the log or as desired.

Almond Torte

This is an intimidating cake at first glance. Most steps may, however, be completed well in advance, lessening the anxiety at assembly time.

The firm Génoise recipe given here is composed of the classic ingredients but is prepared in an unconventional way.

CHOCOLATE GÉNOISE

    ¼ cup clarified, sweet (unsalted) butter*
    ¼ cup cake flour, sifted
    ¼ cup unsweetened, Dutch-process cocoa
      powder, sifted
    3 large eggs, separated
    ½ cup superfine granulated sugar
    ½ teaspoon almond extract

*To clarify butter: Melt more butter than you need in a saucepan. Continue to simmer it over low heat until it appears clear and the sediment on the bottom of the pan turns a light golden brown. Do not allow the butter to brown. Skim the top foam, strain the clear butter, and leave the sediment behind. It will keep refrigerated for several weeks.

Preheat the oven to 350°F. and position the rack so that the cake will bake in the lower third of the oven.

Grease the bottom of a nine-inch round cake pan and line it with parchment or wax paper. Grease and flour the paper as well as the sides of the pan.

Clarify the butter and pour ¼ cup of it into a small bowl.

Sift the flour and cocoa together several times until they are very well blended.

Place the egg whites in a grease-free bowl and beat them until soft peaks form. Add the sugar gradually and continue to beat until the whites are very stiff, but not dry.

Add the unbeaten yolks to the whites and beat them on low speed only until well blended.

Sprinkle the dry ingredients over the egg-sugar mixture, a little at a time. Fold in each addition gently but thoroughly.

Spoon about one cup of the beaten egg mixture into the clarified butter. Mix it vigorously to

blend with the butter. Lightly fold the somewhat thickened butter into the rest of the egg mixture. Add the almond extract.

Pour the batter into the prepared pan, smooth the surface, and bake for 35-40 minutes or until the center of the crust springs back when touched lightly with a finger.

CHOCOLATE MERINGUE LAYERS

1 tablespoon cornstarch
3 tablespoons unsweetened, Dutch-process
    cocoa powder, sifted
¼ cup blanched almonds, finely chopped
3 large egg whites
⅛ teaspoon cream of tartar
⅛ teaspoon salt
1 teaspoon vanilla
¾ cup plus **2 tablespoons** superfine
    granulated sugar

Preheat the oven to 325°F. Grease (generously) and flour the tops of two large, inverted cookie sheets. Mark off a nine-inch circle on each of them with your fingertip, using a nine-inch cake pan as a guide.

Sift the cornstarch and cocoa together several times until well blended. Combine them with the ground almonds and set aside.

Place the egg whites, tartar, salt, and vanilla in a large grease-free bowl and beat until soft peaks form.

Begin adding the sugar very gradually, beating well after each addition. Continue to beat the mixture until the whites are *very* stiff.

Fold the cornstarch-cocoa-almond mixture into the meringue.

Fill a large 12-inch decorating bag fitted with a #12 tube with some of this mixture. Beginning in the center of each circle, the bag elevated ½ inch above the surface, use firm pressure to pipe a ¼-inch-thick spiral of meringue over the whole designated area on each circle.

Bake the meringues in a 325°F. oven for 30-35 minutes or until dry. They may be kept loosely covered for several weeks. Broken and unattractive layers are perfectly acceptable for use in this torte. They will not be visible once the cake is assembled.

BUTTERCREAM ICING

¾ cup granulated sugar
½ cup water

⅛ **teaspoon** cream of tartar
1 ½ **cups** sweet (unsalted) butter, cut up
5 **large** egg yolks
4 **ounces** semisweet chocolate, melted
1 **tablespoon** liqueur (optional)

Cook the sugar, water, and tartar in a small saucepan, stirring only until the sugar dissolves and the mixture comes to a boil. Wash down the sides of the pan with a pastry brush dipped in warm water and continue to cook it undisturbed until the mixture registers 240°F. (soft ball stage) on a candy thermometer. Do not use your chocolate thermometer unless it registers that high. Wash down the sides again.

While the syrup cooks, cream the butter and set it aside.

In another bowl, beat the yolks until they are very thick and creamy. Continue to beat them as you pour a very fine stream of the hot cooked syrup over them. Some of it will splatter onto the sides of the bowl. Ignore it.

Beat the yolk-syrup mixture until it cools to room temperature. Add the melted chocolate and blend well.

Gradually add the creamed butter to the cool mixture and beat only until well blended.

Flavor with liqueur as desired or leave plain. Use at once or refrigerate. Once chilled, it must return to room temperature before being rebeaten.

FLAVORED SUGAR SYRUP

¾ **cup** granulated sugar
¼ **cup** water
3 **tablespoons** Amaretto liqueur

Place the sugar and water in a small saucepan and cook, stirring, until the sugar dissolves. When the mixture boils, remove it from the heat. Wash down the sides with a pastry brush as above.

Cool the syrup to room temperature before adding the liqueur.

Note: Leftover syrup may be strained and kept covered in the refrigerator for future use.

ASSEMBLY

2 **9-inch** chocolate meringue layers
⅔ **cup** seedless red raspberry jam or jelly
1 **9-inch** Chocolate Génoise cake

Amaretto flavored syrup
1 **recipe** chocolate buttercream
1 **cup** toasted sliced almonds
½ **pound** semisweet chocolate
10 freezer-paper cones made from six-inch squares (see pages 87–88).

Secure one of the meringue layers to a nine-inch cake cardboard round with a dab of buttercream.

Spread it with ⅓ cup of raspberry jam.

Torte the génoise in half. Peel the crust off the top of the cake and place that layer on top of the meringue layer. (Use a cake cardboard-round to transfer it, if necessary.) Use a pastry brush to moisten it with the Amaretto syrup. Spread it evenly with a thin layer of chocolate buttercream. Place the second meringue layer on top of it and spread it with the remainder of the jam.

Invert the remaining génoise layer and place it, bottom side up, on the meringue layer. Brush it with syrup.

It may be necessary to trim the slightly oversized meringue layers at this time. To do so, use a knife with a serrated edge to saw away the excess and make the sides of the cake even.

Ice the entire surface of the cake with buttercream, removing the excess as described on page 181.

To coat the sides of the cake with nuts: Hold the cake directly over a large cookie sheet containing the almonds. Take a handful of almonds and press them against the buttercream-coated sides of the cake, allowing the extras to fall back onto the cookie sheet. Continue in this manner, moving the hand up or down, wherever coverage is needed.

Secure the cake to its final serving plate with a dab of buttercream.

Note: See instructions on page 183 for molding a chocolate serving plate.

CHOCOLATE DECORATIONS

1. Temper ½ pound of semisweet chocolate and make chocolate cones.
2. Pipe a line of icing on the backs of each cone and position them carefully on the

cake's surface. Press on them gently to secure them.

3. Pipe a buttercream design between each cone with a #2 tube.

4. Refrigerate the cake for at least several hours to blend the flavors and allow the crisp meringue layers to mellow. Serve at room temperature.

Torta Mexicana

This example of confectionery art—a tribute to Mexico's mellow flavors and the chocolate artist's skilled hands—combines an unusual, delicious flavor with very special, classic beauty. The blend of Kahlúa, cocoa, vanilla, and cinnamon produces an elusive but delectable cappuccino taste that will likely intrigue your guests and give rise to inquiries as to its identity. The pairing of ivory-colored white compound coating and buttery buttercream is a monochromatic combination well suited to the elegance and simplicity of the scroll design.

CHOCOLATE CAKE

1 cup sour cream
4 tablespoons Kahlúa liqueur
1 tablespoon vanilla
2 ½ cups cake flour, sifted
¼ teaspoon salt
1 teaspoon baking soda
½–1 teaspoon cinnamon
½ cup unsweetened, Dutch-process cocoa powder, sifted
5 large eggs, separated
1 cup sweet (unsalted) butter, cut up
2 cups granulated sugar

Preheat the oven to 350°F. Grease the bottom of a 12-by-2-inch round cake pan and line it with parchment or wax paper. Grease and flour the paper and the sides of the pan.

Combine the sour cream, Kahlúa, and vanilla in a small bowl. Mix well.

Sift the flour, salt, soda, cinnamon, and cocoa together at least three times to assure a thorough blend.

Beat the egg yolks until thick and creamy.

In another bowl, cream the butter. Add the sugar gradually and mix well.

Add the beaten yolks to this mixture and beat until thoroughly incorporated.

On low speed add the flour and sour cream mixtures alternately. Beat only until blended after each addition.

Beat the egg whites in a large, grease-free bowl until they are stiff, but not dry. Fold them into the heavy batter in about three additions.

Bake in a 350°F. oven for about 55 minutes. Cool for five minutes in the pan before inverting onto a cooling rack.

KAHLÚA MOUSSE FILLING

8 ounces semisweet chocolate, chopped
⅛ teaspoon cream of tartar
4 large egg whites
2 cups cold whipping cream
5 tablespoons Kahlúa liqueur
2 tablespoons vanilla

Melt the chocolate in the top of a double boiler over warm water. Transfer the chocolate to a large bowl. Cool about 10 minutes.

In the meantime, sprinkle the cream of tartar over the egg whites and beat them until they are stiff but not dry.

In another bowl, beat the whipping cream on low until it begins to thicken; then raise the speed to high and beat until thick. Add the Kahlua and vanilla and mix to blend.

Add about 1½ cups of the beaten whites to the cooled chocolate. Vigorously beat them together. Once incorporated, gradually fold the now lightened chocolate into the rest of the whites.

Fold this mixture into the thick whipped cream and use it to fill the cool cake.

KAHLÚA BUTTERCREAM ICING

1 ½ cups sweet (unsalted) butter, cut up
½ cup white vegetable shortening*
2 cups confectioners' sugar, sifted
2 cups warm milk
6 tablespoons cornstarch
2 teaspoons vanilla
2 teaspoons Kahlúa liqueur
3 tablespoons finely ground almonds (reserve until assembly)

*For a firmer but less tasty icing, use 1 cup

butter and 1 cup white shortening.

Cream the butter and shortening together. Gradually add the confectioners' sugar, mixing well after each addition. Set aside.

In a heavy saucepan, cook the milk and cornstarch together over medium heat, stirring constantly, until the mixture thickens and resembles pudding.

Spoon the hot pudding into a large bowl and beat it until it is cool—about seven minutes.

Add the creamed butter to this cooled mixture, a heaping spoonful at a time, to blend well. Add the flavorings and mix them only briefly. Overbeating will soften the icing excessively.

Note: This icing may be frozen or refrigerated before using. Warm to room temperature before rebeating. Yields approximately 5½ cups.

Scroll pattern for Torta Mexicana. Trace 4.

CHOCOLATE DECORATIONS

Scroll

1. Make four patterns of the scroll given here. Secure them to a flat surface and tape a wax paper sheet over them.
2. Fill a parchment bag with melted white coating and cut an opening in its tip about ⅛ inch wide. Hold the tip about ¼ inch off the surface as you work.
3. Pipe the small scroll that appears at the top of the decoration first. Use one uninterrupted movement. To terminate the flow at the end of the maneuver, remember to cease pressure and backtrack over the previously piped line as you pull away. Add the extra curlicue in a separate movement, drawing its tail into the rest of the piped scroll.
4. Pipe the large part of the scroll in another continuous movement, if possible. It must overlap the small one slightly to assure a solid adhesion. Add the extra curlicues separately, touching other lines wherever possible to strengthen the scroll.
5. Having piped all four sections of the scroll, overpipe each one again. Chill for approximately five minutes or until the coating is set.
6. Use a spatula to release them from the paper. Carefully turn them over and pipe the backs once and then again, as before. Chill to complete the piping procedure.

Scroll Base

1. Make a pattern for the scroll's base. Place the pattern on a flat board, cover it with wax paper, and secure it with tape.
2. Cut a ¼-inch opening in the tip of a parchment bag filled with creamy, smooth white coating. Outline the pattern and fill it in as quickly as possible. Minor outline distortions can be corrected with an artists' brush, if necessary. Use every means to flatten the ripples in the surface. I tap the bottom of the board gently with a staccato touch.

Pattern for base of
Torta Mexicana scroll.

3. Chill the piece only until it is set. Check it periodically. Overchilling will cause it to curl up on the sides; it *must* be flat. Use a long metal spatula to release it from the paper.

CAKE ASSEMBLY

1. Slide a 12-inch cardboard round under the cool cake. Torte it in half and remove the upper layer (the actual bottom of the cake). Reserve it.

2. Heap the mousse onto the cake and spread it to within ¼ inch of the edge. If you use all of it (optional), the filling will be approximately ¾ inch thick.

3. Top it with the remaining cake layer (crumb side down), aligning it properly. The bottom of the cake is now the top of the cake. Use a spatula to smooth the excess mousse from the sides of the cake, if necessary. Chill the filled cake for several hours to facilitate the next step.

4. Follow the icing instructions on pages 180–181, applying a thicker coating than usual in this case because the white icing must conceal a dark cake. Quickly ice the sides without touching the exposed, still-soft mousse with the spatula.

5. To obtain a neat edge along the top rim of the cake, lightly draw the spatula up over the edge and then toward the center. It is not necessary to smooth the actual center of the top of the cake, however, because it will be covered by the decoration.

6. Place the cake on its final serving platter or on a 14-inch or 16-inch glassine doily-covered cardboard round.

ATTACHING AND ASSEMBLING THE SCROLL

1. Pipe a ¼-inch line of coating on the inner edge of the first scroll section in the three spots designated on the pattern and place it on a sheet of wax paper. Lay section 2 on the paper and affix it to section 1 by pressing it up against the three lines of coating. Check for proper alignment before the coating sets.

2. Attach section 3 at a 90-degree angle to the others with more coating in the same designated places. Stand the scroll decoration on the paper to check the alignment.

3. Join the last section opposite section 3 in the same way. Examine all of the joints

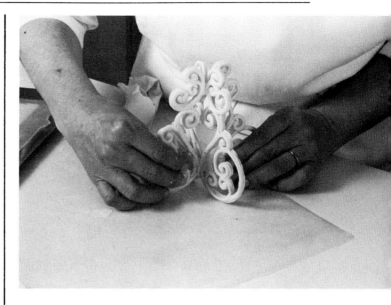

and reinforce any that appear weak. Allow the decoration to set undisturbed.

4. Before positioning the scroll decoration on its base, sprinkle the center of the cake with the reserved ground almonds. This will facilitate the dismantling procedure at serving time. Carefully set the base of the decoration in place.

5. Attach the scroll to the base with coating. Allow it to set undisturbed.

6. To complete the scroll decoration, pipe a simple scroll design around the edge of the base with the same white coating and a small opening in the bag as shown in the pattern. Overpipe it.

7. Make up at least four medium-sized chocolate or compound coating clay roses in advance. To do so, use nine ½-inch balls of clay per rose. Flattened, they will measure approximately ⅞ inch. Position one rose in between each of the four sections of the scroll, attaching each one to the base with coating.

8. Pipe 12 small, pale green coating leaves on the backs of fresh leaves and attach them with coating in and around the roses.

9. Pipe a shell border along the base of the cake with a #22 tube and the same buttercream used to ice the cake.

10. Use a #4 tube to pipe eight 1½-inch-wide scrolls on the surface of the cake. Place them in the 12:00 and 6:00 positions first. Pipe two more at 3:00 and 9:00. Center the remaining four between the rest.

11. Repeat the same design along the center line of the outside wall of the cake, positioning the scrolls in between their counterparts on the surface of the cake.

ADDITIONAL CAKE-DECORATING IDEAS WITH CHOCOLATE

Many of the designs presented in earlier chapters are also suitable for cake decorations. Pattern work, in particular, is highly adaptable to surface or sidewall adornment. The latter requires the use of a curved setting surface for the chocolate pieces that approximates the cake's curvature. Attach the patterns to the sides of deep cake pans, large cans, or buckets, if necessary, and follow the same rules that apply for standard pattern work.

Some flat molded pieces—letters, for example—are simply pressed onto the surface for a neat, tailored look. Other chocolate pieces may be used as stand-up figures on novelty cakes and cupcakes by simply attaching a thin lollipop stick or cocktail stirrer to their backs with a little melted chocolate.

Floral arrangements made up of icing, chocolate, or chocolate clay flowers can, of course, embellish cakes for all occasions. Use the same principles of design discussed on page 55 but enlarge the scale of the arrangement to suit the cake's size.

13
Cookies Decorated with Chocolate and Collectors' Items: Candies and Miscellanea

Chocolate can be used to transform ordinary little cookies into eye-catching morsels in ways that are quick, easy, and practical. Sometimes a simple dipping is all that a cookie needs to elevate it from the ranks of "dropped," "rolled," or "cutout" to the prestigious category of "fancy handcrafted cookies." Regardless of the amount of artistry involved, handcrafted cookies are, in effect, individual works of art as surely as if they had been painted with oil on canvas. The selection of cookies that follows should encourage you to use chocolate artistry as a way of embellishing your own favorite cookie recipes. Once inspired, perhaps you will want to do the same with store-bought varieties.

Bonbon Cookies

These cookies have been popular with students in my decorating classes for years. They are simple to make, easy to dip, and quick to decorate. The version given here is fashioned after the confectionery cherry bonbons, but you may substitute a hazelnut for the cherry, if you wish, or bake them with no filling at all. The recipe is easily doubled.

Approximately **12 ounces** maraschino
   cherries
½ **cup** plus **1 tablespoon** unsalted butter
¼ **cup** confectioners' sugar
1 egg yolk
½ **teaspoon** vanilla
1½ **cups** all-purpose flour, unsifted
¼ **teaspoon** salt
Approximately **2 pounds** semisweet
   chocolate

Yield: 6 ½ dozen
Preheat the oven to 350° F. Set aside several cookie sheets.

Drain the maraschino cherries, rinse under cool water, and dry on paper toweling.

In a large mixing bowl, cream the butter and sugar well; add the egg yolk and vanilla and beat until well blended.

Combine the flour and salt; gradually add to the creamed mixture and mix well.

Flatten about one teaspoon of soft dough between your fingers and wrap it around a drained cherry. Remove the excess dough.

Roll the encased cherry between your palms to

shape it into a ball and place it an inch apart from the others on an ungreased cookie sheet.

Bake for 12–15 minutes in a 350°F. oven.

When the cookies are lightly browned, remove them from the oven, immediately insert a toothpick in the bottom of each one, and set them aside to cool.

DIPPING PROCEDURE

Prepare the cool work area for dipping:

1. The tray of toothpick-speared cookies should be to your left.
2. In the center, position a small, shallow container filled with tempered chocolate to use for dipping the cookies. A larger amount of tempered chocolate and the reserved source of warm chocolate should be positioned nearby to replenish the dipping supply as needed.
Note: The dipping may be done on the marble slab, if preferred. See the truffle-dipping technique later in this chapter.
3. To the right of the dipping chocolate should be an inverted cookie sheet covered with wax paper.
4. Have close at hand a dipping or dinner fork.

Dipping with a toothpick:

This is certainly an unorthodox way to dip, but it produces cookies with perfectly smooth surfaces, which is what is desired here. Caution: Dispose of the toothpicks carefully. Guard against one slipping into the melted chocolate.

1. Brush away any obvious crumbs from the cookies' surfaces.
2. Use the toothpick to maneuver the cookie through the entire dipping procedure. At the point of entry, the position of the toothpick in relation to the surface of the chocolate is important; it should be nearly parallel, not

perpendicular to it. The latter position would tempt fate too much. Use the fork to help ease the chocolate up over the top surface of the cookie, if necessary.

3. Now rest the toothpick on the rim of the bowl or edge of the slab and tap it gently several times to allow the excess chocolate to drain away. Use the fork to encourage the runoff.
4. Position the fork so that the base of the cookie rests on it, the toothpick between the tines. Turn the toothpick counterclockwise as you pull it out. The dipped cookie,

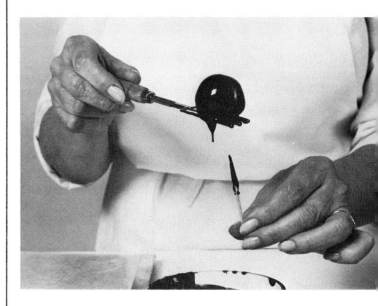

balanced on the bowl of the fork, must now be transferred to the wax paper. Position the fork close to the surface and use the toothpick to help slide the cookie off the fork and onto the paper.

5. Continue with the remainder of the cookies and allow them all to set before decorating them.

Decoration:

1. Half-fill a parchment bag with chocolate and cut a small opening equivalent to a #2 tube in its point.
2. Hold the bag perpendicular to the center of the cookie, elevated slightly. As the string of chocolate emerges, raise the tip a little more and begin to pipe a counterclockwise spiral of chocolate to cover the top and upper sides of the cookies. It is not

necessary to reach all the way to the bottom with the piped string.

Note: These cookies are lovely dipped in pastel-colored coatings and decorated with spirals or dot flowers and leaves.

Viennese Cookies

Cookies as rich and elegant as these deserve a place of honor on any sweets table. They are troublesome to roll out but well worth the extra effort.

> **2 cups** all-purpose flour, sifted
> **1 teaspoon** baking powder
> **1 cup** blanched ground almonds
> **¾ cup** granulated sugar
> **1 cup** cold unsalted butter
> **1 teaspoon** lemon rind
> **2 tablespoons** lemon juice
> **¾ cup** apricot preserves
> Approximately **2 pounds** semisweet chocolate
> *Yield: 40 sandwiched cookies*

Preheat the oven to 350°F. Set aside several cookie sheets.

Combine the dry ingredients in a large bowl. Cut the cold sticks of butter lengthwise, turn

them over on their sides, and cut them lengthwise again. Now cut them vertically into ½-inch slices to form small cubes of butter. Use a pastry blender to cut the butter into the dry ingredients until the mixture has the texture of oatmeal.

Add the lemon rind and juice and begin to knead the very dry mixture. Transfer it to a large work surface and continue to work it until it forms a ball. Be patient.

Divide the dough in half and shape each piece into a flat round. The dough may be used immediately or chilled briefly if you find it too hard to handle. Do not, however, let it get too cold and firm.

Using a floured rolling pin, roll out one piece of the dough on a floured surface to a thickness of ⅛ inch. Frequently throughout the rolling procedure, release the delicate dough from the surface with a long metal spatula to prevent it from sticking.

Cut the dough into two-inch rounds with a cookie cutter. Use a metal spatula to lift and then carefully transfer them to the ungreased cookie sheets. Bake for approximately 10 minutes. They should be barely tan, not brown, when done. Briefly cool the cookies on the baking sheets and then transfer them to a cooling rack.

Chill the scraps and reroll them.

Use a fork to break up the chunks in the apricot preserves. Sandwich the cookies, back to back, with a small amount of preserves and set them aside.

Dipping procedure:

1. Cover several inverted cookie sheets with wax paper. The dipping may be done on a marble slab or in a small deep bowl as just described.

2. Grasp the sandwiched cookie between your fingers, edges down, and immerse it into the chocolate so as to cover half of its surface, including the front, back, and bottom edge. Gently shake the cookie to remove the excess chocolate and carefully lay it on the cookie sheet until the chocolate has set. Chill briefly, if your dipping room is warmer than 65°F.

3. Spoon a small amount of chocolate into a parchment cone, cut a small opening in its tip, and pipe scroll E on page 79 along the edge of the chocolate.

Dipped Fortune Cookies

These are not your typical fortune cookie cookies. They are lightly crisp, delicious, and filled with the most personal of fortunes—the ones you write yourself!

> **2** egg whites
> ¼ **cup** vegetable oil
> ½ **teaspoon** almond extract
> ½ **cup** all-purpose flour
> ¼ **cup** granulated sugar
> **1 tablespoon** cornstarch
> Pinch of salt
> **1 tablespoon** water
> Approximately **40** paper fortunes
> **1½–2 pounds** chocolate

Yield: approximately 40 cookies

Briefly whisk the egg whites, oil, and extract together.

Combine the dry ingredients and gradually add them to the egg white mixture. Beat until well blended.

Add the water, mixing well. Set the batter aside for 30 minutes.

In the meantime, prepare the paper fortunes using lightweight paper cut into 2-inch-by-½-inch strips.

Cut a piece of paper towel or fabric into a three-by-four-inch piece.

Heat a heavyweight griddle and grease it well. It will take some experimenting to get the heat just right. Drops of water should "dance" on it when it is ready.

Spoon one teaspoon of the batter onto the hot griddle (you may eventually be able to handle more than one at a time). Quickly begin to spread it in a circular motion with the back of the spoon until it is about three inches in diameter. If the griddle is too hot, the batter will pull away from it. Lower the heat and keep trying. Press down firmly on the cookie with a metal spatula to flatten it.

After a few seconds, lift the edge to see if it has turned a golden brown. If so, turn it over and flatten it again. The second side should be cooked as long as the first, but it will not brown as evenly.

Working quickly now, transfer the hot cookie, golden brown side down, to the piece of paper towel or fabric. Place a paper fortune in the center of the cookie. Use the paper towel to protect your fingers from the heat as you fold the cookie in half.

Holding it with the open edges up, place the center of the folded cookie over the edge of a bowl and pull down on both sides to form a crease across its center.

Remove the paper towel and immediately place the creased cookie in an ungreased miniature muffin cup to cool. It will retain its shape.

To dip the cookie: Grasp it by one end and immerse it halfway into the chocolate. Shake it back and forth to remove the excess chocolate and place it on a wax-paper-lined cookie sheet. Chill only until set.

The chocolate portion may be decorated with an appropriate Chinese character (see below for examples) or left plain. Use a contrasting shade of chocolate and a small opening in the tip of the parchment bag.

Love　好　祥 Happiness　子 Child or Son　Man 人　女 Woman

Cookie Lollipops

Are you looking for a special classroom treat? Try these heart-shaped cookies. They are as delicious as they are versatile. Try varying their shapes sometime or eliminating the lollipop stick and sandwiching two of them together with ice cream or chocolate mousse.

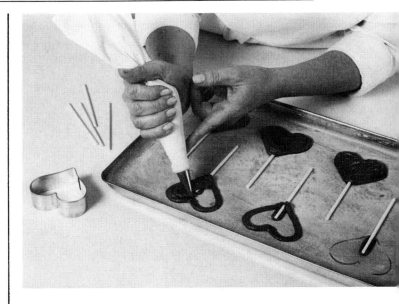

> ½ **cup** unsalted butter
> **1 cup** granulated sugar
> ½ **teaspoon** vanilla
> **2** eggs
> ¼ **cup** unsweetened cocoa
> ¾ **cup** unsifted all-purpose flour
> ¼ **teaspoon** cinnamon
> ¼ **teaspoon** salt
> Approximately **24** lollipop sticks
> **2–2½ pounds** milk chocolate

Yield: approximately 24 lollipops (3 by 2½ inches each)

Preheat the oven to 350° F. Grease and flour three or four cookie sheets.

Cream the butter and sugar together in a large mixing bowl.

Add the vanilla and then the eggs, one at a time, beating well after each addition.

Sift all the dry ingredients together and gradually add them to the creamed mixture, mixing them until thoroughly incorporated.

Piping procedure:
1. A heart-shaped cookie cutter (mine is 2⅞ inches wide by 2½ inches long) is used to mark the patterns on the prepared cookie sheets. Grasp the cutter and press it firmly against the floured surface, jiggling it back and forth, if necessary. Repeat the same procedure three or four times across the top of the cookie sheet, leaving at least one inch of space between them.
2. Fit a 12-inch decorating bag with a #10 tube and half-fill it with the chocolate batter. Use it to pipe a vertical line of batter from the center of the heart down to the tip of its point. Position a lollipop stick on it. Repeat for the remaining marked hearts.
3. Turn the cookie sheet around so that the sticks are facing away from you. Mark the heart patterns as in step 1, positioning them in between the previously marked ones and allowing space for their lollipop sticks.

4. Hold the tube about ¼ inch above the surface and use light pressure to outline the heart. Using the same pressure and elevation, move the tube back and forth across the rest of the heart and exposed stick to completely cover them with batter. The elevation and pressure will determine the thickness of the piped heart. The thicker the piped piece, the more it is likely to run during the baking and distort the shape. Try to maintain a thickness of about ¼ inch. Ignore the rippled appearance of the piped heart. The ripples will all blend together in the baking.
5. Bake the cookies for 10 minutes. Allow them to remain on the cookie sheets briefly; remove them carefully and place them on a cooling rack.
Note: Heat the bottom of the cookie sheet over the lit burner of the stove if you have difficulty releasing any of the cookies.

Dipping:
1. Use the same setting up procedure for dipping as described on page 196.
2. Lightly brush the backs of the cookies to remove any loose crumbs.
3. Lift each cookie by the stick and lay it (back side down) atop the dipping chocolate's surface. Use a candy scraper, metal spatula, or spoon to ladle the chocolate over its face in one slow scoop.
4. Rest the stick on the rim of the bowl or edge of the slab and tap it as described

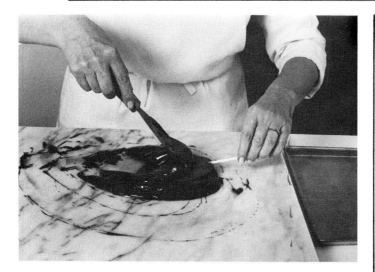

earlier to remove the excess chocolate and flatten the ripples. Use a toothpick to puncture any air bubbles that may appear on the surface of the cookie.

5. Position the dipped cookies on a wax-paper-lined cookie sheet and cool them undisturbed until set. Chill, if necessary.

Note: Milk chocolate (particularly in morsel form) is normally more viscous than semisweet chocolate. As it cools, it becomes more so. Be sure to maintain the proper temperature within the dipping supply throughout the procedure. Excessive air bubbles visible on the dipped cookies sometimes indicate that the dipping chocolate was too cool. If the thickness continues to trouble you, even after you have adjusted the temperature, add a drop or two of lecithin or a very small amount of melted cocoa butter, and mix well. Do not, of course, add cocoa butter to compound coating.

Decoration:

1. Choose a scallop border from those shown on page 79 or create one of your own. Starting at the top, pipe the design along the edge of the heart using a chocolate-filled parchment bag with a small opening.
2. Use the same bag to pipe two filigree scrolls. Personalize the heart as desired.

Mushroom Meringue Cookies

These delectable morsels are always received with enthusiasm, whether presented in a napkin-lined wicker basket or in a delicious chocolate one. I know of at least one thoughtful hostess who was so charmed by them that she personally distributed a mushroom to each of her 200 guests so that nobody would miss getting one!

Meringues are extremely susceptible to humidity and may disappoint you if the weather is uncooperative. As a precaution, bake them ahead but store them unassembled. That way you can dry them in the oven again, if they get soft before you need them.

½ **cup** egg whites at room temperature
⅛ **teaspoon** salt
¼ **teaspoon** cream of tartar
1 cup granulated sugar or **1 cup** plus **3½ teaspoons** superfine granulated sugar
Unsweetened cocoa (approximately **2 tablespoons**)
Chocolate or chocolate-flavored compound coating (approximately ½ **pound**)

Yield: It is difficult to calculate the yield on a recipe like this. It will vary each time that you make it. Expect an average of 35–45 multisized mushrooms.

Note: To make your own superfine granulated sugar, place one cup of regular granulated sugar in a food processor fitted with a steel blade. Process for one minute.

Preheat the oven to 225°F. Test the temperature with an oven thermometer for accuracy. (If in doubt, lower the temperature and bake the meringues a little longer. Do not let them brown; the idea is to dry them.)

Cover two large, inverted cookie sheets with parchment paper or aluminum foil.

Have ready a 12-inch decorating bag fitted with a #7 large-sized plain tube.

Meringue:

1. Place the egg whites in a large, clean, grease-free mixing bowl and beat them at medium speed until foamy. Add the salt and cream of tartar and continue to beat at medium-high speed until they thicken and almost cling to the sides of the bowl.
2. At high speed, begin adding the sugar very, very gradually and continue beating the whites until the sugar is well incorporated and the mixture is *very* stiff. The meringue should be used immediately.

Stems:

Pipe these first, while the meringue is still thick.

1. Half-fill the decorating bag with the meringue. Use it to dot the surface of the cookie sheet to secure the aluminum foil to it.
2. Position the bag perpendicular to the surface, with the tube elevated slightly. Press gently on the bag to pipe stems approximately 1-1½ inches tall and ¾ inch in diameter. Pipe a few smaller ones, too.

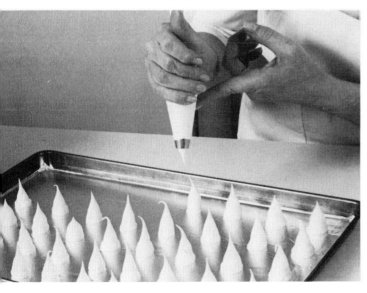

Each stem should be somewhat broader at the base than elsewhere, but guard against piping tall, skinny ones, which are likely to topple over. To terminate the flow of the meringue at the conclusion of each stem, cease pressure and pull the tube straight up and away. Ignore the points caused by this maneuver; they will be removed easily at assembly time. Space the stems ½ inch apart on the cookie sheet. Pipe about 35 stems at this time. Once you see how many caps there are, you may need to pipe a few more.

3. Use a small sieve to dust the stems lightly with cocoa. If desired, direct a quick gust of air from a hand-held hair dryer toward the cocoa-dusted stems. The cocoa will blow and create a soft, natural mushroom coloring on them.
4. Bake the sheet full of stems on the top shelf of the oven for less time than required for the caps (see below).

Caps:

1. Follow the instructions given on page 56 for piping balls, using a #7 large tube to pipe the mushroom caps. Smooth the caps' surfaces with a dampened fingertip, if they need it, but do not overdo it. Pipe caps in different sizes—1½-2 inches in diameter— and space them ½ inch apart on the cookie sheet.
2. Dust the caps as described above and bake them in the lower half of the oven for about one hour. To test for doneness, tap the meringue with your fingertip. It should sound hollow and release easily from the paper. If neither condition is found, it may be necessary to extend the baking time. The meringues may remain in the oven for several hours (or overnight) with heat off and the door ajar.

3. Store the dry caps and stems at room temperature, lightly covered, until needed.

Assembly:

1. Have on hand several miniature cupcake pans or egg cartons to support the mushrooms during their assembly.
2. Trim the points off all of the stems with a sharp knife to leave a flat surface that is broad enough to enable the stem, if inverted, to stand on it unsupported.
3. Use a metal spatula or small spoon to spread a little dark chocolate on the bottom of each cap. Stand the inverted stem in the center of it and position the assembled mushroom in the cupcake tin. If chilling is required to set the chocolate, it must be brief. The moisture in the refrigerator or freezer will soften the meringue.

STORE-BOUGHT COOKIES

Many commercially manufactured cookies on the market today can be treated artistically in much the same way as home-baked ones. A chocolate touch here and there can transform even the most familiar cookies into unique ones—and with half as much work.

Oreo Double-Stuf Chocolate Sandwich Cookies

1. Use a small knife to gently separate the top cookie from the filling-covered bottom cookie. Set it aside.

2. Grasp the bottom cookie firmly against the counter as you press the end of a lollipop stick into the center of the filling, pushing it in as far as it will go. Readjust the filling, if it needs it.
3. When those preliminary steps have been completed on all of the cookies, reattach the top cookies to their mates with a little dab of chocolate. Allow the chocolate to set completely before continuing.
4. Dip each prepared lollipop cookie into melted chocolate. Tap the stick on the rim of the bowl or edge of the marble slab to remove the excess chocolate.

5. Place the lollipop cookies on an inverted cookie sheet covered with wax paper and leave undisturbed until set.
6. To decorate: Trace one or all of the patterns shown here to prepare your own pattern sheet. Position the sheet on a flat board, cover it with wax paper, and attach it with tape.

Patterns for Oreo Double-Stuf cookie lollipops.

Sunshine Face

1. Use yellow coating and a small opening in the parchment bag to pipe the sunburst first. Allow it to set slightly before proceeding.
2. To pipe the round sun, position the bag perpendicular to the center of the figure and press hard. Keep the tip submerged as you squeeze and move it in a circular direction to coax the coating to go where it should. Allow the coating to set completely.
3. Use dark chocolate and a very small opening to pipe the facial features on the face. Personalize the cookie, if desired.

Apple

1. Outline the apple with red coating and a small opening in the parchment bag. Do the same with the rest that you plan to pipe.
2. Immediately enlarge the opening in the bag slightly. Use firm pressure as you flood the outlined apple so that the figure will be puffy, not flat. Allow it to set before proceeding.
3. Pipe the green leaf on the surface of the dry apple with a parchment bag cut specifically for leaf piping. The stem may be added now or at assembly time.

Blue Ribbon

1. Use a parchment bag with a small opening to outline and then flood the medal with yellow coating.
2. Use blue coating and a similar opening to outline and flood the blue ribbons. Set aside to dry thoroughly.
3. Pipe a yellow zigzag border around the dry medal.
4. Personalize the center of the medal with red coating and a very small opening in the bag, as desired.

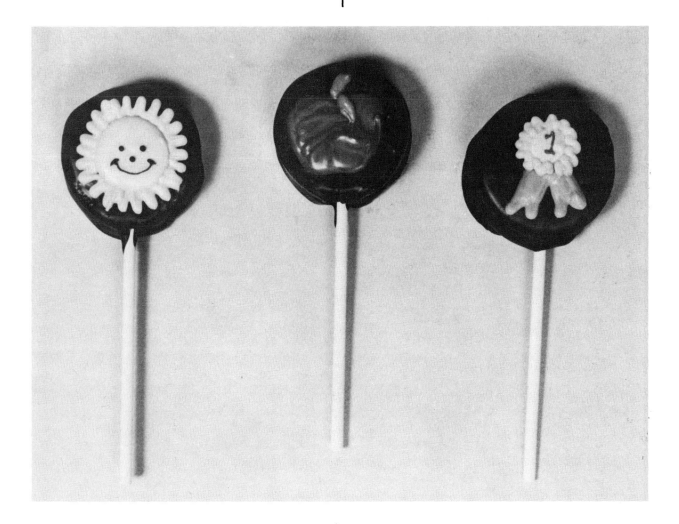

Dipped, store-bought cookies and dipped, dried apricot and pear.

The grocery store cookie shelves are filled with many suitable choices for chocolate embellishment. Examine the selection carefully with an eye to quality, appearance, size, and shape and then start experimenting. Here are a few of my favorites:

Pepperidge Farm, Inc., Chocolate Laced Pirouettes

Dip them halfway in chocolate. Decorate with a scroll, if desired.

Nabisco Famous Chocolate Wafers

Sandwich two together with Ganache. Decorate the top with a Ganache miniature rose spray.

Alsacienne Biscuits S. A. (French) Fan Wafers

Dip the bottom of the fan ½ inch deep into semisweet chocolate. Immediately sprinkle the wet chocolate with finely chopped pecans.

COLLECTORS' ITEMS: CANDIES AND MISCELLANEA

The chocolates presented in this section are a collection of the little extras that I use to fill

boxes, baskets, shells, etc. They include a few bonus items that can be used as party favors as well.

Cashew Tortugas

> ½ **pound** Nestlé bulk caramel or soft, commercially made caramels
> ¼ **pound** roasted cashews, salted or unsalted
> ¾ **pound** white compound coating
> **1 ounce** chocolate-flavored compound coating

Yield: approximately 24

   Note: Real chocolate and cocoa butter coating may be substituted.

   Melt the white compound coating and cool it to 90° F. while you complete the next two steps.

   Roll the soft caramel into ¾-inch balls.

   Flatten each ball between your fingertips and press it over the top of a cashew nut that has been broken into two pieces. Shape the caramel to simulate a turtle's shell—oval and elevated in the center.

   Note: Masochists may choose to position cashews beneath the shell to simulate his four legs.

   Place it on a wax-paper-lined cookie sheet. Reserve a whole cashew for each one that you shape.

   Pour a spoonful of the cool coating over the

back of each turtle shell and immediately press the reserved whole cashew firmly into position—narrow end down—to simulate the head. You will need to brace the opposite side of the body with a finger to do this. (The smudged coating can be smoothed with a spatula.) Chill until set.

Use a very small opening in a parchment bag filled with dark chocolate coating to pipe the design on the tortuga's back, beginning to the left or right of his "neck." Touch the surface with the tip of the bag as you begin to press on the bag. Maintain a light but steady pressure as you lift slightly and move diagonally to the opposite side of the turtle shell, pulling a string of chocolate as you do.

Pull several more strings—about ¼ inch apart—to cover most of the shell's surface.

Turn the tortuga around and repeat the same piping procedure on the opposite side. A diamond pattern will become apparent. Use the same bag and chocolate to pipe his eyes.

CHOCOLATE WALNUTS

4 ounces soft almond paste
1 egg white
1½ cups confectioners' sugar, sifted
1 ounce melted and cooled milk chocolate

1 teaspoon hazelnut liqueur (optional)
½ pound white cocoa butter coating
¼ pound milk chocolate
Whole walnut halves
English walnut mold (Apollo Mold Co. #126)
Note: Substitute all compound coating, if desired.
Yield: approximately 40

CHOCOLATE MARZIPAN FILLING

1. Break the almond paste apart in a mixing bowl. Add the egg white and knead the two together until nearly blended.
2. Cover the work area with the confectioners' sugar. Begin kneading the sugar into the almond paste mixture along with the chocolate and liqueur to form a smooth, evenly colored mass. Set aside.

SHELLS

1. Combine the chocolates and melt and temper them as described in Chapter 1. Place the prepared chocolate in a bowl and maintain the temper as desired.
2. The procedure for molding hollow shells shown on page 29 (Method II) is decidedly easier if you have more than one mold. Each time the mold is emptied, the chocolate must be scooped up immediately (before it cools excessively) and added to the pot of tempered chocolate. Stir well before proceeding.
5. Briefly chill the shells to set the chocolate. Carefully fill each one with a small ball of the previously prepared chocolate marzipan.
6. Immediately press a walnut half into place. Chill again and release from the molds. Keep refrigerated until needed.

Truffles

Truffle recipes generally begin with the same basic ingredients: chocolate, whipping cream, and butter. The proportions vary according to the degree of creaminess desired, and that is often determined by whether or not they are to be hand dipped.

Most truffles are soft and difficult to shape, much less dip. To compensate for that, the mixture must be chilled or frozen to facilitate handling, and that cold temperature must be maintained right up until dipping time. Dipping an ice-cold truffle is a procedure that contradicts every rule in the chocolate dipper's book. Centers made for enrobing (dipping) purposes should be 75° F., not half-frozen!

I feel obliged to tell you that the act in which we are about to engage may cause cracks in the chocolate's surface, leakage, and a finished product that is often dull and subject to eventual bloom if allowed to warm to room temperature. Well, fortunately for us, these intoxicating morsels are also perishable and must be kept refrigerated (for up to two weeks), so none of the above matters much, does it? Let us, then, throw our good senses to the wind and enjoy!

Truffles

> **1 cup** whipping cream
> **12 ounces** semisweet chocolate, chopped
> **4 tablespoons** unsalted butter, cut in small pieces
> **1 cup** chopped pecans
> **1 tablespoon** cognac (optional)
> **2–3 pounds** semisweet chocolate (includes reserve)

Yield: approximately 42

In a medium-sized saucepan, heat the cream until it simmers along the edges.

Add the chocolate and butter and stir until both are melted and the mixture is smooth. Set aside to cool briefly.

When the mixture is lukewarm, add the pecans and cognac and stir to blend.

Pour the mixture onto an ungreased cookie sheet and chill it in the refrigerator or freezer until it is quite firm.

Use a spoon or melon-ball cutter to scoop, and hands dusted with confectioners' sugar to roll, the cold, firm mixture into one-inch balls. Use a light, quick touch when you handle them.

Refrigerate or freeze the balls, uncovered, on a cookie sheet until they are hard. It will not take more than one or two hours.

Dipping procedure:

It is difficult to hold a bowl of chocolate in temper if you are repeatedly dipping ice-cold centers into it. Be sure to have a reheating source nearby. I prefer to use the method that draws warm chocolate from the pot of chocolate in reserve for dipping procedures.

1. Use your left hand to handle the bare truffle and your right hand to dip it. Roll it in the chocolate to coat it completely.

2. Lift the truffle out of the chocolate with your fingertips. Turn your hand over, palm up, fingers apart, and tap the edge of the slab or bowl to shake off the excess chocolate. The coating should be as thin as possible.

3. To transfer the coated truffle from its perched position on your fingertips to the wax-paper-covered cookie sheet, it will be necessary to turn your hand over, depositing the dipped truffle on the sheet, as you do.

4. Allow the excess chocolate on the tip of your thumb to drizzle a circular design on top of the truffle as you conclude the procedure.

Easter Nests

1 pound milk chocolate
2 ounces (or more) coconut
4 ounces tiny jelly beans
Yield: approximately 24

Add the coconut to the tempered chocolate and mix well.

Drop spoonfuls of the mixture onto a wax-paper-covered cookie sheet, spreading them into patties two inches in diameter.

Position three jelly beans in the center of each nest. Chill briefly.

Wrap each nest in plastic wrap and use them to fill Easter baskets or as desired.

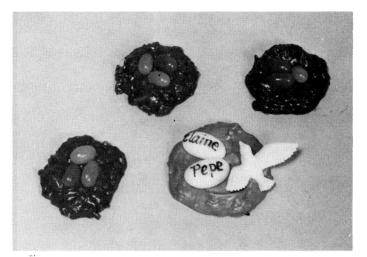

Easter and wedding/ anniversary nests.

Wedding/Anniversary Nests

1 pound pastel-colored coating
2 ounces coconut
Approximately **48** Jordan almonds
Yield: approximately 24

Prepare the nests as described above.

Position two personalized, sugar-coated Jordan almonds in each nest. Use a #1 tube and Royal Icing to write the names of the honored guests.

Personalized Pretzel Sticks

Chocolate
Seven-inch-long salted pretzel sticks
Royal Icing or chocolate

Spoon two or three cupfuls of prepared chocolate into a deep bowl or onto a marble slab.

Dip the pretzel stick ¾ of the way into the chocolate. Use a spoon to coax the chocolate over all surfaces of the pretzel and to remove some of the excess from the back of the pretzel.

Place the dipped pretzel on an inverted wax-paper-lined cookie sheet. Do not handle it until it is completely set.

Once set, the pretzels may be personalized as desired with a contrasting shade of chocolate or with Royal Icing.

Wrap them individually in plastic wrap or serve them in a napkin-lined wicker basket.

Appendix: Sources of Equipment and Chocolate

Standard cake and candy decorating supplies are available throughout the country in the houseware sections of many retail department stores, in cookware shops, and in stores that specialize in cake decorating and candy molding. Check the yellow pages of your local telephone directory for sources in your area.

Chocolate molds may be purchased in many of these same stores, though the largest selections are usually found in cake/candy decorating supply shops. The molds identified by brand names throughout the book are *not* intended to imply exclusivity on the part of any one mold company. Many mold manufacturers produce the same molds. Except where noted, the molds listed are popular, current designs that are readily available.

Chocolate is available wherever candy is sold. Imported brands are often sold by the three-ounce bar at fine candy counters or in gourmet food shops. Bulk compound coating (sometimes

called *bark, confectioners' coating, pastel coating, summer coating,* or *compound chocolate*) and domestic chocolate are available at some candy counters and in shops selling chocolate molds and cake/candy decorating equipment.

RETAIL MAIL-ORDER SOURCES

The mail-order sources that follow specialize in cake/candy decorating equipment as well as chocolate and compound coating and a variety of candy molds. Madame Chocolate specializes in a very wide selection of bulk imported and domestic chocolates and also stocks many Tomric plastic molds. They all will supply you with a descriptive catalog upon request (some charge a fee). In addition to mail-order sales, some also maintain retail outlet stores. It is important to

209

note that most will not ship chocolate during the summer months.

KITCHEN KRAFTS, INC.
2410 West 79th St.
Merrillville, IN 46410

MADAME CHOCOLATE
1940C Lehigh Ave.
Glenview, IL 60025

MAID OF SCANDINAVIA
3244 Raleigh
Minneapolis, MN 55416

THE COUNTRY STORE
2255 CR 27
Waterloo, IN 46793

THE OVEN DOOR
1203 16th Ave. S.
Fargo, ND 58102
          or
Box 6684
Lakeland, FL 33803

PARRISH'S CAKE DECORATING SUPPLIES, INC.
314 West 58th Street
Los Angeles, CA 90037

WILTON ENTERPRISES, INC.
2240 W. 75th St.
Woodridge, IL 60515

Note: Some of the above mail-order houses also maintain a wholesale division.

MOLD DESIGNERS AND MANUFACTURERS

Here is a list of some of the major manufacturers of high-grade plastic candy molds. Please note that these companies sell only to authorized distributors (including those listed above), shop owners, and members of the confectionery trade. They do *not* accept retail orders.

APOLLO MOLD CO.
5546 S. Columbia Ave.
Tulsa, OK 74105

INTERNATIONAL LEISURE ACTIVITIES, INC.
107 Tremont City Road
Springfield, OH 45502

LIFE OF THE PARTY
Sweet 11
Broadway, NJ 08808

EAST COAST MOLD MFG'S.
58A Lamar St.
West Babylon, NY 11704

FISCHER MOLD CO.
831 S. Hwy. 67
Florissant, MO 63031

GEORGE H. HAKE INC.
11154 Broadway
Alden, NY 14004

LINNEA'S CAKE AND CANDY SUPPLIES, INC. — whole
1609 Massillon Rd.
Akron, OH 44342

PARTY WORLD MOLDS
Oriskany Blvd.
PO Box 8
Whitesboro, NY 13492

TOMRIC PLASTICS, INC.
136 Broadway
Buffalo, NY 14203

CHOCOLATE MANUFACTURERS

These are the major chocolate manufacturers of the United States. Except for those that operate retail outlet stores, none sells chocolate directly to the consumer.

AMBROSIA CHOCOLATE CO.
Division W.R. Grace and Co.
1133 N. 5th St.
Milwaukee, WI 53203

BAKER'S CHOCOLATE AND COCONUT
General Foods Corporation
PO Box 600
Dover, DE 19901

COCOLINE CHOCOLATE CO., INC.
689697 Myrtle Ave.
Brooklyn, NY 11205

GHIRARDELLI CHOCOLATE CO.
1111 139th Ave. W.
San Leandro, CA 94578

GUITTARD CHOCOLATE CO.
10 Guittard Rd.
Burlingame, CA 94010

HERSHEY FOOD CORPORATION
Chocolate Ave.
Hershey, PA 17033

MERCKENS CHOCOLATE CO.
810 Main St.
Cambridge, MA 02139

THE BLOMMER CHOCOLATE CO.
600 W. Kinzie St.
Chicago, IL 60610

THE NESTLÉ CO., INC.
100 Bloomingdale Rd.
White Plains, NY 10605

VAN LEER, CHOCOLATE CORPORATION
110 Hoboken Ave.
Jersey City, NJ 07302

WILBUR CHOCOLATE CO.
Lititz, PA 17543

WORLD'S FINEST CHOCOLATE, INC.
2521 W. 48th St.
Chicago, IL 60632

ADDITIONAL WHOLESALE PRODUCT SOURCES

Food Coloring

NESTELLE's CAKE CRAFT
221 N.W. Schuyler St.
Portland, OR 97212

Placecard Cookie Cutter

CREATIVE HOUSE
190 W. Ashland St.
Doylestown, PA 18901

Wet-Dry Food Warmer

MEDALIE MANUFACTURING CO.
4701 Humboldt Ave. N.
Minneapolis, MN 55430

Thermometers

SYBRON/TAYLOR
Arden, NC 28704

Index